GREAT RAILWAY
JOURNEYS
OF THE
WORLD

THE TIMES GREAT RAILWAY JOURNEYS OF THE WORLD

Published by Times Books
An imprint of HarperCollins Publishers
Westerhill Road
Bishopbriggs
Glasgow G64 2QT
www.harpercollins.co.uk

First edition 2014
© HarperCollins Publishers 2014
Text © Julian Holland
Maps © Collins Bartholomew Ltd 2014

A catalogue record for this book is available from the British Library
ISBN 978-0-00-755935-0
ISBN 978-0-00-794254-1
10 9 8 7 6 5 4 3 2 1

Printed and bound in Hong Kong

All mapping in this book is generated from Collins Bartholomew digital databases.
Collins Bartholomew, the UK's leading independent geographical
information supplier, can provide a digital, custom, and premium
mapping service to a variety of markets.
For further information:
Tel: +44 (0)208 307 4515
e-mail: collinsbartholomew@harpercollins.co.uk
or visit our website at: www.collinsbartholomew.com

If you would like to comment on any aspect of this book, please
contact us at the above address or online.
www.timesatlas.com
e-mail: **timesatlases@harpercollins.co.uk**

facebook.com/thetimesatlas

@TimesAtlas

THE TIMES

GREAT RAILWAY JOURNEYS

OF THE

WORLD

Julian Holland

White Pass &
Yukon Railroad

Across the
Canadian Rockies
'Empire Builder'

Durango &
Silverton Railroad

Cumbres &
Toltec
Railroad

Sugar Cane
Steam in Cuba

Guayaquil &
Quito Railway

Ferrocarril
Central Andino

Ferrocarril
del Sur

La Trochita

Settle to Carlisle
West Highland Line
Isle of Man
Welsh Highland Railway
Dublin to Rosslare Harbour
The Jungfrau Railway
Le Petit Train Jaune
The Douro Valley
Ferrocarril de Sóller

Bergen Railway
Flåm Railway
Harz Mountains Narrow Gauge
Wolsztyn to Poznań
and Leszno
Thuringian Forest
Albula Railway
Chemins de Fer de la Corse
Trenino
Verde
Hedjaz Railway

Sudan's Railway

Massawa
to Asmara

Swakopmund to
Windhoek

Cape Town
to Kimberley

21st Century Steam
in Northeast China

Changbai
Mountain Region

Qinghai-Tibet
Railway

Jitong Railway

Khyber Pass
Railway

Kalka to
Shimla
Railway

Nilgiri
Mountain
Railway

Janakpur Railway

Darjeeling
Himalayan Railway

Yangôn(Rangoon)
to Mandalay

'Seven Stars'
on Kyushu

21st Century
Steam in Java

Ghan Railway

Madagascar's
Railways

Trans-Australian
Railway

CONTENTS

INTRODUCTION

Back in 1959, as a young British railway enthusiast, I borrowed a book from my local library. It was called 'Far Wheels' and was written by C. S. Small, an American oil man whose duty and service had taken him all over the world, from Japan to Mozambique, from Port Sudan to Peru, and everywhere he sought out and rode on local trains. The jacket blurb succinctly summed up this wonderful book: '*In a manner informal but well-informed, he sketches the setting of these lines, and their sometimes farcical history. This book is assured of a permanent place in world railway literature – but just as a highly unusual travel book it will be very much to many people's taste*'. I was transfixed by it and a rare copy today sits proudly on my bookshelf alongside my latest volume, 'Great Railway Journeys of the World'.

In this new book I leave my native country and spread my wings to discover not only the awesome spectacle of some of the most remote and rugged railways in the world but also some of the lesser-known and idiosyncratic lines that are still kept alive by loving admirers, steam enthusiasts, tourists and governments keen to protect their country's heritage.

In the Horn of Africa, the fledgling government of Eritrea pledged in 1993 to prioritize the reopening of the Italian-built narrow-gauge railway between the Red Sea port of Massawa and the capital Asmara that had been wrecked during the country's war of independence. After rejecting offers of foreign aid, the project started by using domestic skills and veteran railway workers to recover track, rebuild workshops and stations, and restore the motley collection of Italian railcars, locomotives and rolling stock. The highly scenic 73-mile line up through the mountains to Asmara reopened in 2003.

The surviving narrow-gauge railways on the Italian island of Sardinia were saved from certain closure in 1995 by a European Union project that saw the majority of regular services replaced by a seasonal tourist operation. Known collectively as 'Trenino Verde', these popular tourist lines are operated by restored vintage diesel railcars and steam locomotives.

In South America the narrow-gauge Guayaquil & Quito Railway was virtually destroyed by floods and landslides in the late twentieth century but its reopening by the Ecuadorian government in 2013 restores it as one of the most spectacular train journeys in the world.

PREVIOUS PAGE: Hauled by a TransNamib diesel, the 'Desert Express' heads out across the arid Namibian landscape on its journey between Swakopmund and Windhoek.

Two Italian-built Mallet 0-4-4-0Ts pound up the grade near Shegerini in the Eritrean mountains on the reopened narrow-gauge line between Massawa and Asmara in 2005.

Even UNESCO has got in on the act by protecting the narrow-gauge hill railways in India as World Heritage sites.

Many of the lines featured in this book were built by incredible human endeavour in some of the most inhospitable and inaccessible regions on Earth – by the early twentieth century their steel rails were spreading like gleaming ribbons across continents, through previously untouched mountain ranges and rainforests, and across high plateaux, deserts and frozen tundra. Others were more local affairs built to serve isolated rural communities and provide a lifeline to the outside world.

The story of these railways in far-off places starts in the late nineteenth century when British, European and American entrepreneurs and visionaries such as Cecil Rhodes and Henry Meiggs pushed the boundaries of rail transport in order to exert power and influence over distant lands. By the early twentieth century – from the mighty Andes, Rocky Mountains, Middle Eastern deserts and African wilderness to the Australian outback, the jungles of Burma, the hill stations of India and the Highlands of Scotland – virtually no part of the globe was left untouched. These strategic railways gave access to valuable minerals and other raw materials, opened up trade routes from remote hinterlands to ports and allowed the free movement of people in countries where there had previously been no reliable transport infrastructure.

With a magnificent Himalayan backdrop, Darjeeling Himalayan Railway locomotive No. 788B heads a Kurseong to Darjeeling service around the Batasia loop. Together with two other Indian hill railways it has the status of a UNESCO World Heritage site.

Nearer to home, European railway builders had conquered the Alps and opened up stunning vistas for a growing number of tourists in a new age of travel and prosperity.

Today, aided by modern technology, the railway builders are still opening up new wildernesses – the completion of the 1,215-mile Qinghai to Lhasa railway across the frozen tundra of the high Tibetan plateau in 2006 marked another milestone in human achievement. The statistics are staggering – 675 bridges; 340 miles laid on permafrost; the highest tunnel in the world, Fenghuoshan, at 16,093 ft; the highest railway line in the world, the Tanggula Pass, at 16,640 ft; the highest station in the world, Tanggula, at 16,627 ft. Needless to say, all passenger trains carry a doctor and there is an oxygen supply for every traveller!

Ranging far and wide over six continents, 'Great Railway Journeys of the World' features fifty of these fascinating railways, some well known to globe-trotting railway travellers, others not so well known but still much loved. Some, such as the Durango & Silverton Railroad and the Cumbres & Toltec Railroad in the US, are leftovers from a bygone age, still using vintage steam locomotives to haul their trains of passengers along twisting narrow-gauge tracks on exhilarating journeys into the mountains, while others, such as the Trans-Australian Railway and the Qinghai-Tibet Railway, are served by long, modern air-conditioned trains hauled by powerful diesel-electric locomotives that cross vast distances in a wild and desolate landscape. Electric haulage is not forgotten either, with the quaint third-rail 'Le Petit Train Jaune' winding up into the French Pyrenees, the vintage trains of the Ferrocarril de Soller crossing the mountains on the island of Majorca and the steeply graded Flåm Railway in Norway.

While the future of the vast majority of the railways featured in this book looks positive, the same cannot be said for all. In Syria the bloody civil war has put an end to the tourist steam trains on the Hedjaz Railway while in Sudan years of civil war, US economic sanctions, labour unrest and lack of maintenance and investment have brought the country's railways to its knees. The steam-operated Khyber Pass Railway on the Pakistan/Afghanistan border closed in 2006 following severe flooding but its reopening in this volatile region may be some years away. Their stories still need to be told, however, with the hope that one day they will be resurrected.

No book on world railway journeys would be complete without one last look at steam's mainline swansong, which ended in China as recently as late 2005. While the Jitong

Railway across the wilds of Inner Mongolia is still open for business today, albeit with diesel traction, the images of double-headed 'QJ' 2-10-2s struggling in sub-zero temperatures to haul their 3,000-ton coal trains through the mountains in the early years of the twenty-first century are certainly worth including as a memorial to the awesome brute power of these machines battling against the elements.

'Great Railway Journeys of the World' features a detailed history of fifty of these railways along with up-to-date information on the journey today and detailed route maps. To satiate the appetite of every intrepid armchair traveller the book is illustrated with stunning colour photographs supplied by some of the best railway photographers in the world.

Enjoy this book from your armchair or use it as a springboard to visit these enticing and off-the-beaten-track destinations. When considering the latter, remember that there are numerous specialist travel companies offering very attractive accompanied tours to visit many of the railways featured in this book.

LEFT: Steam's magnificent swansong on the Jitong Railway - with Siming Yi viaduct in the background, two Chinese Class 'QJ' 2-10-2s slog upgrade towards Reshui with a heavy coal train in April 2004.

The Settle-Carlisle Line in northern England is a triumph of Victorian engineering. Here, with the evening sun casting its spell on the Pennine Fells, a southbound steam-hauled charter train climbs through Mallerstang, north of Garsdale.

EUROPE

HARZ MOUNTAINS NARROW GAUGE
GERMANY

GAUGE: 1,000 MM (3 FT 3⅜ IN.) • **LENGTH:** 87 MILES •
ROUTES:
1. TRANS-HARZ LINE – WERNIGERODE TO NORDHAUSEN
2. BROCKEN RAILWAY – DREI ANNEN HOHNE TO THE BROCKEN
3. SELKE VALLEY RAILWAY –QUEDLINBURG TO EISFELDER TALMÜHLE

Located in Germany's highest mountain range, the scenic Harz narrow-gauge railways were once at the frontline of the Cold War. Today, massive steam locomotives still haul some of the trains on the three different routes including the steeply graded line up to the summit of the Brocken.

Located in central Germany and once on the frontline between East Germany and West Germany, the Harz Mountains are the highest range in the country. The Brocken, at 3,743 ft above sea level, is the highest point and was once the site of Russian and East German listening posts during the Cold War. The region is crossed by many rivers, of which twelve were dammed during the 1920s and 1930s to form lakes and provide drinking water and hydroelectric power.

The first narrow-gauge railway to be built in the Harz was a metre-gauge line from Gernrode to Mägdesprung which was opened to serve mines and local communities along the Selke Valley by the Gernrode-Harzgerode Railway in 1887. A standard-gauge railway had already reached Gernrode in 1885. Over the following years it was extended westwards along the valley to Stiege, from where a branch line went north to Hasselfelde, and by 1905 it had reached Eisfelder Talmühle. Increased competition from road vehicles saw the introduction of the company's own feeder bus routes in 1925 and diesel rail buses in the 1930s.

Following the Soviet invasion of eastern Germany in 1945 the railway ceased operating and much of its track was torn up as war reparations to the Soviet Union. Rebuilding the line was completed in 1949 by which time the railway had been nationalized under the control of Deutsche Reichsbahn.

The second railway to be built in the Harz was also a metre-gauge line that was opened between Wernigerode and Drei Annen Hohne by the Nordhausen-Wenigerode Railway in 1896. Two years later the 11¾-mile branch line from Drei Annen Hohne up to the summit of the Brocken was opened, followed by the main line southwards from Drei Annen Hohne to Benneckenstein, Eisfelder Talmühle and Nordhausen in 1899. At its northern and southern termini the railway met the standard-gauge lines of the Prussian State Railway, at Sorge it met the South Harz metre-gauge line (since closed) and at Eisfelder Talmühle it formed a junction with the metre-gauge Gernrode-Harzgerode Railway. Like the latter, the Nordhausen-Wenigerode Railway also started running feeder bus routes in the mid-1920s and became part of the state-owned Deutsche Reichsbahn (DR) in 1949.

Under DR management the two railways ordered seventeen of the massive, by narrow-gauge standards, DR Class 99.23 2-10-2T locomotives to work the heavy mineral trains on these steeply graded and scenic routes. Delivered between 1954 and 1956 they were built by VEB Locomotivbau 'Karl Marx' of Babelsburg and were modified to operate on the sharp curves that abound on these lines. They were the most powerful narrow-gauge German locomotives ever built and the majority are still in service.

Following the unification of Germany in 1990, the Harz narrow-gauge lines were taken over by a new private railway company, the Harzer Schmalspurbahnen GmbH (HSB).

Since 1993 the HSB has operated three distinct but interconnected routes:

1. **The Trans-Harz Railway** between Wernigerode and Nordhausen

2. **The Brocken Railway** between Drei Annen Hohne and the summit of the Brocken

3. **The Selke Valley Railway** between Gernrode to Eisfelder Talmühle and branches to Hasselfelde and Harzgerode

In 2006 the Selke Valley Railway was extended five miles northwards along the track bed of the former standard-gauge line to Quedlinburg where trains connect with the standard-gauge Harz-Elbe Express to Halberstadt.

With some timetabled trains still steam hauled, the 87-mile railway serves forty-four stations and halts and has its headquarters and main workshops at Wernigerode. In addition to operating passenger services the railway also carries freight traffic with standard-gauge wagons being carried from Nordhausen on specially adapted narrow-gauge transporter wagons.

TRANS-HARZ RAILWAY

Passengers wishing to travel from Nordhausen to Wernigerode usually have to change trains at either Eisfelder Talmühle or Drei Annen Hohne. There are normally four trains a day in each direction in the summer, two of which are operated either totally or partially by steam and the others by diesel railcar. The 37-mile journey

PREVIOUS PAGE: HSB 2-10-2 tank No.99 7236 climbing up to Drei Annen Hohne near Thumkuhlenkopf tunnel on 28 October 2008.

northwards begins at Nordhausen Nord station with trains calling at Bahnhofplatz, the connecting station for the modern Nordhausen electric tramway. Continuing northwards the railway climbs into the Harz Mountains beyond the village of Ilfeld before reaching Eisfelder Talmühle, the junction station for the Selke Valley Railway.

Still climbing into the mountains north of Eisfelder Talmühle the railway passes through forests to Benneckenstein station, 1,739 ft above sea level and the first summit of the line. After dipping down into the Warm Brode Valley it begins to climb again to the next summit (1,827 ft) between the villages of Sorge and Elend. The junction for the Brocken Railway at Drei Annen Hohne station is next before the line heads down to the Thumkuhlenkopf Tunnel, the only one on the entire Harz network. Still heading north, the line encounters a series of tight curves between Steinerne Renne and Wernigerode-Hasserode stations. The journey ends at Wernigerode, a town nestling in the Harz Mountains famous for its unspoilt medieval town centre and castle and also the headquarters of the HSB. The station is also an interchange for the standard-gauge railway line that links the cities of Halle and Hanover.

The famous 'double departure' from Alexisbad is recreated on 3 February 2007, as (left) 0-6-0T No. 99.6001-4 leaves with a service train to Eisfelder Talmühle paralleling No. 99.5906-5 with a charter to Harzgerode.

THE BROCKEN RAILWAY

The Brocken Railway runs through the Harz National Park from Drei Annen Hohne station on the Trans-Harz Railway to the summit of the Brocken – climbing nearly 2,000 ft over a distance of 11¾ miles with gradients as steep as 1-in-30. The line was closed to the public between 1961 and 1989 when the Brocken, close to the border with West Germany, was home to a Soviet listening post. From Drei Annen Hohne trains hauled by powerful DR Class 99.23 2-10-2T locomotives start their climb to Schierke, the only intermediate station on the line, before climbing high above the heavily forested Cold Bode valley. The railway makes its final, dramatic approach to the summit station up a steeply graded spiral around the mountain top.

THE SELKE VALLEY RAILWAY

This line between Quedlinburg and Eisfelder Talmühle is the least known and least used of the three routes operated by HSB. It has two branch lines, from Alexisbad to Harzgerode and from Stiege to Hasselfelde. Steam-hauled trains along the route in summer are limited to one during weekdays and two at weekends but none operate between Stiege and Eisfelder Talmühle. Services normally hauled by 1939-built Krupp 0-6-0 tank 99 6001-4 depart southwards from the town of Quedlinburg, its old town and medieval court now a UNESCO World Heritage site. En route, along the Selke Valley, trains call at the medieval town of Gernrode, the village of Mägdesprung, once home to an ironworks, and the spa town of Alexisbad, junction for the branch line to the ancient town of Harzgerode.

From Alexisbad the railway continues southwards into the Harz Mountains sometimes encountering gradients as steep as 1-in-25, calling at the village of Straßberg, once an important centre for fluorspar and silver mining. After calling at Stiege, junction for the connecting line to the Trans-Harz Railway, trains terminate at the town of Hasselfelde. North of Stiege station there is a sharply curved loop where complete trains can be turned.

OVERLEAF: On the 8 February 2013 the cloud lifted on the Brocken for a few minutes as the train No. 8927, the 13:39 from Drei Annen Hohne, hauled by 2-10-2 tank No. 99 7241, climbs the last section to the summit station at 1,125 metres above sea level.

THE THURINGIAN FOREST (THÜRINGERWALD)

GERMANY

GAUGE: 4 FT 8½ IN. • **LENGTH:** 115 MILES •
ROUTE: EISENACH-MEININGEN-ARNSTADT-KATZHÜTTE

The network of scenic standard-gauge railways that crisscross the Thuringian Forest and mountains in central Germany is one of the forgotten railway delights of Europe. Several of the routes operate regular steam-hauled trains during special events each year.

The Thuringian Forest area of Central Germany has been labelled as 'Steam Railway Country', a brand name collectively used by the German National regional railway company DB Regio, the Thuringian regional railway company and the various heritage railway organizations established in the district. The chief towns of particular interest in Thuringia are Eisenach, Arnstadt and Meiningen. There are in effect four different railway routes of special interest, three chosen on the merit of the heritage trains that are frequently on offer, and the fourth as an interconnecting route through the equally scenic landscape of the Thuringian Forest (Thüringerwald). This district is crisscrossed by a rich network of national main and branch lines, all offering equally splendid panoramas. Highlights of the district include: the Eiben Forest near Dermbach; a fairytale sandstone cave at Walldorf; the deepest lake in Germany formed by land subsidence, near Bernshausen; and the Krayenburg, the ruins of a castle dating back to the year 786, with a spectacular outlook from a tower at Tiefenort across the Werra Valley.

The most appropriate starting point when visiting the area by rail is Eisenach, which is located on the main 130-mile-long standard-gauge railway line running from

PREVIOUS PAGE: Ex-Deutsche Reichsbahn class 03.10 Pacific No. 03 1010-2 storms along near Schwallungen, Werratal, heading an Eisenach-Meiningen service on 31 October 2008.

Ex-Prussian Railways class 'T16' class 0-10-0 tank No. 94 1538 climbs away from Rottenbach with a special service for Katzhütte on the Schwartzatalbahn on 14 October 2007.

Halle (Saale) via Erfurt and Gerstungen to Bebra, mainly through the Thuringian Forest. Originally constructed between 1846 and 1849, the route between Halle and Gerstungen was formally part of the Thuringian Railway Company, while between Gerstungen and Bebra was part of the Friedrich-Wilhelms-Nordbahn, named after the Prussian King Frederick Wilhelm IV. Eisenach, the birthplace of the composer Johann Sebastian Bach and once the centre of the East German automotive industry, is situated on the northwest fringe of the Thuringian Forest district, situated at the junction of the Thuringian and Werra railways, and forty-four miles west from Weimar. The town boasts one of the region's finest castles, the Wartburg, designated a UNESCO World Heritage site, and a ring of half-timbered houses around the market square. Most visitors visit Eisenach for its historical significance; Martin Luther lived there in the sixteenth century.

The Werra Railway (Werrabahn) branches off at Eisenach, a former main-line railway between north and south Germany via Meiningen to Eisfeld and connecting Thuringia with Bavaria. Following the division of Germany after the Second War War it was downgraded to a single-track secondary main line. Opened in 1858, it is one of the oldest railways in Germany, running predominantly alongside the river Werra and with a number of branch lines radiating from it. The company that built it located their head offices at the theatre town of Meiningen and the main workshops of the Prussian State Railways were consequently established there. This stately town is considered the cultural, judicial and financial centre of southern Thuringia. Splendid prestigious buildings, wide avenues and extensive parks give this former seat of the Dukes of Saxe-Meiningen a special atmosphere. Its Franconian-style timber-framed houses, the Bleichgräben (moat) and the remains of the old town walls are reminders of the late Middle Ages when the town was in its heyday. Evidence of Meiningen's rich cultural history can be seen in the English-style park with its wealth of statuary, as well as in the town's museums and Elisabethenburg Castle. The Meiningen steam locomotive works is also located in the town and since 1990 has specialized in the maintenance of locomotives from heritage railways and museums throughout Europe. The newly built British Peppercorn 'A1' class steam locomotive No. 60163 'Tornado' that was delivered in 2008 had her all-steel, high-performance boiler made at Meiningen; the only part that was not made in Britain. There are guided tours of the factory every first and third Saturday in the month at 10.00 a.m. A tour lasts about 1½ hours and booking is not necessary. Since 1995 the Meiningen Steam Festival has taken place annually on the first weekend in September, with a number of special steam-hauled visiting charter trains making an appearance.

A change of train at Meiningen with the Ritschenhausen-Neudietendorf railway provides connections with services to Arnstadt. This scenic route, opened by the Prussian State Railway in 1884, is exceptionally steeply graded across the Thuringian Forest Mountains and passes through the 1-mile-long Brandleite tunnel which took just under four years to build. Arnstadt, one of the oldest towns in Thuringia and where Johann Sebastian Bach lived as an organist from 1703 to 1707, lies along the Gera River at the northern foothills of the Thuringian Forest Mountains. A working railway museum has been established in Arnstadt for over fifteen years in the former locomotive semi-roundhouse. This museum houses a collection of locomotives that have a special significance with Thuringia over the last forty years, however it is not just a museum but a fully functional depot servicing locomotives involved in special charter trains on the main line, including the 'Rodelblitz' winter steam-hauled services from Eisenach and special steam-hauled trains on the Schwarzatalbahn via Rottenbach to Katzhütte.

In 1895 the Prussian Railway administration was granted permission to construct the Schwarzatalbahn. The 18½-mile-long line opened in 1900 and passes through typical Thuringian forest and mountain terrain from Rinnetal, through the romantic Tal der Schwarza, before reaching the terminus at Katzhütte. At the half-way point from Rottenbach can be found the valley station of the Oberweißbacher funicular railway, which offers the opportunity of taking in the magnificent views from atop the Oberweißenbach hill. This mountain railway, which was opened in 1923, possesses listed status and has a 1,531-yd-long continuous rope haulage system. It is the only broad-gauge cable railway in Germany and climbs at a 45-degree incline using the Swiss Abt rack and pinion system.

The main line between Erfurt and Bebra via Eisenach is an electrified route operated by DB Netze with most types of train using the line, including InterCity Express, serving four of the six largest cities in Thuringia with connections to and from Berlin and Frankfurt am Main.

The Sud-Thüringen Bahn operates diesel multiple units on an hourly basis along the Werrabahn from Eisenach to Meiningen. A special Plandampf event takes place most years, currently in April, whereby former German State Railway (Deutsche Reichsbahn) steam locomotives take over some scheduled passenger and freight services along the entire route, including heavy timber and gravel trains originating from loading points at Walldorf and Immelborn. This event, along with other steam-hauled passenger charter trains operating throughout the year, is administered by IGE Eisenach, a heritage railway society with locomotive and rolling stock facilities based in Eisenach. The popular Rodelblitz passenger services have been operating for the past sixteen years between Eisenach and Arnstadt over weekends in February, using the steeply graded and scenic route via Wernshausen and Oberhof, where a popular winter sports centre is located. These trains are normally hauled by former DR class '41' 2-8-2 No. 41 1144-9, which was built in 1939 and designed as a 56-mph mixed-traffic locomotive. Having had a complete overhaul between 2001 and 2003 at the Meiningen workshops, it is now the key locomotive featuring in DB Regio's and the Thuringian regional railway company's programme of excursions throughout the year. Coaching stock used on these services comprises up to eight carriages originating from the 1960s German State Railway era for use on long-distance services and, in latter years, by the German Federal Railway (DB) as suburban coaches.

Between Meiningen and Arnstadt an hourly service is offered between DB Regional Express and Süd-Thüringen-Bahn services. From Arnstadt to Katzhütte, along the Schwarzatalbahn route, class 641 railcars are used, offering an hourly service. Additionally, the Schwarzatalexpress from Leipzig operates once daily on Saturdays, Sundays and public holidays from May to October. Special excursions are also operated using a 1922 Prussian State Railways 'T16' class 0-10-0 tank No. 94 1538, this type being a familiar sight on steeply graded sections of the railways in the Thüringerwald between the 1920s and 1960s. Historical diesel railbuses, nicknamed 'Piglet Taxis' Nos. 772 140-0 and 772 141-8 of the Oberweißbacher Berg-und Schwarzatalbahn (OBS) have been sympathetically restored to their 1969 condition and are retained for special excursions on the Schwarzatalbahn.

Ex-Deutsche Reichsbahn class 44 'Jumbo' 2-10-0 No. 44 2546 heading a log train near Breitungen, Werratal, on 8 October 2010.

WOLSZTYN TO POZNAŃ AND LESZNO

POLAND

GAUGE: 4 FT 8½ IN. • **LENGTH:** 76 MILES •
ROUTES:
1. WOLSZTYN – POZNAŃ
2. WOLSZTYN – LESZNO

Located in Poland's Wielkopolska National Park, these routes both operated a regular steam-hauled passenger service until the end of 2013. However, the Wolsztyn to Leszno route still sees daily steam-hauled trains, the only remaining service of its kind in the world.

With an economic upturn in Prussia, the Parliament approved an act in 1880 specifying the principles of construction of secondary railway lines in the Province of Poznań which were to enhance the already established mainline routes. The so-called local lines serving Wolsztyn came under this act and the lines were built to transport mainly agricultural produce from the numerous landed properties in the area. These secondary lines were built by the state, the Wolsztyn-Leszno line opening in 1896 and the Wolsztyn-Grodzisk Wielkopolski (for Poznań via Opalenica) line opening in 1898, connecting with an existing route from Zbąszynek to Wolsztyn which had been established in 1886. After the First World War and the Wielkopolska Uprising of 1918-1919, the Treaty of Versailles set the Polish State border with Germany at just over six miles from Wolsztyn, which had a severe influence and subsequent decline on the railway traffic serving the town due to the lines being truncated to short local sections.

With the Second World War breaking out in September 1939 and upon an order from the Polish Army High Command, the main station building at Wolsztyn was set alight and destroyed and the railway control operations were subsequently established in a wooden building on the station platform, still there today, and also in the locomotive shed. Much of the railway infrastructure in the region was also destroyed in order to hamper the advance of the German troops. Upon occupation by Germany, Wolsztyn's railway infrastructure was entirely rebuilt with a new station, extended locomotive shed, maintenance and servicing facilities and signalling, the town being considered a strategic junction on the network in the district. In the region of thirty locomotives were based there with 300 footplate crew and supporting engineers, providing services to and from the Soviet border as well as locally.

After the Second World War the status of Wolsztyn as an important railway centre in the Wielkopolska region remained unchanged. The entire infrastructure established by the German occupation also remained in situ, as it does to this day. Wolsztyn remained a strategic centre for military equipment, supplies and troops in transit between the Soviet Union and the German Democratic Republic right up until the early 1990s, predominantly in the hands

of 'Kriegslok' 'Ty2' class 2-10-0s and Polish rebuilt version of the 'Kriegslok', the 'Ty43' and 'Ty45' classes. Although freight services, especially those once using the minor routes radiating from Wolsztyn and Grodzisk Wielkopolski, have contracted over the last twenty years, the historic town of Wolsztyn remains a key railway centre with services to Poznań, Leszno and Zbąszynek, some being steam hauled with locomotives maintained at the historic 'half roundhouse' locomotive depot.

Wolsztyn can trace its roots back to the Cistercians in 1285 and started to expand from the fifteenth century as a crafts and commerce centre, famous for its cloth industry and wool fairs. In 1793 Wolsztyn came under Prussian rule (Wollstein in the Province of Ostbrandenburg) and later from 1807–1813 became part of the Duchy of Warsaw. By virtue of the ruling of the Congress of Vienna the town came within the borders of the Great Duchy of Poznań. The Wielkopolska Uprising involved the town, which was liberated in January 1919, after which it experienced an economic upturn until the onset of the Second World War. In 1989 Wolsztyn was returned to its historic administrative borders, quickly developing into an expanding town in the province of Greater Poland.

PKP 'Ol49' class 2-6-2 No. 111 heads a Wolsztyn-Poznań service away from Steszew on 7 april 2007.

PREVIOUS PAGE: The train guard of the 06:07 from Wolsztyn to Leszno converses with the driver of 'Ol49' class 2-6-2 No. 59 just before departure on a misty Saturday, 18 January 2014.

Although Wolsztyn is the key centre for travel on the two lines, the starting point for any visit to the area is usually the city of Poznań (formerly Posen); Euro-City trains provide convenient rail connections, for example the journey from Berlin to Poznań takes just three hours.

Situated on the Warta River, Poznań is one of the oldest cities in Poland and a world tourist attraction of note. Its impressive cathedral is the earliest church in the country, containing the tombs of the first Polish rulers. Today it is a vibrant centre for trade, industry and education and is Poland's fifth largest city.

Modern diesel multiple units operated by Wielkopolska Railways (Koleje Wielkopolskie) now form the nucleus of the passenger services operating between Poznań and Wolsztyn (with sixteen intermediate stations) and Wolsztyn and Leszno (with eleven intermediate stations). This company also operates the world's only main-line regular steam-hauled passenger services, maintained at Wolsztyn's historic locomotive depot and museum. The only freight services seen today on the two lines are a weekly cement train for the cement works at Powodowo, just west of Wolsztyn, and coal delivery for the locomotive depot. This is usually worked by a PKP Cargo 'SU46' class diesel-electric locomotive allocated at the region's main Leszno depot, where some steam locomotive repairs are still carried out.

Until December 2013 there were two return timetabled steam services per weekday on the Wolsztyn-Poznań route, although the steam-hauled services are now concentrated on the Wolsztyn-Leszno line, with two trains per day, seven days a week in addition to other services employing diesel multiple units. There are three locomotives available for the steam services, two 2-6-2s of class 'Ol49' Nos. Ol49-59 and Ol49-69 built at the Chrzanów locomotive factory in the mid-1950s, a once 115-strong class of mixed traffic locomotive, and a 'Pt47' class express passenger 2-8-2 No. Pt47-65 built at Chrzanów in 1949. Additionally, locomotives of various classes stored out of service or on display can be found in the adjacent goods yard and at the locomotive depot. The depot consists of a semi-roundhouse and turntable, but was originally constructed in 1907 as a four-road building, enlarged to eight roads in 1909. It is now unique as the last everyday operating steam motive power depot in the world and is open to the public upon payment of a small fee at the shedmaster's office. A visit between 11.00 a.m. and midday will usually reward the visitor with the sight of a steam locomotive between its two daily Leszno diagrams being

serviced, coaled and watered in the traditional manner, as well as being turned on the shed's turntable. At the beginning of 2014 the future of the steam operation was in some doubt, but the rail operating company has allowed continued operation, pending a long-term operational arrangement being established to assure its future.

Wolsztyn hosts one of Poland's two annual mainline steam galas, usually on the last Saturday in April or the first Saturday in May, when around a dozen or more locomotives are found in steam, some visiting with heritage charter trains from Poznań, Wroclaw, Berlin and Cottbus. In addition to visiting locomotives drawn from across Poland, locomotives from other countries also appear in the parade, traditionally from the Czech Republic and Germany. It is a main event in the local calendar and is visited by thousands of people, both from the surrounding regions and afar.

Key to the continued operation of steam locomotives from Wolsztyn depot is The Wolsztyn Experience, a mutual trust society which was set up and run by British steam train enthusiasts to offer financial support for the continued use of scheduled steam services in Poland. It has been running footplate experience courses for the last sixteen years, which have proved popular with enthusiasts from around the world.

Both lines to Poznań and Leszno boast small architecturally elegant railway stations typical of the Prussian style. The bridges, viaducts, semaphore signalling, water cranes and signal boxes, which date back several decades, give the two lines, along with the steam passenger services, a unique character and travel experience. The station buildings and signal boxes at Wolsztyn date back to 1895, still with much original functioning equipment in daily use. Although the Wolsztyn-Poznań line has recently been subject to modernization with new platforms and station lighting, the original station buildings and control rooms remain, with some of the wayside structures now being used as private dwellings. Both lines run through the Wielkopolska National Park, an area of lakes, wooded plains and moraine hills, which is a popular holiday destination in Poland, located in the Warta River basin.

OVERLEAF: The 08:45 Poznań to Wolsztyn service, with an unusually long trailing load for the line comprising double-deck stock and ex-Deutsche Reichsbahn coaches for onward transit to Cottbus, heads away towards Wolsztyn near Grodzisk on 2 January 2000.

CHEMINS DE FER DE LA CORSE
CORSICA, FRANCE

GAUGE: 1,000 MM (3 FT 3⅜ IN.) • **LENGTH:** 144 MILES •
ROUTE: AJACCIO TO BASTIA/PONTE-LECCIA TO CALVI

Surviving several threats of closure, the steeply graded and highly scenic metre-gauge railway of Corsica threads its way up through the island's mountainous interior via a series of tunnels, horseshoe curves and impressive viaducts.

LIGURIAN

SEA

*Isola
di Capraia
(Italy)*

*Parco Nazionale dell'
Arcipélago Toscano*

Capraia Isola

ITALY

Isola d'Elba

Portoferraic

Cap Corse

Marciana Marina

Marciana

Monte Capanne

*Parco Nazionale
dell' Arcipelago Toscano*

Rogliano

*Monte
Stello
1307*

Brando

Santa-Maria-di-Lota

San-Martino-di-Lota

Ville-di-
Pietrabugno

Bastia

Furiani

Désert des Agriates

St-Florent

Oletta

L'Île-Rousse

Biguglia

Belgodère

Murato

Borgo

Lucciana

Poretta

Calvi

Calenzana

Campitello

Golo

Vescovato

Venzolasca

Penta-di-Casinca

*Monte
Padro* 2393

Figarella

Ponte-Leccia

Parc

Morosaglia

*Monte
Cinto
2706*

La Porta

Fango

Calacuccia

Piedicroce

Naturel

Corte

San-Nicolao

Cervione

*Col de
Vergio
1477*

Sermano

Moïta

Piana

1101

*Col de
Sevi*

*Monte
Rotondo
2622*

Venaco

Vezzani

CORSE

(CORSICA)

(France)

Vico

Tallone

Régional

*Monte
d'Oro
2389*

Ghisoni

Fium'Orbo

Aléria

Liamone

Bocognano

*Monte
Rénoso
2352*

Sari-d'Orcino

de

Prunelli-
di-Fiumorbo

Ghisonaccia

Sarrola-Carcopino

Bastelica

la

Gravona

Cuttoli-Corticchiato

Ventiseri

Ajaccio

Campo dell'Oro

Bastelicaccia

Zicavo

Travo

Corse

Santa-Maria-Siché

Golfe d'Ajaccio

Grosseto-Prugna

*Monte
Incudine* 2134

1218

*Col de
Bavella*

Taravo

Petreto-
Bicchisano

Zonza

TYRRHENIAN

Olmeto

Levie

Rizzanese

Propriano

Porto-Vecchio

Sartène

Montagne de Cagna

*Punta
d'Ovace
1340*

Ortolo

SEA

Figari

*Capo Pertusato
Réserve Naturelle des Îles Lavezzi*

Bonifacio

*Parco Nazionale dell' Arcipélago
de la Maddalena*

S t r a i t   o f   B o n i f a c i o

SARDEGNA

(SARDINIA)

(Italy)

Santa Teresa
di Gallura

La Maddalena

*Serra
Paoloni
361*

Palau

Costa Smeralda

Arzachena

Liscia

*Monte Morro
421*

*Isola
Asinara* 391

Aglientu

640

Bassacutena

Arzachena

Luogosanto

*Monte dell
Fortezza
645*

Oletta

irthplace of Napoleon Bonaparte and for centuries home to groups of warring bandits, the rocky and mountainous island of Corsica has been a 'région' of France since 1769. A close northern neighbour of the larger Italian island of Sardinia (*see* page 36), it is located in the Mediterranean Sea to the west of Italy and southeast of the French mainland. The capital, Ajaccio, is located on the west coast of the island while the island's main port, Bastia, is on the northeast coast.

A proposal to build a network of metre-gauge railway lines on the island was first put forward in 1877 – the narrow gauge was selected as it was more suitable for the mountainous terrain, allowing the railway to follow contours with sharper curves than would be possible with standard gauge. Construction of the heavily engineered line started in 1879 and by 1888 the northeastern section of the railway had opened between Bastia and Corte along with the southwestern section from Ajaccio to Bocognano. In between lay the mountainous heart of the island which held up completion for another six years.

The steeply graded section between Bocognano and Corte, which finally opened in 1894, had involved the building of numerous tunnels, bridges and viaducts: the longest tunnel, near Vizzavona, is nearly 2½ miles long and almost

PREVIOUS PAGE: A 2-car diesel train slowly crosses Gustave Eiffel's impressive 300-ft-high viaduct at Vecchio in in the Parc Naturel in Corsica's mountainous interior.

A 1949-built Renault railcar and trailer skirt the sandy bay at Calvi with a train for L'île-Rousse.

3,000 ft above sea level; the largest and most impressive viaduct, at Vecchio, was designed by Gustav Eiffel and is 459 ft long and just over 300 ft high. To gain height, the engineers built a series of dramatic reverse curves up to Vivario station – from here the railway can be seen far below looping back and forth as it climbs up to the summit. A branch line from Ponte-Leccia to Calvi on the north coast followed but the 81-mile line down the east coast from Casamozza to Porto-Vecchio was not completed until 1935. The latter had a short life as it was seriously damaged by bombing during the Second World War when it was closed south of Folleli. The remaining northern stub from Casamozza to Folleli closed in 1953.

Apart from the Porto-Vecchio line the rest of the Corsican railway network has survived into the twenty-first century despite threats of complete closure during the 1950s and 1970s. Steam haulage in the shape of French-built 0-6-2Ts and powerful 0-4-4-0T articulated Mallets began to decline in the 1930s and 1940s when railcars and trailers built by Billard and Renault were introduced. These in turn have been replaced by more modern diesel multiple units built between the 1970s and 1990s and recently introduced AMG800 panoramic twin railcars.

Today operated by the state-owned Chemins de Fer de la Corse (CFC), the highly scenic network of railways on Corsica is centred on the town of Ponte-Leccia in the north of the island, from where lines radiate out to Ajaccio, Bastia and Calvi. While there are currently four return trains each day on the main line between Ajaccio and Bastia with a journey time of 3 hours 25 minutes, there is a more frequent service, especially during the summer months, on the northeast coast route between Bastia and Casamozza and on the northwest coast route between Calvi and L'île-Rousse – the latter runs close to beaches and is very popular with holidaymakers and passengers from visiting cruise liners. A suburban service operates from the harbour station at Ajaccio to Mezzana. Assisted by major track improvements, the recently introduced AMG 800 panoramic twin railcars have cut the Ajaccio to Bastia journey time by one hour.

AJACCIO TO BASTIA

Ajaccio, the birthplace of Napoleon Bonaparte in 1769, is the largest city in Corsica and is located in a sheltered position on the shores of the Gulf of Ajaccio. An important trading port since Ancient Greek times, its rich cultural and architectural heritage makes it a popular destination for today's modern cruise liners. Located close to the port, Ajaccio railway station is the departure point for trains to Bastia. Departing from here in an easterly direction, trains first follow the coastline before heading inland up the Gravona Valley. Climbing continually the railway reaches Bocognano (2100 ft above sea level) before passing through the longest tunnel on the line to reach Vizzavona (2953 ft above sea level). From here it climbs up through spectacular mountain scenery in the Parc Naturel on a series of dramatic reverse curves to Vivario before crossing Eiffel's viaduct at Vecchio. After reaching Riventosa the line descends steeply through tunnels and reverse curves to reach the hillside town of Corte (1312 ft above sea level) before arriving at Ponte-Leccia, junction for the Calvi branch.

From Ponte-Leccia trains head eastwards down the Golo Valley to reach the coastal plain at Casamozza, once the junction for the coastal line south to Porto-Vecchio before heading north through flat agricultural land to reach the coast at Bastia. Sandwiched between the sea and mountains, the historic port of Bastia was the capital of Corsica until 1791 while today its modern ferry terminal is kept busy with the comings and goings of vehicle ferries to and from the French mainland.

PONTE-LECCIA TO CALVI

From the village of Ponte-Leccia trains heads northwards through a rocky and mountainous landscape, before descending to the northwest coast down the Navaccia Valley through a series of tunnels and reverse curves. At L'île-Rousse the railway meets the coastline and follows it westwards past sandy beaches and coves, popular with sun worshippers in the summer, before rounding the bay to Calvi. Home to a regiment of the French Foreign Legion, Calvi's other claim to fame is that it was possibly the birthplace of Christopher Columbus. Today, its beaches around the Gulf of Calvi are popular destinations for the holidaymakers who arrive at its airport on flights from Europe during the summer months.

OVERLEAF: The metre-gauge railway between Ajaccio and Bastia serves many villages in as it winds its way through Sardinia's mountainous interior.

TRENINO VERDE – SARDINIAN NARROW GAUGE
SARDINIA, ITALY

GAUGE: 950 MM (3 FT 1½ IN.) • **LENGTH**: 259 MILES •
ROUTES:
1. MACOMER TO BOSA – 28½ MILES
2. NULVI TO PALAU – 71½ MILES
3. MANDAS TO ARBATAX – 99 MILES
4. MANDAS TO SORGONO – 60 MILES

'A strange railroad. Would like to know who built it. Scooting up the hills and down the valleys and around sharp turns with the utmost nonchalance... advancing in deep trenches and grunting while polluting the air in the tunnels, but it runs up a hill like a little dog panting...'
D. H. Lawrence. 'Sea and Sardinia', 1921

The second largest island in the Mediterranean after Sicily, Sardinia measures about 160 miles from north to south and 75 miles from east to west and is significantly larger in area than Israel. It has a mountainous interior – the highest peak, Punta La Marmora, is 6,017 ft above sea level – and few rivers. Inhabited for over 10,000 years, the island bore the brunt of attacks by Muslim pirates for 1,000 years and has, in more recent centuries, been a pawn in the game played out by the European powers, being occupied by Spain for 400 years and for a short period by Austria until, in 1861, it became part of the newly formed Kingdom of Italy. Today, Sardinia is one of five Italian autonomous regions, giving it wide-ranging legal and administrative powers. The two largest cities on the island are the capital Cagliari (population 150,000), on the south coast, and Sassari (population 125,000) in the northwest, while the island's rugged east coast remains sparsely populated.

Reliable communications across the mountainous island were always poor and even in the 1860s there were few roads, with travellers often subject to attack by roving gangs of bandits. Many parts of the island were isolated from the capital, Cagliari, only able to access it via a long and often rough sea voyage around the coast. Avoiding the mountainous interior, the first railway to be built on Sardinia opened between Cagliari and the west coast town of Oristano in 1872. In the same year a railway opened from Decimomannu, on the Cagliari to Oristano line, to the southwestern industrial town of Iglesias in 1872. Oristano was joined in 1878 by a line from Porto Torres on the northwest coast and the city of Sassari in 1878. Opening throughout in 1883, another line struck out from a junction at Ozieri, on the Sassari to Oristano line, to the northeastern city of Olbia and the port of Golfo Aranci. All these were built to the standard gauge of 4 ft 8½ in.

While the standard-gauge railways provided much-needed communication between the north, west and south coasts, the mountainous interior and the east coast remained very isolated. However, during the latter part of the nineteenth century the building of narrow-gauge railways in mountainous regions of Europe had proved to be both economical and successful.

The first to be built in Sardinia was the 5-ft $5^{21}/_{32}$-in.-gauge, 25-mile railway between Monti, on the standard-gauge line to Olbia, northwestwards across the Gallura Mountains to Tempio Pausania which opened in 1889. This was followed over the next four years by a total of 354 miles of more similarly gauged lines through demanding terrain: between Cagliari, Mandas and Sorgono in 1889; between Bosa on the west coast, Macomor and Nuoro in 1889; between Sassari and Alghero in 1889; between Chilivani and Tirso in 1893; and between Mandas and Arbatax on the east coast, with a branch from Gairo to Jerzu, in 1894.

A further 56 miles of narrow-gauge lines were opened between 1913 and 1915, including a route between Sarcidano, north of Mandas, to Villacidro along with a branch line to Ales. This wasn't quite the end of narrow-gauge railway building in Sardinia: in the southwest a 70-mile route was opened between Siliqua, Calasetta and Carbonia in 1926 to serve coal mines; the final route was the 93-mile line across the Gallura Mountains between Sassari and the small northeastern port of Palau which opened in 1932.

The austerity years of the 1930s along with modest, but growing, competition from road transport saw the introduction of diesel railcars on many of Sardinia's narrow-gauge lines. The Second World War effectively bypassed the island but the narrow-gauge railways suffered from lack of maintenance and spare parts, and by 1945 they were in a poor state. While the standard-gauge lines had been nationalized in 1920, the privately owned narrow-gauge system struggled to make ends meet until it was thrown a lifeline by the state in the form of subsidies for modernization including the upgrading of track, ironing out of some of the sharpest curves and new equipment. Despite this, some of the least economical lines were subsequently closed: Sarcidona to Villacidro and the Ales branch in 1956; Monti to Tempio Pausania in 1958; Chilivani to Tirso in 1969; and Siliqua to Calasetta and Carbonia in stages between 1969 and 1975. The private company that operated the surviving routes went into receivership in 1971 but the Italian Government stepped in, administering them until they were taken under state control as the Ferrovie della Sardegna (FdS) in 1989.

The 1990s saw traffic still in decline on the surviving narrow-gauge system. Major improvements to Sardinia's road system funded by European Union handouts only made matters worse: freight traffic was withdrawn and many routes were reduced to operating only during the tourist season from May to October. On the positive side, the more economically viable lines also received EU funding to modernize stations, track and signalling. In 1995 four of the lines were saved from closure by another EU project that saw the majority of regular services replaced by a seasonal tourist service. Known collectively as 'Trenino Verde', these popular tourist lines are operated by restored vintage diesel railcars and steam locomotives.

In 2010 the FdS narrow-gauge system became totally integrated in the island's regional transport company, the Azienda Regionale Sard Transport (ARST). Apart from the four 'Trenino Verde' routes, it operates regular services on 126 miles of narrow-gauge lines using modern diesel locomotives and multiple units. The Ferrovie dello Stato operates the standard-gauge lines on the island.

MACOMER TO BOSA

This 28½-mile route starts in the historic town of Macomer, which is also served by trains operating on the south-north standard-gauge mainline between Cagliari and Sassari, and the narrow-gauge line eastwards to Nuoro. Trains for Bosa depart from Macomer station in a westerly direction, first climbing over the standard-gauge line before shortly reaching the summit of the line, 1,762 ft above sea level. From here the railway descends westwards to the coast, passing through a landscape of pastureland cut by stone walls and dominated by bronze-age towers known as *nuraghi*. After passing the twelfth-century Cistercian Abbey of Santa Maria Court and calling at Sindia station, the train heads into flat, cultivated countryside to reach Tinnura station. The nearby village is famous for the murals that have been painted on its houses, shops, walls and practically everything else.

Continuing its descent, the railway winds around the hillsides to reach the village of Tresnurages – literally meaning 'three Bronze Age towers' – which is famous for its Feast of Saint Mark, held every year on 25 April. Trains then make a circuitous descent to Magomadas, from where there is the first glimpse of the sea, before plunging into the Modolo Valley, well known for its fine local Malvasia wine. The final approach to Bosa takes the railway northwards along the cliffs above a pebble beach

before heading inland along the Temo Valley to the ancient town's terminus station.

NULVI TO PALAU

Nulvi, the starting point for this 71½-mile journey, is still served by regular narrow-gauge trains from Sassari. Trains depart from Nulvi in a northeasterly direction, passing en route many of the Bronze Age sacred wells and water temples that abound on the island and descending through a landscape more typical of the mesas in the American West. The first stop is at Martis followed by the village of Laerru, famous for its religious festivals, caverns and petrified forest. Continuing its descent through this rich and fertile region the railway reaches Perfugas, where the church of Santa Maria degli Angeli houses the largest collection of religious wooden paintings in Sardinia. Continuing northeastwards, the railway soon starts to climb out of the green, cultivated valley into the Gallura Mountains, passing over the Coghinas River on a viaduct en route.

Crossing the mountains was a major engineering feat for the railway builders, requiring the construction of numerous viaducts and tunnels, including the spiral Bortigiadas Tunnel. The railway reaches its summit at Tempio Pausania, once the terminus of the line from Monti which closed in 1958. With an elevation of 1,857 ft, the town is the largest in the region and is famous for its numerous eighteenth-century granite buildings.

From Tempio the line begins its scenic descent through the mountains to the coast and Palau, serving stations at Calangianus and San Leonardo before crossing the Rio Piatto on a modern concrete viaduct. After calling at Arzachena, passengers are treated to fine views of the Gallura coastline and the La Maddalena archipelago before their train terminates at the pier-side station in Palau.

MANDAS TO ARBATAX

This tortuous 99-mile railway is the longest tourist line in Italy, if not in Europe, and is also one of the most spectacular. Much of its steeply graded, highly engineered, twisting and turning route to the east coast takes it across the forested Gennargentu Mountains. Trains depart from Mandas station – also served by regular narrow-gauge trains from Cagliari – in a northwards direction before branching off eastwards at the junction of the line to Sorgono (see below). Twisting and turning through the hills the railway reaches its first stop at the village of Orroli, so-named after the downy oak trees that grow in this area. The village lies in a hollow on the Pranemuru Plateau and is rich in archaeological sites including five Bronze Age towers, or *nuraghi*, From Orroli the railway heads north to Nurri then swings east again to Villanovatulo station before crossing the man-made Lake Flumendosa on a long road/rail bridge. After climbing out of the Flumendosa Valley on a gradient of 1-in-30 the railway winds round the hills to head north up to Betilli, Esterzili and Sadali-Seulo, the latter a medieval village famous for its magnificent waterfall.

Continuing on its tortuous route through the Gennargentu Mountains the railway then heads east through a series of tunnels and across viaducts to Seui, famous for its Art Nouveau museum and also a lunch stop for the tourist trains, followed by Anulu, Ussassi and Gairo. Once the junction for the short branch line to Jerzu, which closed in 1956, much of the historic centre of Gairo still lies ruined following a disastrous flood in 1951. From here the railway heads north through a lunar landscape to Villagrande before turning southeastwards down the side of the Siccaderba Valley to Arzana from where passengers first glimpse the sea to the east. Set below the highest mountain peaks in Sardinia, the ancient village of Arzana lies at the centre of numerous archaeological sites and is famous for its *culurgionis* (tasty ravioli made with local cheese).

From Arzana the railway continues its descent from the mountains via a 360-degree spiral and a horseshoe curve to reach the attractive hill town of Lanusei. After crossing a curving viaduct the railway descends to the coast, first northwards to Elini-Ilboso and Sella-Elecci and then eastwards to meet the coastal plain at the town of Tortoli. From here it is but a short distance to the harbour-side terminus at Arbatax, a small coastal town famous for its distinctive red rocks and porphyritic granite.

from Mandas to Isili. Surrounded by Neolithic archaeological sites, the small town of Isili lies on the edge of a plateau overlooking the Sarcidano Valley and is famous for its feast of San Giovanni Battista in June. The 'Trenino Verde' train heads north from here along the Mannu Valley to Sarcidano, the junction of the line to Villacidro until 1956 – much of this long-closed route is now a footpath and cycleway.

Continuing to climb northwards into the mountains the railway serves the isolated settlements of Nurallo – a centre of bronze casting several thousand years ago – followed by Cignoni and Sulau, before reaching the village of Laconi – birthplace of St Ignatius, the Saint of the Sardinians. Here, surrounded by ilex and oak woods, the grounds of Aymerich Park contain the remains of an ancient ruined castle. Leaving Laconi the railway twists and turns along the hillsides, climbing to Funtanameia, the first summit at Ortuabis, then descending to the ancient hill town of Meana Sardo. Set amidst hills rich with vineyards, the town is famous for its Bronze Age *nuraghi* and Roman archaeological sites.

Leaving Meana Sardo the railway levels out through S'Arcu Tunnel, at 3,277 ft the longest on the line, before reaching the pretty station at Belvi-Aritzo, nestled at the foot of the Gennargentu Mountains. A popular tourist centre, the nearby village of Aritzo is famous for its pure mountain springs and mineral water while the village of Belvi, set on a wooded ridge thick with hazelnut, walnut and chestnut trees, is home to a natural history museum. After reaching the summit of the line at Desulo-Tonara the railway twists and turns through tunnels and across viaducts before reaching the end of the line at Sorgono. Set amidst dense woodland on the western edge of the Gennargentu National Park, this ancient village is renowned for its numerous archaeological sites and its locally produced wines including the famous Mandrolisai.

MANDAS TO SORGONO

The first part of this 60-mile railway journey through the woods and mountains of Barbagia and Mandrolisai is taken using the regular narrow-gauge service northwards

RIGHT: Reggiane 2-6-2T No. 402 crosses the viaduct at San Cristofolo between Seri and Gairo with a mixed train on the mountainous route between Mandas and Arbatax on 8 April 2003.

FERROCARRIL DE SÓLLER
MAJORCA, SPAIN

GAUGE: 3 FT • **LENGTH:** 17 MILES •
ROUTE: PALMA TO SÓLLER

Originally steam-operated and opened on the same day that the *'Titanic'* sank, the picturesque and heavily engineered railway between the capital of Majorca, Palma, and the north coast port of Sóller was electrified in 1929. Tunnelling deep under the Alfabia mountains, the railway offers visitors to the island a memorable journey in 85-year-old rolling stock.

SPAIN

MENORCA
(MINORCA)

Pta Nati
Cap Menorca
Ciutadella de Menorca
Sant Joan Gran ○ Ferreries
Cap d'Artrutx Cala Santa
Galdana

MALLORCA
(MAJORCA)

Punta Beca
Cap de Formentor

Morro   Port de Pollença
de sa Vaca   Pollença   *Badia de Pollença*
                 (Pollensa)   *Cap des Pinar*
         Escorca   Alcúdia
Port de Sóller   *Puig Major*   ○ Lago Menor
         Sóller   1445   *Cap*
                                   Sa Pobla   *Ferrutx*
Valldemossa   Selva (La Puebla) *Badia*   *Cap*
                                      Muro   *d'Alcúdia* *des Freu*
Banyalbufar   Bunyola   Alaró   ○   ○ Can Picafort   *Punta*
Esporles   ○ Consell Lloseta Llubí Colònia   *de Capdepera*
Puig de Galatzó   Binissalem   de Sant Pere Cala Ratjada
    △ 1026   Sencelles ○ Sineu   Santa Margalida Artà Capdepera
Sa Dragonera   La Cabaneta Petra Son Servera
Sant Elm   Calvià   □ **Palma de Mallorca** Sant Llorenç Cala
Port d'Andratx Andratx   Montuïri des Cardassar Millor *Badia*
                                                         de Son Servera
Cap de sa Mola Peguera Palmanova ✈ Algaida Vilafranca Manacor *Punta Amer*
          Magalluf Can Pastilla *Badia* Porreres de Bonany   Porto Cristo
          ○ Portals Vells S'Arenal *de Palma*
Cap de Cala   Llucmajor   Felanitx   *Puig*
Figuera   (Lluchmayor)   *de Sant Salvador*
                           ○ Badia Gran   Campos   △ 510 Cala Murada
                  S'Estanyol   Portocolom
                  de Migjorn   Santanyí   Cala d'Or
Cap Blanc   Ses   Porto Petro
                   Colònia   Salines   Cala Figuera
                   de Sant Jordi
                              Cap de ses
                              Salines

Serra de Tramuntana

Borges

Es Cap Enderrocat

Sa Punta Plana

ISLAS BALEARES
(BALEARIC ISLANDS)

ILLES
BALEARS

Freu de Cabrera
Es Cap des Llebeig   *Illa des Conills*
Illa de Cabrera
      Parc Nacional
      Archipiélago de Cabrera

The first railway to be built on the Spanish Mediterranean island of Majorca opened over a distance of eighteen miles between the capital, Palma, and Inca in 1875. By 1921 there was a network of 3-ft-gauge lines radiating out from Palma to Arta, La Puebla, Felanixt and Santanay. Meanwhile, in the north of the island, the growing town and port of Sóller, the centre of a booming orange and lemon trade, remained isolated from the capital by the Alfabia mountain range. The journey involved a stagecoach trip along a steep, winding and narrow dirt track across the mountains via the Sóller Pass. Inns were provided along the route, where travellers and horses rested and received refreshment.

The growing clamour for a Palma to Sóller railway led to several proposals being put forward by leading local businessmen at the end of the nineteenth and beginning of the twentieth centuries. Eventually a direct route was chosen that would take the railway northwards from Palma and across the plains before tunnelling under the Alfabia mountains directly below the Sóller Pass. Construction work started from both ends of the line in 1907 and by the following year the work team, which started from Palma, had reached the mountains. Here a 9,370-ft-long tunnel (a total of thirteen tunnels were excavated along the entire route of the railway) was excavated under Sóller Pass and in August 1911 the contractor's steam locomotive 'Maria Luisa' (built by the Falcon Works at Loughborough, England in 1891) had reached the Mirador de's Pujol de'n Banya viewing point. From here the railway dropped down to Sóller through a series of sharp curves, the Cinc-Ponts Viaduct and the Cinc-Cents Tunnel.

The completed railway was opened on 16 April 1912, the same day that the *'Titanic'* sank after hitting an iceberg in the Atlantic Ocean. Motive power for the railway was provided by three powerful 2-6-0 tank locomotives manufactured by Maquinista Terrestre y Marítima of Barcelona, which were named 'Sóller', 'Palma' and 'Buñola'. A fourth locomotive, 'Son Sardina' was delivered from the same manufacturers in 1913. By that time the railway's rolling stock consisted of ten carriages built by Carde & Escoriaza of Zaragoza. A 3-mile long 3-ft-gauge electric tramway opened between Sóller station and Port de Sóller on 4 October 1913 (*see* page 45).

(*see* page 45)

PREVIOUS PAGE: A 1929-built electric train slowly crosses the Cinc-Ponts Viaduct in the mountains of northern Majorca on the scenic Ferrocarril de Sóller between Palma and the port of Sóller.

The Ferrocarril de Sóller was electrified in 1929 using the 1,200 V DC system with current collected from an overhead conductor. The current for the railway is carried from Palma in a high-tension line to Buñola, midway on the route, where it is transformed from 15,000 V to 1,200 V. Four electric driving cars and ten trailers were built for this new service by Carde y Escoriaza of Zaragoza and they are still in use today. Another transformer at Sóller further reduces the voltage to 500 for the Sóller Tram.

Despite past closures one of Majorca's other railways is still operational. Now operated by Serveis Ferroviaris de Mallorca, the recently electrified metre-gauge line from Palma to Manacor is currently being extended to Artà while a proposed extension of the Sa Pobla branch to Alcudia is under consideration. With a total of 53 route miles, the company also operates the Palma Metro which opened in 2007.

The Ferrocarril de Sóller still operates the original electric driving cars and coaches that were supplied to the railway in 1929. Trains operate all year round with a more intensive service between March and October. Palma railway station – considered by many to be one of the most beautiful buildings on Majorca – is located alongside a park close to the Plaça de Espanya, and from here trains head northwards across the plains to Buñola, calling en route at the little halts of Son Sardina, Apeadero de Son Reus, Apeadero de Santa Maria and Apeadero de Caubet. Nine miles from Palma in the foothills of the Alfabia mountain range, the small town of Buñola features a picturesque square.

North of Buñola the railway starts its climb up into the Alfabia mountains, passing under the Sóller Pass via the long Túnel Major, the longest of the thirteen tunnels on the line. From here it begins its descent to Sóller, first calling at the famous viewing point of Mirador des Pujol d'En Banya, from where there are panoramic views of the Sóller Valley and the mountains, before heading west to cross the Cinc-Ponts viaduct which carries the line across the Monreals torrent. The line then follows a winding route through the 1,739-ft-long Son Angelats Tunnel, the second longest on the line, before doubling back on itself on the descent to Ca'n Tambor Halt and Sóller station. Here the railway company has its offices and workshops while a museum dedicated to Picasso and Joan Miró is located inside the attractive station building. The Sóller electric tramway connects the station with the Port de Sóller.

THE SÓLLER TRAM
MAJORCA, SPAIN
GAUGE: 3 FT · LENGTH: 3 MILES
ROUTE: SÓLLER TO PORT DE SÓLLER

Construction of the single-track electric Sóller tramway began after the opening of the railway from Palma. Opened on 4 October 1913, the only major engineering feature along its 3-mile route is an iron bridge over the Torrent Major. Three motor trams and two trailers were supplied originally by Carde & Escoriaza in Zaragoza but these were supplemented by open trailers purchased from the Palma street tramway in 1954. The tramway also owns five re-gauged motor trams from the Lisbon tramway in Portugal.

Although designed to carry passengers the tramway was also used to transport fish from the Port to Sóller station and coal in the opposite direction. The tramway has fourteen intermediate wayside halts between Sóller station and the terminus at La Payesa. The first, at Mercat, lies opposite the market and from there trams pass through orchards and gardens to Ca'n Guida where there is a passing loop. Ca'n Reus, named after the adjacent bar is next, followed by L'Horta, Monument, Ca'n Llimó, Ca n'Aí, Roca Roja and Es Control. Before the Spanish Civil War, the latter was a checkpoint to prevent smuggling and, later, when the port was a military base, became a security control point. Today, it is the jumping-off point for walks to Muleta, the lighthouse and Deià.

At Sa Torre the tramway reaches the coastline to continue its route around the Port along a promenade overlooking the beach. S'Espléndido, Las Palmeras, S'Eden and Ca'n Generós halts all follow before trams reach the penultimate halt at Marysol. This was the original tramway terminus, which was taken over during the Civil War as lodgings for Italian submarine officers who were based at the nearby dock. It now houses a restaurant.

Located close to the entrance to the military base, La Payasa is the present terminus of the tramway. Until 1975 the line extended into the base and was used exclusively by marines but before the Civil War it went even further onto the dockside for carrying oranges, lemons, locally made textiles and passengers that were then shipped from Port de Sóller to Marseilles and other Mediterranean ports.

The quaint Sóller Tramway hugs the sea wall along much of its 3-mile route between the station and the port.

THE DOURO VALLEY
PORTUGAL
GAUGE: 1,668 MM (5 FT 5 $^{21}/_{32}$ IN.) • **LENGTH:** 101 MILES •
ROUTE: ERMESINDE TO POCINHO

Home to the world-famous Port-wine industry, the highly scenic Douro Valley is served by a broad-gauge railway from Porto. Giving passengers breathtaking views of the river valley and its steep-sided vineyards, the railway carried international traffic to and from Spain until 1984 when the Spanish rail link was closed.

At 557 miles in length, the Douro River is the third longest in the Iberian Peninsula. It flows westwards from its source in Soria Province in northern Spain and into Portugal where it meets the Atlantic Ocean at the city of Porto. For seventy miles it forms the border between Spain and Portugal along a series of narrow canyons. In Portugal the Douro Valley supports the growing of almonds and olives but it is better known for its grapes, which grow on the steep sides of the valley and are used in making Port wine. The area around Pinhão and São João da Pesqueira is the centre of the Port-wine industry and part of the valley has been given World Heritage site status by UNESCO.

For centuries the river provided the main form of transport for wine growers but after the Second World War a series of five dams was built along it to generate hydroelectric power. Boats can still operate along the river via a series of five locks.

Portugal's first railway was opened between Lisbon and Carregado in 1856. Porto was eventually reached from Lisbon in 1877 when Gustave Eiffel's dramatic wrought-iron bridge over the Douro River was completed. The earliest railways in Portugal were built to the standard gauge of 4 ft 8½ in. but these were regauged in the late 1860s to be compatible with the Spanish gauge of 1,668 mm (5 ft 5²¹/₃₂ in.). The country also once had an extensive network of rural metre-gauge lines but the vast majority have now closed.

Meanwhile the railway from Viana do Castelo in northern Portugal had reached Porto in 1868. The first nineteen miles to Penafiel were opened on 29 July 1875 and by July 1879 it had crossed the Tâmega Valley (a tributary of the Douro) and reached the north bank of the Douro River in September 1878. The railway's route took it eastwards from here alongside the river on a series of spectacular ledges and through tunnels, reaching Peso da Régua in July 1879. Once inhabited by Roman settlers, the town grew in importance after 1836 when the products of the Douro Valley vineyards were recognized as a quality brand suitable for export.

From Peso da Régua the railway builders continued along the north bank of the narrowing Douro Valley reaching

Pinhão in June 1880, Tua in September 1883 and Pocinho in January 1887. Between Tua and Pocinho it crosses to the river's south bank on a spectacular viaduct. The final seventeen miles to the Spanish border near Barca D'Alva was opened in December 1887 and allowed through running of trains to and from the Spanish city of Salamanca via La Fuente de San Esteban.

The Douro Valley railway carried international traffic between Portugal and Spain until 1984 when the Spanish state-owned rail company RENFE closed the connecting line from La Fuente de San Esteban to the Portuguese border. The line terminated at Barca d'Alva until 1988 when it was further cut back to its present terminus at Pocinho.

The Douro Valley line remained steam operated until the late 1960s when a new fleet of diesel-electric locomotives were introduced. Still in service today, the first ten Class 1400 Bo-Bo locomotives were built by English Electric at its Vulcan Foundry in Lancashire, UK and a further fifty-seven were assembled in Portugal.

A journey by train along the Douro line offers passengers breathtaking views of the river valley and its vineyards. The valley is classified as a UNESCO World Heritage site and the train journey along it is considered to be the most scenic in Portugal.

Today's diesel-hauled trains for the Douro Valley depart from the impressive São Bento terminus in Porto. Opened in 1916, the station is beautifully decorated with large tile panels depicting landscapes and historical events. There are five return services to Pocinho with journey times varying from 3¾ hours to 3 hours 53 minutes.

A restored 2-8-4T steam locomotive built by Henschel in 1925 operates a tourist train of five vintage wooden coaches between Peso da Régua and Tua on Saturdays from the end of June to mid-October. The train also stops at Pinhão, allowing passengers time to visit the award-winning Wine House and admire the twenty-five blue-glazed tile panels that cover the main station building.

RIGHT: A single diesel railcar hugs the steep-sided upper Douro Valley near Tua.

OVERLEAF: A flashback to steam days with 4-6-0 No. 284 crossing the impressive viaduct over the Douro at Ferradosa with a long freight train from Barca d'Alva and Pocinho to Porto on on 10 June 1970.

PREVIOUS PAGE: A steam-hauled heritage train of vintage carriages crosses one of the many fine viaducts on the Douro Valley line in Portugal.

THE JUNGFRAU RAILWAY
SWITZERLAND

GAUGE: 1,000 MM (3 FT 3⅜ IN.) • **LENGTH:** 6 MILES •
ROUTE: KLEINE SCHEIDEGG TO JUNGFRAUJOCH

The Jungfrau railway was the brainchild of Swiss industrialist Adolf
Guyer-Zeller and since its completion in 1912 it has been Europe's
highest railway. Although most of the electric rack railway is in a tunnel,
passengers are treated to stunning vistas of the Bernese Alps and the
Aletsch Glacier from the summit station.

Located in the Bernese Alps, the Eiger (13,025 ft), the Mönch (13,474 ft) and the Jungfrau (13,642 ft) mountains are a formidable ridge of Alpine peaks that were first climbed in the nineteenth century. Lying between the Mönch and the Jungfrau is the Jungfraujoch, a mountain pass at the lowest point of the ridge which, today, can be reached only by experienced mountaineers or on the Jungfrau Railway.

Although there had been earlier proposals to build a mountain railway on the Jungfrau it took until 1894 before wealthy Swiss industrialist and engineer Adolf Guyer-Zeller came up with a viable proposition. His ambitious plan was to build an electric rack railway with around 80 per cent of its route in a tunnel inside the Mönch and Eiger mountains to a station at the summit of the Jungfrau. To finance this Guyer-Zeler founded the Bank Guyerzeller AG.

Meanwhile, the 800-mm-gauge Wengernalp rack-and-pinion railway had opened from Lauterbrunnen to Grindelwald via Kleine Scheidegg in 1893. Although originally steam operated, the 12-mile railway – the longest rack railway in the world – was electrified in 1909. At 6,782 ft, Kleine Scheidegg is a high mountain pass located below the Eiger and it was from the station here that construction work on the Jungfrau Railway started in 1896. Built to a gauge of 1,000 mm, the line was designed to be electrified with 3-phase electric power collected from two separate overhead supplies and a rail. With gradients as steep as 1-in-4, the Strub rack-and-pinion system was fitted: a toothed driving wheel beneath the locomotive engages a rail fitted with rack teeth positioned centrally between the tracks. In addition to this safety feature, the 3-phase electrical system also provides regenerative braking with the power fed back into the system. Electricity to drive the railway was generated by a hydroelectric power plant built by Guyer-Zeller near Kleine Scheidegg.

By 1898 the railway had opened as far as Eigergletscher station, at the foot of the Eiger. From here, construction of the tunnel was started using dynamite but the project was continually dogged by accidents, explosions, deaths of workers, labour unrest and bad weather. Adolf Guyer-

PREVIOUS PAGE: The lower terminus of the Jungfrau Railway at Kleine Scheidegg is dwarfed by the twin peaks of the Mönch and Eiger.

A 2-car electric train heads away from Kleine Scheidegg station on the first part of its steep journey up to Jungfraujoch station.

Zeller died in April 1899 but progress continued albeit slowly. The railway opened to a temporary station at Rotstock in August 1899 followed by viewing platforms at Eigerwand station in 1903 and Eismeer station in 1905. A massive accidental dynamite explosion at Eismeer station in 1908 killed a number of workers.

Finally, sixteen years after construction work began, the tunnel to Jungfraujoch station was opened in 1912: at 11,332 ft above sea level the station was, and still is, the highest railway station in Europe. After Guyer-Zeller had died the goal of reaching the summit of the Jungfrau had been quietly dropped.

Once the railway had opened there were further developments on the Jungfraujoch including a tourist mountain house that opened in 1924, a research station in 1931 and the Sphinx Observatory in 1937. In more recent years an atmospheric research station, a radio relay station and a restaurant and exhibition centre have also opened near the station.

Railway travellers to the Jungfraujoch on Europe's highest railway are treated to sensational views of the eastern Bernese Alps and the Aletsch Glacier which, as part of the Jungfrau-Aletsch Protected Area, was declared a UNESCO World Heritage site in 2001.

Electric trains for Jungfraujoch depart from Kleine Scheidegg station, which can be reached from

Nestling beneath the Eiger, Kleine Scheidegg station is the lower terminus of the Jungfrau Railway and is also served by trains from Grindelwald and Lauterbrunnen on the Wengernalp Railway.

Grindelwald and Lauterbrunnen on the Wengernalp Railway. Overall journey time on the Jungfrau Railway to the summit station is around fifty minutes and snow-blowing equipment is used to keep the lower open-air section of the line functioning in winter. After calling at Eigergletscher station, where the railway has its workshop, trains climb steeply into the tunnel before calling at Eigerwand station where passengers alight to enjoy the scenery from the glass-fronted viewing platform which was used as a location in the 1975 action film 'The Eiger Sanction'. From here the train continues its steep climb up through the tunnel to another glass-fronted viewing platform at Eismeer station. The final stretch to Jungfraujoch is less steep and was worked purely by adhesion until 1951 when the rack system was extended.

A series of tunnels and a lift link the station with the Jungfraujoch's tourist attractions such as the summit of the Sphinx, the Top of Europe building, the Ice Palace and the Alpine Sensation.

OVERLEAF: Europe's highest-altitude railway station was opened on 1 August (Swiss National Day) in 1912. At 11,333 ft above sea level, the scenically spectacular Jungfrau Railway carries passengers up to Jungfraujoch station in all weathers.

ALBULA RAILWAY
SWITZERLAND

GAUGE: 1,000 MM (3 FT ⅜ IN.) • **LENGTH:** 55 MILES •
ROUTE: CHUR TO ST MORITZ

A remarkable feat of railway engineering, the electrified metre-gauge route from Chur to the ski resort of St Moritz must rate as one of the most spectacular railway journeys in the world. Featuring numerous spiral tunnels and soaring viaducts, the railway burrows through the mountains in a 3-mile 1,056-yd-long tunnel beneath the Albula Pass.

The city of Chur, the capital of the Canton of Graubunden in southeast Switzerland, was first reached by the United Swiss Railways (USR), which opened a standard-gauge line from Rorschach on the southern shore of Lake Constance and along the Upper Rhine Valley via Landquart in 1858. It then took nearly forty years before a railway penetrated the mountainous terrain of the canton, which by then was becoming a popular destination for well-heeled Europeans. The first railway to overcome this physical barrier was the metre-gauge Landquart-Davos Railway, which opened up the Landquart Valley to Klosters and Davos in 1890. Initially steam hauled, it was an instant success turning both towns it served into popular year-round tourist destinations. The USR changed its name to Rhaetian Railway in 1895 and was nationalized in 1902.

The success of the new railway to Davos soon led to proposals for a line to connect Chur with the growing winter resort of St Moritz in the south of the canton, which even at the end of the nineteenth century could only be reached by a long and tiring stagecoach journey. Between Chur and St Moritz lay deep valleys and the Albula Alps which have sixteen peaks over 10,000 ft high, the highest being Piz Kesch (11,288 ft).

After considering various proposals for narrow- and standard-gauge lines the Swiss Government finally decided to build a metre-gauge railway up the Albula Valley from Thusis and through the Albula Alps to St Moritz. The first part of the route had already been opened from Landquart, the Rhaetian Railway's headquarters, to Chur and then southwards along the Hinterrhein Valley to Thusis in 1896. Construction work on the new railway started in 1898 and as steam power was to be used the maximum gradient allowed was 1-in-35. To stay within this limit, the ambitious railway engineers planned to build curving and spiral tunnels and numerous viaducts.

A remarkable feat of railway engineering, the single-track line opened between Thusis and Celerina, on the outskirts of St Moritz, in 1903 with the final section into the resort being opened one year later. Climbing over 3,500 ft in thirty-eight miles, the railway has a total of thirty-nine tunnels, including the 3-mile 1,056-yd-long Albula Tunnel

and the 2,165-ft-long Rugnux Spiral Tunnel, and fifty-five bridges and viaducts, of which the iconic 213-ft-high curving Landwasser Viaduct is by far the most famous.

The Albula Railway was a great success but shortages of coal during the First World War and the availability of cheap hydroelectric power led to the line's electrification with overhead power lines in 1919. In 1930 the 'Glacier Express' was introduced between Zermatt and St Moritz during the summer months, its route taking it via the Albula Railway. After the Second World War the 'Bernina Express' was introduced between Chur and St Moritz and thence on to Tirano in northern Italy via the Bernina Railway.

Between 1921 and the early 1980s the famous 'Crocodile' electric locomotives were the mainstay of services on the Albula line. Although officially withdrawn from service, two examples have been preserved to haul occasional special trains along the route.

Both owned and operated by the Rhaetian Railway, the Albula Railway and the Bernina Railway were jointly listed as a UNESCO World Heritage site in 2008.

In addition to the 'Bernina Express' and the 'Glacier Express' and a regular interval passenger service that operates all year round between Chur and St Moritz, the Albula line also carries significant freight traffic. Other passenger trains include car transporter wagons between Thusis and Samedan, near St Moritz, while glass-topped panorama cars were introduced on the popular 'Glacier Express' in 1986.

Electric trains depart from Thusis station to cross the Hinterrhein River and head east up the Albula Valley, first passing Sils im Domleschg station before burrowing through a series of nine tunnels over less than four miles to reach Solis station. From here trains continue up the narrowing steep-sided valley, crossing Solis Viaduct and passing through four more tunnels to reach Tiefencastel station, followed by stations at the villages of Surava and Alvaneu. Continuing eastwards the line takes a dramatic route across the 115-ft-high Schmittentobal Viaduct, the curving 213-ft-high Landwasser Viaduct and through two tunnels to reach Filisur, junction for the electrified metre-gauge line to Davos.

After the stop at Filisur the railway heads southeastwards on its climb through the mountains, passing through no

Autumn in the Alps - a passenger train on the metre-gauge Albula Railway passes the village of Bergün, 4,501 ft above sea level, on its journey between Chur and St Moritz.

less than thirteen tunnels including one spiral tunnel before reaching Bergün station, 4,501 ft above sea level. The following four miles to Preda become even more dramatic with the railway climbing up through no less than ten tunnels including three spiral tunnels and across seven viaducts. After Preda the railway enters the 3-mile 1,056-yd-long Albula Tunnel, taking it below the Albula Pass and reaching the summit of the line at 5,954 ft above sea level, before emerging at Spinas. Beyond here the railway descends to Bever, where the Engadine Line from

Scuol joins from the east, and then to Samedan, junction for Pontresina and the Bernina Railway to Tirano.

From Samedan, trains heads off southwestwards for the final leg through Celerina and two more tunnels before ending their spectacular journey at St Moritz. The resort town has grown from its early beginnings in the 1860s to become, thanks to the coming of the railway at the beginning of the twentieth century, one of the most popular (and expensive) winter ski resorts in the world.

OVERLEAF: Located in a UNESCO World Heritage site and on the route of the Glacier Express, the iconic, curving Landwasser Viaduct carries the Albula Railway 213 ft above the Landwasser River between Schmitten and Filisur.

LE PETIT TRAIN JAUNE/ LIGNE DE CERDANGE

FRANCE

GAUGE: 1,000 MM (3 FT 3⅜ IN.) • **LENGTH:** 39 MILES •
ROUTE: VILLEFRANCHE-DE-CONFLENT TO LATOUR DE CAROL

Yellow-painted electric trains take passengers on a highly scenic journey along this narrow-gauge line that climbs up the steep-sided and wooded Têt Valley into the French Pyrenees. Never far from the border with Spain, the railway, which opened throughout in 1927, features France's highest railway station.

Set in the region of Catalonia that straddles the French/Spanish border, the historic walled town of Villefranche-de-Conflent lies in the foothills of the eastern Pyrenees in southwest France at an altitude of 1,444 ft above sea level. With its source in the Pyrenees, the River Têt flows past the town in a northwesterly direction on its 72-mile journey to the Mediterranean Sea which it joins to the west of the city of Perpignan. Villefranche-de-Conflent is also connected to Perpignan by a standard-gauge railway operated by SNCF.

By the end of the nineteenth century the boom in tourism across Europe had led to the building of numerous scenic mountain railways in countries as far apart as Switzerland and North Wales. Building a railway up into the Pyrenees through the Cerdagne from Villefranche-de-Conflent was first proposed at this time and construction work started in 1903. Unusually, the metre-gauge line was electrified using power generated by small hydroelectric power stations on the River Têt – the 850 V DC current is collected via the train's pick-up shoes running on a separate conductor rail.

Construction of the steeply graded line up the steep-sided Têt Valley was slow and involved the building of nineteen tunnels, the unusual suspension bridge at Pont Gisclard

between Sauto and Planès and the curving stone Viaduc Séjourné. By 1910 the railway had reached the small commune of Mont-Louis, 4,974 ft above sea level. Further work on the line was delayed by the onset of the First World War but after its end construction continued up through the mountains to the summit of the line at Bolquère-Eyne – at 5,226 ft above sea level the highest station in France. From here the railway drops down to a Pyrenean plateau to terminate at the commune of Latour-de-Carol, reached in 1927. Here, on the French/Spanish border, the Spanish broad-gauge line from Barcelona also met the now-closed French standard-gauge line from Toulouse. Before the closure of the French line the station was the only one in the world to be served by three different gauges.

The electric train has been a great success with tourists both in summer and winter and also provided a lifeline for some of the Cerdagne's isolated villages. Trains operate as multiple units, including some of the original versions, which are painted a canary yellow with a red horizontal band, the colours of the Catalan flag, giving rise to the nickname Le Petit Train Jaune. During the summer months open carriages are coupled between two sets of multiple units.

PREVIOUS PAGE: A yellow electric train on the Ligne de Cerdagne in the French Pyrenees crosses the unusual Pont Gisclard suspension bridge in the heavily wooded Têt Valley.

A 4-car electric train crosses the suspension bridge at Fontpedrouse between Thuès-Caranca and Sauto stations on the metre-gauge Ligne de Cerdagne in the French Pyrenees.

During the summer months the third-rail electric trains of the Ligne de Cerdagne, seen here near the historic village of Mont Louis, include an open passenger car.

Popular with walkers and mountain bikers in the summer and skiers in the winter, this highly scenic 39-mile railway is today operated by the French state-owned railway SNCF. The starting point is at the town of Villefranche-de-Conflent, which is now listed as a UNESCO World Heritage site for its defensive town walls built by the military engineer Vauban in the early eighteenth century. The most spectacular part of the railway is from Villefranche up to the ski resort of Font-Romeu-Odeillo-Via as the line closely hugs the steep sides of the Têt Valley, winding up between forests, gorges and mountain streams. From Villefranche the railway heads southwestwards up the valley calling at the small villages of Serdinya, Joncet, Nyer, Thuès-Entre-Valls, Thuès-Caranca (for a precarious trail and walkway along the gorge), Fontpédrouse, and Sauto, then crosses the unusual Pont Gisclard suspension bridge en route to Planès and Mont-Louis. Here, the castle and fortified walls (the highest in France) built by Vauban in the early eighteenth century are also listed as a UNESCO World Heritage site. The nearby Mont-Louis Solar Furnace, built in 1949, was the first to be built in the world.

From Mont-Louis the railway continues its climb to the summit at Bolquère-Eyne station before calling at Font-Romeu-Odeillo-Via, the oldest ski resort in the Pyrenees and home to the world's largest solar furnace. It then parallels the border with Spain, descending to the villages of Estavar, Saillagouse, Err, Sainte-Léocadie, Osséja, the border town of Bourg-Madame (about half a mile from the twelfth-century Spanish town of Puigcerda), Ur-les-Escalade and Béna Fanès before ending at Latour-de-Carol. Journey time along the entire route is around three hours.

OVERLEAF: The wonderfully ornate, castellated viaduct at Sejourne carries Le Petit Train Jaune high across the steep-sided Têt Valley in the French Pyrenees.

OSLO TO BERGEN
NORWAY

GAUGE: 4 FT 8½ IN. • **LENGTH:** 308 MILES •
ROUTE: OSLO TO BERGEN

Connecting Norway's two largest cities and the highest mainline railway
in Northern Europe, the Bergen to Oslo railway has had its route
modified several times since it opened in 1909. Electrified since 1964,
the railway was always at the mercy of heavy winter snowfalls on the
high and exposed Hardangervidda Plateau until the opening of a
6½-mile tunnel in 1993.

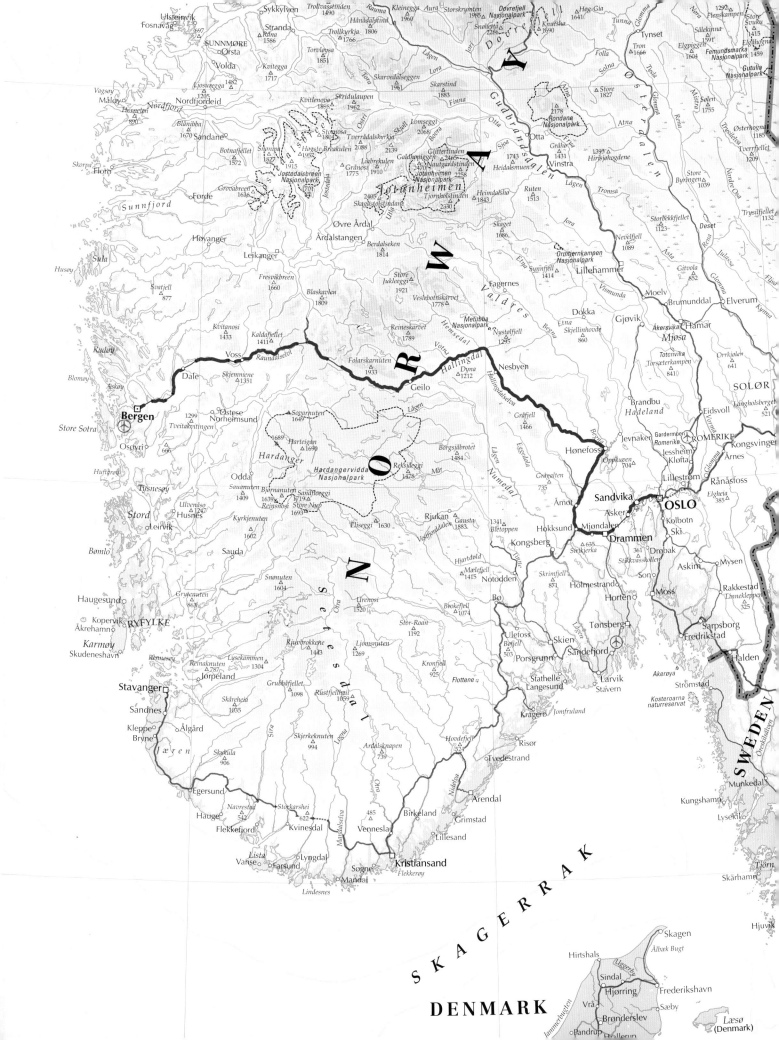

Bergen is the second largest city in Norway and for centuries has been the country's principal port, its sheltered harbour one of the busiest in Europe with important links across the North Sea to Britain. The 308-mile mainline between the city, on the west coast of Norway, to the capital, Oslo, began life as a 66-mile narrow-gauge railway built by gangs of Swedish navvies. Construction of the 3-ft 6-in.-gauge Voss Line, as it was known, started in 1876 with completion eastwards from Bergen to Voss in 1883. In the same year the railway became part of the newly formed Norwegian State Railways.

Meanwhile there had been several proposals put forward to build a railway between Norway's two largest cities but the country's economic woes of the 1880s and early 1890s saw no progress until the Norwegian Parliament voted in favour of a standard-gauge line in 1894. From west to east the route that was chosen was from Bergen to Voss, rebuilding the existing Voss Line to standard gauge, from Voss to Roa via Honefoss on a new line, and from Roa to Oslo, on the existing Gjovik Line.

With surveying and finance in place, construction work started from both ends in 1902. Progress was slow through the difficult terrain, there were no roads and during the winter heavy snowfalls held up work for months. The heavily engineered single-track line required over 100 tunnels, including the 3-mile 528-yd Gravehalsen Tunnel which had to be excavated through extremely hard rock. The railway was eventually opened throughout by King Haakon VII in 1909.

During the Second World War a 12-mile steeply graded branch line was opened from Myrdal, on the Bergen Line, to the port of Flåm at the head of Sognefjord. Surviving threatened closure in the 1990s, this highly scenic route is now one of the most popular tourist attractions in Norway (see pages 74-79).

While steam power had been replaced by diesels in 1958, electrification of the railway using the abundant natural resource of hydroelectric power took until 1964 when the whole route was 'switched on' using overhead current collected by pantographs on the locomotives' roofs.

When built, the western section of the line inland from Bergen took a very circuitous route to avoid what was then an impassable mountain barrier. However, with modern tunnelling techniques the route was considerably shortened after the opening of the 4-mile 1,320-yd Ulriken Tunnel and two shorter tunnels in 1964. An 11-mile section of the original route is now operated as a heritage railway (see feature box on page 73).

At the eastern end of the Bergen Line the Oslo Tunnel was opened in 1980 but, while serving a more populated area, trains between Oslo and Bergen had their journeys extended by 14 miles through Drammen via the tunnel instead of along the more direct route via Roa.

The 4,268-ft summit of the Bergen Line lay between Finse and Hallingskeid and this heavily exposed section had always caused operating problems during winter months when snowfall often blocked the line. This was overcome in 1993 when the 14-mile section was replaced by a 6½-mile tunnel which, along with line upgrades either side, allowed operating speeds to be substantially increased. The track of the original route across the Hardangervidda Plateau can be seen from the Rallarvegen, the old railway navvies' road built in 1902 which, since 1974, has become a popular route for mountain bikers during the snow-free months between July and October.

The Bergen Line is not only one of the most scenic standard-gauge railways in Europe, it is also the highest mainline in the north of the continent. The electrified line is used by Norwegian State Railways' express trains (including an overnight service), mainly locomotive-hauled, between Bergen and Oslo via Drammen and commuter services between Bergen and Voss with some of the latter extended to Myrdal for passengers wishing to travel on the Flåm Line. Freight services between Bergen and Oslo are operated by CargoNet but these travel along the original route via Roa.

The passenger termini at each end of the line are grand affairs. Opened in 1913 to replace an earlier station, Bergen station has a large overall glass curved roof and four platforms. The much larger and modern Oslo Central station, which opened in 1980, incorporates the original Oslo East station built in 1882. The highest and remotest station on the line is at Finse (4,010 ft above sea level) where there is a museum dedicated to the navvies who built the railway. With no road access, the station is popular with walkers on the Aurlandsdalen hiking trail that ends in the UNESCO World Heritage site of Næoyfjord.

PREVIOUS PAGE: Viewed from the Rallarvegan – the old railway navvies road - the route of the Bergen Railway across the high Hardangervidda Plateau was bypassed by the opening of a 6½-mile tunnel in 1993.

OLD VOSS LINE

The opening of the Ulriken Tunnel near Bergen in 1964 shortened journeys between the city and Oslo by fourteen miles. The original circuitous route was then closed but since then eleven miles of the line between Games and Midtun have been reopened as a steam-operated heritage railway. Known as the 'Old Voss Line', it operates vintage tourist trains between June and September, hauled by restored Norwegian State Railways Class 18 4-6-0 No. 255 that was built for use on the Bergen Line in 1913.

FLOIBANEN

Opened in 1918, the Floibanen is a ½-mile, metre-gauge, cable-operated funicular railway that runs from Bergen up to the Floyen from where, at 1,394 ft above sea level, there are panoramic views across the city and its harbour.

Seen in this night shot with the lights of Bergen harbour far below, the Floibanen is a funicular railway giving access to the Floyen, a local viewpoint.

THE FLÅM RAILWAY
NORWAY/AURLAND
GAUGE: 4 FT 8½ IN. • **LENGTH:** 12½ MILES •
ROUTE: MYRDAL TO FLÅM

The most steeply graded standard-gauge adhesion railway in Europe, the Flåm Railway took eighteen years to build and features twenty tunnels on its electrified route down to Aurlandsfjord. Today it is one of the most popular tourist attractions in Norway and a regular onshore destination for cruise liner passengers.

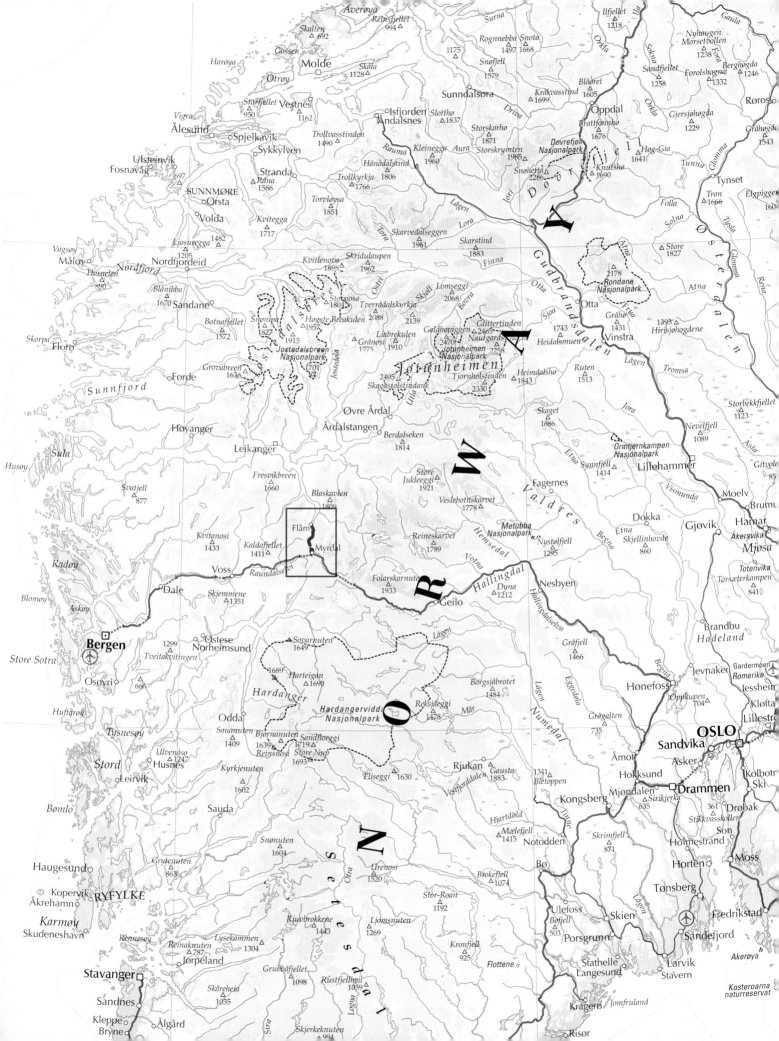

The village of Flåm is located in western Norway at the inner end of Aurlandsfjord, itself an arm of the Sognefjord. A popular tourist destination since the nineteenth century, Flåm remained virtually inaccessible overland until the Second World War, when the heavily engineered railway from Myrdal, 12½ miles over the mountains to the south, was completed. Myrdal is a station on the 231-mile Bergen Line (*see* pages 70-73) that was opened in 1909 between Norway's two major cities, Oslo and Bergen. A feat of engineering in itself, the Bergen Line crossed the Hardangervidda plateau at a height of over 4,000 ft above sea level, making it the highest mainline railway in Northern Europe. The single-track line had been electrified by 1964.

Even before the Bergen Line was completed, engineering surveys had been carried out in 1893 for a narrow-gauge railway to Flåm. The steeply graded line would have included a rack section with a gradient of 1-in-10. This proposal came to nothing and nor did two other alternatives that were put forward in the early twentieth century. The route of the Flåm Line that we know today was finally approved by the Norwegian Parliament in 1916, but it was not until 1923 that construction work started, by which time the estimated cost had rocketed thanks to high inflation during the First World War. Despite the steep gradients involved the decision was also taken to build a purely adhesion standard-gauge line using electric traction.

From Myrdal to Flåm the railway had to descend 2,833 ft through difficult mountainous terrain with a maximum gradient of 1-in-18 via a series of twenty tunnels. This was no mean feat, especially as the vast majority of tunnels were dug by hand through solid rock aided by dynamite for blasting. Landslides and avalanches were common and often involved diverting the railway along a new course. Progress therefore was incredibly slow, especially as the workforce averaged only 200 men – the first tunnel was completed in 1926 and the final one in 1935. A total of ten stations were finally built with the only passing loop on the single-track line being installed at Berekvam.

Once the tunnels had been completed, work commenced on laying track in 1936, but the German invasion of Norway in April 1940 temporarily brought a halt to

proceedings. The Germans were keen to complete the line so track laying was speeded up, allowing a freight service to start in August 1940 followed by a passenger service in February 1941. Trains were initially steam-hauled until electric traction was introduced in November 1944 when a new hydroelectric scheme came into operation. Following the end of the Second World War the Flåm Line (as it was then officially known) saw a rapid increase in traffic. Post-war tourism was in its infancy but by the mid-1950s the Flåm Line had become a popular destination with its rail connections from Bergen and Oslo. Passengers from cruise ships that called at Flåm also took a ride on the line while a sleeping car train was introduced in 1958 between Oslo and Flåm. Passenger traffic continued to increase through the 1960s and 1970s until levelling out during the 1980s but by then freight traffic had been lost to road transport.

By the early 1990s the Norwegian State Railways was losing money on the Flåm Line so ticket prices were doubled and threatened closure was narrowly averted. Day-to-day operations of the line were privatized in 1997 and a new cruise ship terminal was built adjacent to Flåm station.

Today, the highly scenic Flåm Line operates mainly for tourists and is the third most popular tourist attraction in the country. The service operates throughout the year with a more frequent pattern between May and September. All trains are topped and tailed by Class El 17 locomotives built by Thyssen-Henschel in 1987 – these Bo-Bo locomotives have a combined power output of 8,000 hp and consequently have no problem tackling the gradients on what is the steepest standard-gauge adhesion railway in Europe.

From Myrdal's remote junction station (2,833 ft above sea level) trains for Flåm first parallel the Oslo main line then head down into the Flåmsdalen Valley, passing through two tunnels before reaching Vatnahalsen station. From here they loop around a horseshoe curve to Reinunga station before burrowing through the 2,890-ft-long Vatnahalsen Tunnel to emerge on a mountainside ledge hundreds of feet above the valley floor. Three more tunnels follow in quick succession before trains halt at Kjosfossen, jumping-off point for a spectacular 738-ft-high waterfall.

From Kjosfossen trains pass through two tunnels, the second of which is Nåli Tunnel, the longest on the line at 4,401 ft. Kardal station, Blomheller Tunnel,

PREVIOUS PAGE: Hauled by a powerful Class El 17 electric locomotive a train heads up the steeply-graded Flåm Railway close to the 482-ft-high Rjoandefossen waterfall.

76   EUROPE

Cruise ships calling at a new terminal adjacent to the railway station at Flåm provide the majority of customers for the Flåm Railway.

Blomheller station and four more tunnels follow before the train arrives at Berekvam station (1,129 ft above sea level), where up and down trains cross on the only passing loop. From Berekvam the train continues downhill through five more tunnels and over the Hoga River to arrive at Dalsbotn station. The valley then starts to widen out as trains pass through the last two tunnels on the line, close to the 482-ft-high Rjoandefossen waterfall. Håreina and Lunden station then follow before the train ends its spectacular journey at Flåm station. The adjacent cruise liner terminal is visited by over 150 ships each year, which along with the railway ensure the economic survival of the small village. The original station building here is now a railway museum.

OVERLEAF: Justifiably, the Flåm Railway is one of Norway's top tourist attractions. To cope with gradients as steep as 1-in-18 the passenger trains are topped and tailed by powerful Class E1 17 electric locomotives.

WEST HIGHLAND LINE
SCOTLAND, UNITED KINGDOM

GAUGE: 4 FT 8½ IN. • **LENGTH:** 123 MILES •
ROUTE: GLASGOW TO FORT WILLIAM

Opened in 1894, the West Highland Line traverses some of the most remote, inaccessible and untamed countryside in Britain and rightly deserves the title of one of the most scenic railway journeys in the world.

Justifiably rated as one of the most scenic railway journeys in the world, the West Highland Line was a latecomer to the railway scene in Britain. By the latter part of the nineteenth century railways had spread their tentacles to virtually every part of the land except the West Highlands in Scotland. Crossed by glens and lochs, this sparsely populated mountainous region was first tamed by the Victorian railway builders in 1863 when the Inverness & Perth Junction Railway (later to become the Highland Railway) opened between Perth and Inverness. This was followed in 1880 by the Caledonian Railway-backed Callander & Oban Railway (C&OR), the first railway to serve the rugged west coast of Scotland, which previously could only be reached by a long and difficult boat journey from Glasgow. The railway brought enormous benefits to the region; for the first time fresh fish and livestock could be transported in under a day to Scotland's industrial central belt and tourism boomed, with Oban becoming the gateway to the Western Isles.

None of this success was lost on the rival North British Railway, which also had its eye on conquering the Highlands by building a railway from Glasgow to Inverness via Fort William. The proposed route would have taken the line northwards from Glasgow alongside Loch Lomond and then across the wilderness of Rannoch Moor to Fort William, from where it would have continued northwards up the Great Glen to Inverness. The NBR-backed scheme, the Glasgow & North Western Railway, was put before Parliament in 1882 but, following strong opposition from the rival Caledonian and Highland railways who saw it as an invasion of their territories, was rejected the following year.

However, the NBR did not give up easily and in 1888 backed the West Highland Railway's proposed route from Glasgow to Fort William. This time it had better fortune and, despite opposition from its two rivals, the new railway was incorporated by an Act of Parliament the following year. Construction at the southern end of the new line started from Craigendoran, then the terminus of the NBR's suburban line along the north bank of the Clyde from Glasgow Queen Street. The steeply graded route took the new railway along the shores of Gare Loch before climbing high above Loch Long to a summit at Glen Douglas and descending to Arrochar & Tarbet. From here it followed the west shore of Loch Lomond northwards and then tracked Glen Falloch to Crianlarich, where the new line crossed over the Callander & Oban Railway at a higher level.

Construction of the railway, especially during the harsh winters, across this difficult terrain was slow, with the thousands of mainly Irish navvies employed on the project living in makeshift camps along the route. From Crianlarich construction continued northwards, with the new railway climbing continually up through Strath Fillan over a series of viaducts before looping around the 3,524-ft mass of Beinn Dorain to the edge of Rannoch Moor. Here, in 1892, the new line came to an abrupt but temporary halt – crossing the twenty miles of bog that stretched northwards held up proceedings for two more years.

Meanwhile, construction of the northern section of the railway eastwards from Fort William through the Monessie Gorge was also proceeding slowly. Climbing almost continuously with gradients as steep as 1-in-59, the line turned south at Tulloch to follow the east shore of Loch Treig and up to the summit of the line at Corrour. The railway was now complete apart from the missing section across Rannoch Moor.

Crossing the inhospitable and remote Rannoch Moor was no mean feat for the Victorian railway engineers. Labour disputes and appalling winter weather conditions constantly held up progress, while in many places the railway had to be supported on a raft of brushwood, turf and ash that literally floated on the saturated bog. A similar solution had already been used by George Stephenson during the building of the Liverpool & Manchester Railway across Chat Moss in the late 1820s.

Finally, Rannoch Moor was conquered and the completed railway officially opened on 15 August 1894. Even after the opening of the line, Rannoch Moor continued to present major problems for the railway's operators – during winter it was often blocked by heavy snowdrifts until a snow shed and snow fences were erected at the worst black spots.

A 38-mile extension of the West Highland Line from Fort William to the west coast fishing port of Mallaig opened

PREVIOUS PAGE: Loch Lomond is the largest inland stretch of water in Great Britain by surface area. Here a ScotRail diesel multiple unit heads along the west shore at Pulpit Rock with a Glasgow to Fort William train.

in 1901. The heavily engineered route, much of it carved through solid rock, was built by Robert McAlpine & Sons who pioneered the large-scale use of concrete to build the famous curving Glenfinnan Viaduct and other structures along the line.

Until diesels took over in 1962, trains on the steeply graded West Highland Line were double headed by steam locomotives such as the NBR 'Glen' Class 4-4-0s and LNER purpose-built Class 'K2' and 'K4' 2-6-0s, while in the last years of steam haulage LMS Stanier 'Black 5' 4-6-0s were the mainstay of operations. Fortunately for us today, both the West Highland Line and the Mallaig Extension escaped the mass railway closures following the implementation of the 1963 'Beeching Report'.

Living up to its status as one of the most scenic railways in the world, the single-track West Highland Line is alive and well today. In addition to the three daily return passenger trains that are operated by diesel multiple units between Glasgow and Fort William, the line is served daily (except Saturday evenings) by the diesel-hauled Highland Caledonian sleeping car train to and from London Euston. The line also carries freight traffic to and from the aluminium smelter at Fort William. A tourist steam-hauled train, 'The Jacobite', operates from mid-May to October between Fort William and Mallaig.

Trains for Fort William depart from the confined space of Glasgow Queen Street station in a northerly direction and, after climbing up through up through Queen Street Tunnel to Cowlairs, branch off westwards to follow the suburban route through Westerton to Dalmuir. From here, they follow the north bank of the River Clyde through Bowling and Dumbarton to Craigendoran Junction where the line becomes single-track. Now heading north alongside Gare Loch, trains reach Garelochhead station before climbing up to the first summit of the line alongside Loch Long at Glen Douglas.

From the summit, the line heads down to Arrochar & Tarbet station before heading north on a ledge alongside Loch Lomond to Ardlui and then up Glen Falloch to Crianlarich. Here the train is divided, with one half continuing to Fort William along the West Highland Line and the other half to Oban. In common with all the stations on the line, Crianlarich station has an island platform with an attractive Swiss chalet-style waiting room which also features a tea room. Diesel trains for Fort William head northwards from the station, first crossing a viaduct before starting to climb up Strath Fillan to Upper Tyndrum station. From here, the line continues to climb to County March Summit (1,024 ft above sea level) before following the contours of Beinn Dorain around the famous Horseshoe Curve and viaduct to Bridge of Orchy, where the station building is now a bunk house for walkers on the West Highland Way.

Heading northwards up Glen Orchy, the line continues its contour-hugging route high above Loch Tulla, then heads away from all human habitation up Glen Tulla to reach wild and remote Rannoch Moor. Civilization is briefly touched at lonely Rannoch station, where a tea room and visitor centre is located in the station building, before the line plunges into Cruach Cutting and Britain's only railway snow shed, then heads northwestwards across remote terrain to Corrour station. At 1,339 ft above sea level, Corrour is the highest standard-gauge station in Britain and one of the very few with no road access – although it is served by the Highland Caledonian Sleeper train from London, it is one of the loneliest spots on Britain's rail network. Its claim to fame is that it featured in Danny Boyle's famous black comedy film 'Trainspotting', released in 1996 and starring Ewan McGregor. Beautiful and remote Loch Ossian is a short walk away while the best of hill-walking countryside beckons the more adventurous.

From Corrour the railway begins its continuous descent to Fort William, hugging the eastern shore of Loch Treig on a ledge to Tulloch station, before turning westward through the narrow confines of Monessie Gorge to skirt round the Nevis Range of mountains. After emerging from the gorge, trains call at Roy Bridge station followed by Spean Bridge, once the junction for the short-lived branch line up the Great Glen to Fort Augustus. With the 4,406-ft-high summit of Ben Nevis (Britain's highest mountain) looming to the south, the railway makes its final southwestward approach to Fort William. The modern terminus here replaced the original station, half a mile further on alongside Loch Linnhe, in 1975 to make way for a new road.

OVERLEAF: Stanier 'Black 5' 4-6-0 No. 45407 'The Lancashire Fusilier', having just negotiated the horseshoe curve, crosses Glen Coralan on the Gleann Viaduct heading a charter train from Fort William on 19 October 2013.

WELSH HIGHLAND RAILWAY
WALES, UNITED KINGDOM

GAUGE: 1 FT 11½ IN. • **LENGTH:** 25 MILES •
ROUTE: PORTHMADOG TO CAERNARFON

The reopening of the 25-mile narrow-gauge Welsh Highland Railway between Porthmadog and Caernarfon in North Wales in 2011 marked the completion of one of the most ambitious railway restoration schemes in Europe. Hauled by restored South African steam locomotives, trains take a highly scenic route through the Snowdonia National Park.

THE FIRST WELSH HIGHLAND RAILWAY

Even before the opening of primitive railways, the mountainous region of North Wales known as Snowdonia had been quarried for slate and mined for minerals for centuries. However, transport in this harsh terrain was slow with packhorses, mules and horse-drawn sledges employed to carry the output of mines and quarries down to harbours on the coast.

One of the region's first railways was the narrow-gauge Nantlle Tramway, which opened between slate quarries at Nantlle and the harbour at Caernarfon in 1828. Like many early railways the Nantlle Tramway was operated using horse power and gravity – loaded wagons of slate controlled by brakemen would travel downhill to the coast while the empty wagons were hauled by horse back uphill to the quarries. This was soon followed by other horse and gravity railways, all of which used non-standard narrow-gauge track: the Nantlle Tramway's gauge was 3 ft 6 in.; the Ffestiniog Railway (FR) which opened from slate quarries at Blaenau Ffestiniog to Porthmadog in 1836 employed a 1 ft 11½ in. gauge; and the Croesor Tramway which opened in 1864 between slate quarries at Croesor and Porthmadog had a 2-ft gauge.

In 1863 the Ffestiniog Railway was the first narrow-gauge railway in the world to introduce steam haulage. While the first locomotives used were diminutive 0-4-0STT engines built by George England, these were supplemented by more powerful Double Fairlie 0-4-4-0T locomotives, the first of which, 'Little Wonder', was introduced in 1869. These articulated locomotives were an instant success and their trials on the railway were witnessed by railway engineers from as far afield as Russia and the USA.

Buoyed by the success of the Ffestiniog Railway, the company's chief engineer, Charles Spooner, came up with an ambitious plan for a whole network of 1-ft 11½-in.-gauge lines across Snowdonia. In reality the new company, the North Wales Narrow Gauge Railway (NWNGR), opened just two lines: from Dinas Junction, south of Caernarfon, to Spooner's slate quarries at Bryngwyn in 1877 with a branch to Rhyd Ddu following in 1881. The new railway

met the London & North Western Railway's standard-gauge line at Dinas Junction where slate had to be trans-shipped by hand from narrow-gauge to standard-gauge wagons. The new railway was not a financial success and the company soon went into receivership with Charles Spooner stepping down just before his death in 1889.

Despite these financial problems the NWNGR remained operational and in 1900 obtained a Light Railway Order to extend its line from Rhyd Ddu to Beddgelert. To the south of here a new railway, the Portmadoc, Beddgelert & South Snowdon Railway purchased the Croesor Tramway in 1901 and began the construction of a new narrow-gauge line northwards to link up with the NWNGR. Money ran out and the scheme was soon abandoned, and in 1916 the NWNGR ceased its passenger service, having only previously reached South Snowdon station on its extension from Rhyd Ddu. Complete closure was imminent but an eleventh-hour rescue by local councils backed by Government funding saw the new Welsh Highland Railway (WHR) formed in 1922.

The WHR took over the existing NWNGR's route from Dinas Junction to South Snowdon and built a new line southwards from here to Beddgelert, Croesor Juncton and Porthmadog. Opening throughout in 1923, the WHR appointed the 'father of light railways', Colonel Holman F. Stephens, as its locomotive superintendent and Chairman. Despite being used to running railways on a shoestring, the innovative Colonel Stephens struggled to make the line pay its way and by 1933 it was in mortal danger of closure. The railway was temporarily saved by its more successful neighbour, the Ffestiniog Railway, which leased it in 1934, but despite the latter's best efforts passenger services were finally withdrawn in 1936. Freight services ceased the following year and by the end of the Second World War the track had been lifted and the WHR had ceased to exist.

PHOENIX FROM THE ASHES

Despite closure, the trackbed of the railway remained fairly intact with the most scenic section through the tunnels in the Aberglaslyn Pass, south of Beddgelert, remaining open as a footpath. The standard-gauge line south from Caernarfon through Dinas Junction to Afon Wen became a victim of Dr Beeching's Axe when it was closed in 1964 but was later reopened as a footpath and cycleway known as Lôn Eifion.

By the 1970s the railway preservation movement in Britain was moving into top gear. The first railway preservation scheme in the country (and the world) had come in 1951 with the saving from closure of the narrow-gauge Talyllyn Railway in west Wales. This was followed by the gradual reopening of the Ffestiniog Railway which had closed in 1946 and which, by 1982, was once again running passenger trains between Porthmadog and Blaenau Ffestiniog. A group of enthusiasts formed the Welsh Highland Railway (1964) Company with a proposal to reopen the WHR route from Porthmadog to Dinas Junction, and thence northwards along the trackbed of the closed standard-gauge line to Caernarfon. They based themselves at Gelert's Farm in Porthmadog, where a short length of narrow-gauge track was laid and the only surviving WHR locomotive, 'Russell', was restored to run trains.

The WHR (1964) didn't have it all their own way however, as in 1989 the Ffestiniog Railway (FR) made a secret bid to buy the trackbed of the defunct WHR from the Official Receiver. Following years of legal wrangling the FR won the right to reopen the line that would connect with its own system in Porthmadog, creating a 40-mile-long narrow-gauge railway through the Snowdonia National Park from Caernarfon to Blaenau Ffestiniog.

With major funding from the National Lottery, the Welsh Assembly and the European Regional Development Fund, the line was reopened in stages; Caernarfon to Waunfawr in 2000, Waunfawr to Rhyd-ddu in 2003, Rhyd-ddu to Hafod y Llyn in 2009, Hafod y Llyn to Pont Croesor in 2010 and Pont Croesor to Porthmadog Harbour in 2011.

Trains on the Welsh Highland Railway are hauled by some of the most powerful narrow-gauge steam locomotives in the world. Saved from the scrapyard in South Africa, four Beyer-Garratt 2-6-2+2-6-2 articulated locomotives are now in service with one more awaiting restoration. Two ex-South African Railways 2-8-2s also await restoration. The world's first Garratt locomotive, a 0-4-0+0-4-0 originally built for the Tasmanian Government Railways in 1909 is also in service.

Trains for Caernarfon depart from the recently enlarged joint harbour station at Porthmadog Harbour. After threading behind the town and crossing the standard-gauge Cambrian Line on the level, trains head northeastwards across flat reclaimed pastureland to reach Pont Croesor before heading up the Glaslyn Valley and into the Snowdonia

Ex-South African Railways NGG16 Class 2-6-2+2-6-2 Garratt No. 143, built by Beyer-Peacock of Manchester in 1958, hauls a passenger train around the curve near Rhy-Ddu.

National Park to Nantmor. They then enter the dramatic Pass of Aberglaslyn, with its three rock-cut tunnels on the most spectacular part of this journey.

After crossing the Glaslyn on a bridge, the railway reaches the picturesque tourist village of Beddgelert, once an important centre for copper mining, before climbing steadily through tortuous reverse curves to the summit of the line at Pitts Head and paralleling the A4085 road to the remote station of Rhyd Ddu.

From Rhyd Ddu the line heads down along the shore of Llyn Cwellyn where Snowdon Ranger station is the starting point of a steep path to the summit of Snowdon. Heading down the Gwyfrai Valley, trains call at Plas-y-Nant and the former slate-mining village of Waunfawr before heading west through Tryfan Junction to Dinas, with its workshops and engine and carriage sheds. The rest of the journey follows the route of the standard-gauge Afonwen to Caernarfon line that closed in 1964. The Lon Eifion cycleway parallels the WHR along this section. With an intermediate station at Bontnewydd, the railway ends at Caernarfon station, a short distance from the harbour, medieval city walls and the castle, which are designated a UNESCO World Heritage site.

OVERLEAF: Beneath the shadow of the snow-capped peak of Snowdon, ex-South African Railways 'NG/G16' class Garratts Nos. 87 and 138 head a freight train around the horseshoe curve near Rhyd Dhu on the Welsh Highland Railway, on 3 November 2013.

SETTLE-CARLISLE LINE
ENGLAND, UNITED KINGDOM

GAUGE: 4 FT 8½ IN. • **LENGTH:** 72 MILES •
ROUTE: SETTLE JUNCTION TO CARLISLE

Built by thousands of navvies living in temporary camps on the bleak Pennine Hills, the Settle-Carlisle Line is one of the wonders of the Victorian era. Featuring thirteen tunnels and twenty-three viaducts, its opening in 1876 gave the Midland Railway its own independent mainline route to Scotland.

By the mid-nineteenth century England and Scotland had been linked by two competing railway routes: the West Coast Main Line had been completed between London Euston and Glasgow by the London & North Western Railway (LNWR) and the Caledonian Railway in 1849, while the East Coast Main Line had been completed between London King's Cross and Edinburgh by the Great Northern, North Eastern and North British railways in 1850. However, the mighty Midland Railway (MR) also sought a slice of this lucrative traffic but was denied running powers from its northern outpost of Ingleton in the Yorkshire Dales by the LNWR.

Despite this blocking move by its rival, the MR was intent on reaching Carlisle by its own route, where it would link up with the North British Railway's Waverley Route from Edinburgh and the Glasgow & South Western Railway's route from Glasgow. To achieve this goal the MR planned to build a 72-mile mainline across the wild and remote Pennine Hills from Settle Junction, thirty-five miles northwest of the city of Leeds, to Carlisle. This highly ambitious project was given Parliamentary approval in 1866 but construction was initially delayed by a banking crisis in the UK. In 1868, with growing concerns about competition from the new line, the LNWR belatedly gave permission for running rights north of Ingleton. The MR would probably have agreed to this but their partners – the Lancashire & Yorkshire Railway, the North British Railway and the Glasgow & South Western Railway – successfully petitioned Parliament against abandonment of the project.

With engineer John Crossley in charge, construction work started in 1870 with an army of 6,000 unruly navvies housed in a motley collection of remote camps spread out over the bleak Pennine Hills. Finally opened in 1876, several years behind schedule and with a 50 per cent overrun in costs, the railway was a triumph of Victorian engineering in a time before mechanical steam shovels had been invented, and involved the building of thirteen tunnels and twenty-three viaducts. With a ruling gradient of 1-in-100, the first fifteen miles northwards from Settle up to Blea Moor Tunnel was nicknamed 'The Long Drag' by steam locomotive crews.

Costly to maintain and operate and with negligible intermediate traffic, the line was listed for closure in the 1963 'Beeching Report'. It not only survived this threat but also another, thanks to a well-organized national campaign in the 1980s. Two named trains also once used this route: the 'Thames-Clyde Express' operated between London St Pancras and Glasgow from 1927 to 1974; and

PREVIOUS PAGE: The 6M11 Hunterston to Fiddlers Ferry loaded coal hoppers with Freightliner Heavyhaul 66526 in charge powers through Dentdale near the abandoned farmhouse of Rotten Bottom on Wednesday 7 August 2013.

The Lancaster to Carlisle 'The Fellsman' charter train, with Stanier 'Jubilee' 45699 'Galatea' in charge, passes High Scale farmhouse near Garsdale on Wednesday 18 July 2013.

'The Waverley' operated between London St Pancras and Edinburgh from 1923 (when it was named the 'Thames-Forth Express') to 1968.

The perfect summer's evening showcases the mass of Ingleborough looming over Chapel-le-Dale and Ribblehead viaduct. DB Schenker 66103 powers up the 1-in-100 grade past Blea Moor signalbox heading the 4S00 loaded cement tankers from Clitheroe to Mossend on 17 July 2013.

Today, the Settle-Carlisle line is a major freight and diversionary route, taking pressure off the congested electrified West Coast Main Line, while local passenger traffic, served by diesel multiple unit trains running between Leeds and Carlisle, has increased with the reopening of eight stations previously closed in 1970. Steam-hauled charter trains also regularly use the line, testing engine crews and their locomotives to the limit on this demanding route. Manually operated signal boxes and semaphore signalling are still a feature although their replacement by more modern signalling is due soon.

En route, trains first pass through Stainforth Tunnel before calling at Horton-in-Ribblesdale and Ribblehead stations. From here, the railway crosses the iconic 24-arch Ribblehead Viaduct, burrows through the 1-mile 869-yds Blea Moor Tunnel and crosses Dent Head and Arten Gill viaducts to reach remote Dent station (the highest mainline station in England). Continuing to climb northwards through a series of tunnels, trains call at Garsdale to reach the summit of the line at Ais Gill (1,169 ft above sea level).

From Ais Gill the railway begins its descent into the Eden Valley, through Birkett Tunnel, to Kirkby Stephen before crossing Smardale Viaduct and cutting across the hills through Crosby Garrett and Helm tunnels to rejoin the valley south of Appleby. The station here still retains a booking office and is the busiest intermediate station on the line. From Appleby, the railway descends along the Eden Valley all the way to Carlisle. En route, trains pass through six more tunnels, calling at Langwathby, Lazonby & Kirkoswald and Armathwaite, before joining the main line from Newcastle at Petterill Bridge Junction for the final mile into Carlisle's centrally located station.

OVERLEAF: The dark clouds hanging over Angram Common and the limestone ridge of Hangingstone Scar set the scene for Gresley 'K4' No. 61994 'The Great Marquess' heading the return 'The Fellsman' charter train to Lancaster from Carlisle over Ais Gill viaduct on 8 August 2012.

DOUGLAS TO PORT ERIN
ISLE OF MAN, UNITED KINGDOM

GAUGE: 3 FT • **LENGTH:** 15½ MILES •
ROUTE: DOUGLAS TO PORT ERIN

Once part of a 46-mile steam-operated network of narrow-gauge lines that operated around the island, the Isle of Man Steam Railway was rescued from oblivion when it was nationalized by the Manx Government in 1978. Passengers travel in restored original Victorian coaches hauled by equally old original steam locomotives.

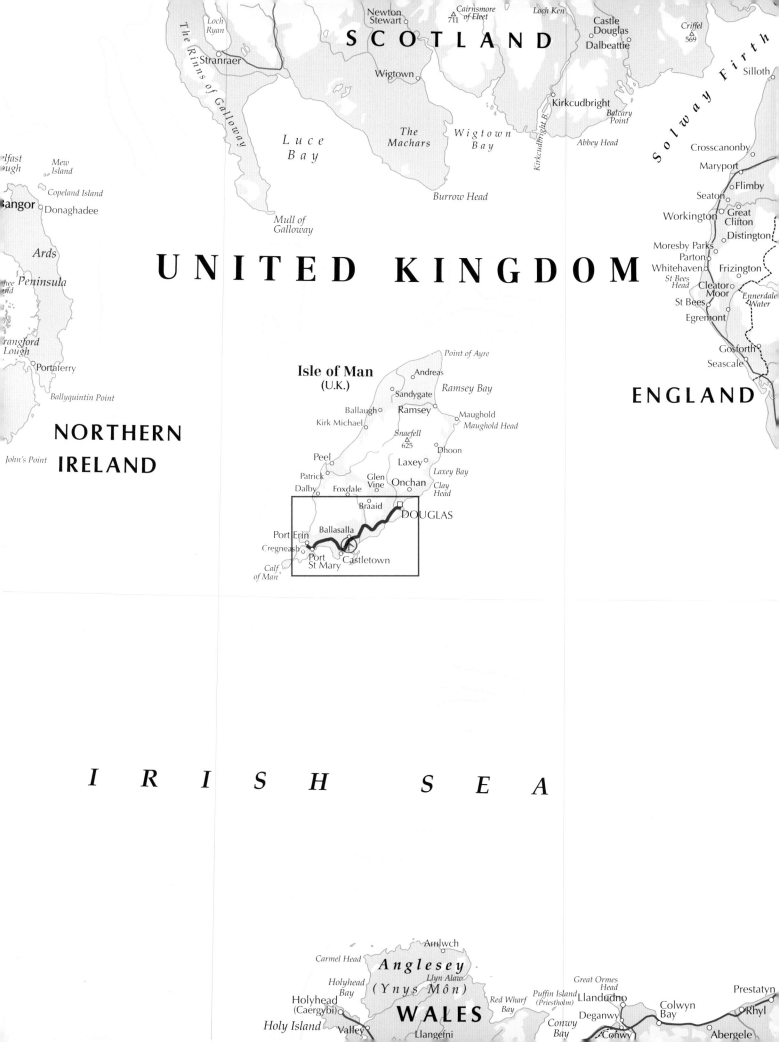

The Isle of Man is located in the Irish Sea, roughly equidistant from Ireland, England, Wales and Scotland. With a long and often turbulent history, it has been a self-governing British Crown dependency since 1863 and, more recently, a member of the British Commonwealth. With the royal stamp of approval following visits from Queen Victoria and the introduction of a regular steam ferry service from Liverpool in the early nineteenth century, the island became a popular holiday destination for thousands of workers and their families from the industrial North of England. Victorian entrepreneurs soon moved in, building grand hotels along the seafront in the capital Douglas and establishing resorts at Port Erin and Ramsey. To cater for this influx of visitors the Victorians were also eager to build railways on the island but its mountainous interior precluded the construction of standard-gauge lines. Instead, the narrow gauge of 3 ft was chosen as this allowed the railway to follow the topography of the terrain with sharper curves – it was also cheaper to build. This gauge was also widely adopted for Irish narrow-gauge lines built at the end of the nineteenth century.

Appointing Henry Vignoles as its chief engineer, the Isle of Man Railway (IOMR) was first on the island railway scene. Registered in 1870, the company planned to build lines from the capital, Douglas, to Peel on the west coast and thence from a junction at St John's up the west coast and across to Ramsey on the east coast. A further extension of the railway from Douglas to Castletown was also proposed.

In Henry Vignoles, the IOMR had an extremely experienced chief engineer as he had previously worked in this capacity on early railway lines in Russia, Germany, Switzerland, Spain and Poland. The first line to be completed on the Isle of Man was the 11½-mile route from Douglas to Peel which followed river valleys across the centre of the island, opening in July 1873. This was soon followed by the steeply graded 15½-mile line from Douglas to Castletown (later extended to Port Erin), which opened in August 1874. Motive power for both lines were diminutive 2-4-0T locomotives built by Beyer Peacock of Manchester.

PREVIOUS PAGE: A late winter's scene is conveyed in this image of Isle of Man Railway's No. 12 'Hutchinson' in the woods above Port Soderick Glen, heading the 11:50 Douglas to Port Erin service train on Monday 8 April 2013.

Although the IOMR decided not to go ahead with the St John's to Ramsey line, a separate company, the Manx Northern Railway (MNR), was formed and the 16½-mile route with its two viaducts was opened in September 1879. A further railway company, the Foxdale Railway, opened a 2½-mile branch line from St John's to lead mines at Foxdale in 1886. It was taken over by the MNR in 1891.

The final piece in the island's jigsaw of railways came in 1893 when the 3-ft-gauge Manx Electric Railway opened up the east coast between Douglas and Laxey. It was extended to Ramsey in 1899. A steeply graded branch line from Laxey to the summit of the island's highest mountain, Snaefell, opened in 1895 but, curiously, this was built to a 3-ft 6-in. gauge. Nationalized by the Manx Government in 1957, both lines are still operating today.

In 1905 the IOMR absorbed the MNR giving the enlarged company a total of 46 route miles of railway on the island. The years immediately following the end of the First World War saw a surge in holidaymakers visiting the Isle of Man from Britain and the railway system was stretched to capacity. However, by the 1930s increasing competition from buses on the island brought a decline in traffic, although the onset of the Second World War brought some relief with the railways carrying large numbers of military personnel along with prisoners of war and aliens to internment camps located on the island.

The immediate post-war years brought an upsurge in holidaymakers visiting the Isle of Man and, along with it, welcome but temporary business for the railways. However, the IOMR was in a pretty decrepit state by then, with vintage steam locomotives and rolling stock, and poorly maintained track. With passenger numbers staring to decline once more, the St John's to Ramsey line closed in 1961 while the Douglas to Peel/Douglas to Port Erin lines continued in operation until they were closed without warning in 1965.

For nearly two years the closed IOMR slumbered on, its rusting track being overtaken by nature until a saviour, in the person of the Marquess of Ailsa (a Scottish peer who once worked as a steam locomotive fireman), took over the railway on a 21-year lease. His intention was to operate it as a tourist attraction during the summer months and by July 1967 all three routes had reopened. This rebirth was short-lived as both the Douglas to Peel and the St John's to Ramsey lines closed for good in September 1968. The only remaining line from Douglas to Port Erin continued to operate during the summer months until it was nationalized by the Manx Government in 1978. It is now known as the Isle of Man Steam Railway.

Today, the Isle of Man Steam Railway operates restored vintage steam trains between Douglas and Port Erin from mid-February to early November. Journey time for the 15½-mile journey is a leisurely one hour. Passengers are carried in a fleet of original wooden bogie coaches hauled by locomotives supplied for the railway between 1874 and 1910. Two locomotives, No. 6 'Peveril' and No. 16 'Mannin', are on static display at the Port Erin Railway Museum. Additionally, two railcars, bought from the long-closed County Donegal Railways Joint Committee in the early 1960s, are currently awaiting restoration in Douglas.

Trains for Port Erin depart westwards from the red-brick terminus in Douglas, which despite losing some of its platforms since closure of the Peel and Ramsey lines still retains much of its Victorian atmosphere. On leaving Douglas trains pass the railway's locomotive shed and workshops before crossing the River Glass to take a southwesterly climb to the first station at Port Soderick, passing close to the coast en route. The railway then loops inland to the summit of the line (588 ft above sea level) before descending across Glen Grenaugh on the approach to Santon station. Continuing its descent the railway then serves Santon station before reaching Ballasalla station where service trains pass on a loop. From here the meandering railway levels out through Ronaldsway Halt (for Isle of Man Airport) before arriving at the island's ancient capital of Castletown. The station here is a good jumping-off point for visits to medieval Castle Rushen, the town's harbour, the welcoming George Hotel and coastal walks around Scarlett Point.

From Castletown trains head back inland on a fairly level route through Ballabeg Halt, Colby and Port St Mary, offering fine views to the north of Bradda Head and the South Barrule Hills en route. The journey ends at the delightful red-brick terminus station in Port Erin. Here there is a locomotive shed and the Port Erin Railway Museum (housed in a converted bus garage), which contains two IOMR locomotives, two royal coaches and other railway relics dating back to 1873. It is but a short walk from the station to the sheltered sandy beach, the Victorian promenade and the coastal cliff path to rugged Bradda Head. From the summit (382 ft above sea level), the Mourne Mountains in Ireland can be seen on a clear day.

No. 8 'Fenella' heads a special charter train of vintage rolling stock near the coast at Keristal during the early evening of 9 April 2013.

OVERLEAF: Built by Beyer Peacock in 1908, Isle of Man Railway 2-4-0T No. 12 'Hutchinson' approaches Port St Mary station with the 11.50 Douglas to Port Erin service in May 2007.

DUBLIN TO ROSSLARE HARBOUR
REPUBLIC OF IRELAND

GAUGE: 5 FT 3 IN. • **LENGTH:** 100 MILES •
ROUTE: DUBLIN TO ROSSLARE HARBOUR

Incorporating Ireland's first railway, the Dublin to Rosslare line features a scenic coast-hugging route that was engineered by Isambard Kingdom Brunel. At the mercy of the sea and geological instability, this section has required constant attention since it opened over 150 years ago.

Built to the English standard gauge of 4 ft 8½ in., Ireland's first railway was the 6-mile Dublin & Kingstown Railway (D&KR) that opened in 1834 between Dublin Westland Row and the east coast port of Kingstown (today known as Dún Laoghaire). The engineering consultants for this very early railway included such famous names as George Stephenson, Thomas Telford and Charles Vignoles. A short extension from Kingstown to Dalkey which opened in 1844 was operated by atmospheric traction until 1856 when the D&KR was leased to the Waterford, Wexford, Wicklow & Dublin Railway.

Meanwhile a Royal Commission had been set up to standardize railway gauges in Ireland, which by 1845 consisted of a confusing mixture of 4 ft 8½ in., 5 ft 3 in. and 6 ft 2 in. In the end the 5-ft 3-in. gauge was chosen and this went on to be used for all new railways in Ireland (excluding later narrow-gauge light railways) as well as in the Australian states of Victoria and South Australia, and in Brazil.

Incorporated in 1846, the Waterford, Wexford, Wicklow & Dublin Railway (WWW&DR) was the brainchild of Britain's Great Western Railway and its chief engineer, Isambard Kingdom Brunel, who saw it as a link in the chain for a cross-Channel service from Fishguard in southwest Wales to Dublin. William Dargan, the ambitious contractor who had already built the D&KR, then bought the GWR's shares in the new company. In 1849 the WWW&DR changed its name to the Dublin Wicklow & Wexford Railway (DW&WR).

To the south of Kingstown the coastal town of Bray was reached simultaneously by two railways in 1854: the Dublin & Bray Railway reached it from a new terminus at Harcourt Street in Dublin, while the DW&WR – which by then had changed its name to the Dublin & Wicklow Railway (D&WR) – extended its existing line southwards from Dalkey. Both lines were built to a gauge of 5 ft 3 in. with the original Westland Row to Kingstown and Dalkey section being converted from the English gauge. Soon after opening in 1854 the D&BR was absorbed by the D&WR.

Extending the D&WR southwards down the coast to Wicklow was a major engineering feat. With Brunel in

charge as the chief engineer, the single-track line followed a coast-hugging route that necessitated building several viaducts and excavating four tunnels through solid rock at Bray Head. The Bray to Wicklow section opened in 1855. In 1860 the company was renamed once again, this time back to its 1849 title as the Dublin, Wicklow & Wexford Railway (DW&WR) with the obvious intent of reaching Wexford on the southeast coast. Taking an inland route from Wicklow the railway opened to Rathdrum in 1861, to Enniscorthy in 1863 and to Wexford in 1872. A 16½-mile branch line from Woodenbridge to Shillelagh opened in 1865 and a branch from Macmine Junction to New Ross in 1887 – this was later extended to Waterford in 1904. Rosslare Strand was reached from Wexford in 1882 and Rosslare Harbour, connecting with the GWR's new steamship service to and from Fishguard, was finally reached in 1906. Both Fishguard and Rosslare harbours had been built by the Fishguard & Rosslare Railways & Harbours Company, a joint venture between the British Great Western Railway and the Irish Great Southern & Western Railway. The joint company also built the 3½ miles of line between Rosslare Harbour and Rosslare Strand and the remaining 34½ miles to Waterford.

Since its opening in 1855 the coastal section of the railway between Bray and Wicklow has been subject to numerous realignments due to rock slippage around Bray Head and coastal erosion to the south of here. Connecting two of the tunnels at Bray Head over a ravine, the timber Brandy Hole Viaduct collapsed in 1867 and new tunnels were excavated further inland in 1876, 1879 and 1917.

In 1906 the DW&WR changed its name once again, this time becoming the Dublin & South Eastern Railway, which in turn was amalgamated by the Great Southern Railways in 1925. In 1945 all railways and other transport operators in the Republic of Ireland were nationalized as Coras Iompair Éireann (CIE). By the mid-1950s the CIE's ageing fleet of steam locomotives was being replaced by British-built diesel locomotives, which were in turn replaced by American locomotives supplied by General Motors. In recent years diesel multiple units have replaced most of the locomotive-hauled passenger trains while, around Dublin, the electrified Dublin Area Rapid Transit (DART) system now operates thirty-three route miles of suburban lines including the route from Dublin to Bray via Dún Laoghaire, which came into service in 1984 and was extended under Bray Head to Greystones in 2000.

PREVIOUS PAGE: Building the coast-hugging route through Bray Head to Greystones was a major engineering feat. This embankment, sandwiched between two tunnels, replaced an earlier timber viaduct that collapsed in 1867.

A Dublin Area Rapid Transit (DART) electric train from Greystones heads along the coast-hugging route at Bray Head.

Former Northern Counties Committee 2-6-4T No. 4 crosses the River Slaney as it leaves Enniscorthy on 14 May 2005 with an Railway Preservation Society of Ireland railtour from Dublin to Rosslare.

While the original mainline from Dublin to Rosslare Harbour is still operational today, all its branches have long since closed: Woodenbridge to Shillelagh closed in 1944; Harcourt Street to Bray closed in 1958; Macmine Junction to New Ross closed completely in 1963; and the last freight train ran between New Ross and Waterford in 1995.

Diesel trains for Rosslare Harbour depart from Dublin Connolly station, crossing the River Liffey to Dublin Pearse station, the original terminus (then named Westland Row) of Ireland's first railway, the Dublin & Kingstown. The first part of the journey follows the route of this railway, now electrified as part of the DART system to Greystones, through numerous suburban stations before reaching the coast at Booterstown. From here the coastal double-track route heads through Dún Laoghaire (formerly Kingstown), for the Stena Line fast ferry services to Holyhead in North Wales, Dalkey, Killiney and Shankhill before arriving at Bray.

Hugging the coastline southwards into County Wicklow, this highly scenic railway then becomes single track, passing through four tunnels under Bray Head to reach Greystones, the current limit of DART electric services from Dublin. Continuing southwards down the coastline, trains call at Kilcoole before arriving at Wicklow station where there is a passing loop. Here, as was typical practice at other stations on the line, the signal box is located on the footbridge although semaphore signalling on the route was replaced by a Centralized Traffic Control (CTC) system in 2008.

From Wicklow the railway makes a long loop inland through the wooded foothills of the Wicklow Mountains to the village of Rathdrum before heading back towards the coast to reach Arklow. Located at the mouth of the River Avoca, Arklow is famous for its Nineteen Arches Bridge that links the two parts of the town across the wide river.

From Arklow the railway heads inland into County Wexford to reach Gorey before following the Bann Valley to Enniscorthy, once an important station for cattle and agricultural traffic to Dublin. During the Easter Rising of 1916, hundreds of Irish Republican volunteers briefly took control of the railway line here to prevent British troop reinforcements reaching Dublin. From Enniscorthy it heads south through Enniscorthy Tunnel and along the lush Slaney Valley to Wexford station. Trains then clatter along the quayside on the last part of their journey to Rosslare Strand and Rosslare Harbour where there are connections with the ferry crossing to Fishguard in Wales.

AFRICA

MASSAWA TO ASMARA
ERITREA, NORTHEAST AFRICA

GAUGE: 950 MM (3 FT 1³/₈ IN.) • **LENGTH**: 73 MILES •
ROUTE: MASSAWA TO ASMARA

Built by the Italian colonial rulers of Eritrea, the heavily engineered narrow-gauge railway from the Red Sea port of Massawa to the new capital, Asmara, took twenty years to build. The steeply graded line was virtually destroyed during the Eritrean War of Independence but has since been reopened by the Eritreans as a tourist railway.

Located on the Red Sea coast in the Horn of Africa, and bordered to the north and west by Sudan and to the south by Ethiopia and Djibouti, Eritrea only became an independent country in 1993 after years of Italian domination and rule and then, following liberation by the British during the Second World War, thirty more years of struggle in a vicious civil war with its new boss, the Marxist state of Ethiopia.

As the European 'Scramble for Land' in Africa gathered pace following the opening of the Suez Canal in 1869, the Italians soon moved into the region and by 1889 were in control of Eritrea, ruling it as part of an Italian empire. It was during this period that construction started on a 950-mm narrow-gauge railway between the Red Sea port of Massawa and the capital Asmara, located on a plateau 7,854 ft above sea level. Not only did the railway have strategic importance for moving supplies to Italian forward army positions, it had a commercial

PREVIOUS PAGE: Built by Ansaldo in 1938, Mallet 0-4-4-0T locomotive No. 442.54 heads a short train over the curving viaduct at milepost Km112 above Shegerini in 2005, on one of the most spectacular sections of the metre-gauge railway between Massawa and Asmara.

purpose in conveying raw materials mined in the Eritrean highlands down to the port of Massawa. Progress was very slow along this heavily engineered and steeply graded route, which required thirty-nine tunnels and sixty-five bridges and viaducts. Asmara, seventy-three miles from Massawa, was finally reached in 1911. The railway did not end here but continued westwards reaching Keren in 1922, Agat in 1925, Agordat in 1928 and Bishia, 164 miles from Massawa, in 1932. Plans to continue westwards to Teseney, where it would have met the Sudanese railway network, never materialized. The new railway opened up new markets for farm products however, and towns along the route prospered. It was also the region's largest employer, with well-equipped workshops at Asmara.

In 1935, Mussolini's Italy invaded Abyssinia (now known as Ethiopia) and decreed that Eritrea, Abyssinia and Italian Somaliland were to be henceforth known collectively as Italian East Africa. Although the railway carried enormous amounts of supplies to support this invasion – operating up to thirty trains a day – it was soon stretched to capacity and, in 1938, the Italians built a cableway between Massawa and Asmara. The longest of its kind in the world, it had thirteen intermediate stations each fitted with stationary diesel engines and carried food, supplies and war materials for the Italian army.

On 10 June 1940 Italy declared war on Britain and France. In East Africa the Italians based a fleet of destroyers and submarines at Massawa, threatening British convoys in the Red Sea, and successfully invaded British Somaliland. Retribution soon followed and in January 1941 two British-led Indian infantry divisions attacked eastwards from the Sudan while three South African divisions attacked northwards from Kenya. By November of that year the Italians had been beaten and Italian East Africa came under British control, although some Italian civilian officials were kept on to help run the territory. British control continued until 1951 when Eritrea was federated with Ethiopia under a UN resolution. Ethiopia's annexation of Eritrea in 1962 then led to a bloody 30-year civil war in the country that ended in 1991. Finally, following a UN-supervised referendum, the Eritrean people gained their well-earned independence in 1993.

Meanwhile, the railway carried on operating although the section from Agordat to Bishia was closed in 1942. The cableway between Massawa and Asmara was dismantled as war reparations in 1944 and moved to Kenya. The railway prospered through the 1950s and 1960s but the onset of the civil war between Eritrean separatists and the Ethiopian army soon led to its downfall. During the fighting much of its infrastructure was destroyed by both sides and it ceased operations in 1976. The rolling stock and locomotives were left to rot and this appeared to be the end of the line for the railway.

However, this was not the end for the Massawa to Asmara section! Following independence in 1993, the new Eritrean Government pledged to prioritize the reopening of the railway. After rejecting offers of foreign aid, the project started by using domestic skills and veteran railway workers to recover track, rebuild workshops and stations and restore the motley collection of Italian railcars, locomotives and rolling stock.

The line reopened between Massawa and Ghinda in 1996 and was completed to Asmara in 2003. The final twisting stretch up through the mountains between Nefasit and Asmara was the most challenging as it included gradients as steep as 1-in-30 and many tunnels and bridges.

Built by Ansaldo in 1938, Mallet 0-4-4-0T locomotive No. 442.55 heads a short mixed train in the mountainous country above Nefasit in 2010.

Today the Eritrean Railway provides a regular Sunday return service along the highly scenic section between Asmara, Arbaroba and Nefasit. It also operates a customized charter train for tourists along the entire route from Massawa to Asmara, a journey which takes six hours at an average speed of 12 mph. Trains are operated by restored vintage steam and diesel locomotives and also by the 1930s-vintage Italian 'Littorina' railcars.

Eleven steam locomotives have survived, of which six have been restored to working order. Stars of this fleet are the three restored 0-4-4-0 compound Mallet locomotives built by Ansaldo in Italy in 1938. These powerful locomotives, often double-headed, operate many of the tourist services. Also in operation are two Bo-Bo diesels built by Krupps of Germany in 1957, which will be used on freight trains in the future. There are also two restored 28-seat Fiat 'Littorina' diesel railcars that were built in the 1930s – their curved Art Deco styling and large front radiator make them a popular form of travel with tourists.

The port of Massawa is built on three islands surrounded by the clear blue waters of the Red Sea. The oldest, predominantly Arab, part of the city is on the Island of Massawa. The railway station is on the Island of Tallud, which is dominated by Italian colonial buildings. From here trains cross to the mainland on a causcway and head out into a flat coastal desert where the thorn bush is the only vegetation. After about six miles the line, keeping company with a road, starts to climb gradually to Moncullo then crosses a dry river bed at Dogali on an impressive 13-arch viaduct. The climb steepens and at Mai Atal the railway and road part company, the former entering a broad valley alongside a dry river bed – this is remote and barren country inhabited by herds of camels that survive by eating the leaves of thorn bushes. At Damas the railway has climbed 1,365 ft and from here it winds in and out of the lava rock formations through a succession of sharp curves and tunnels, crossing the Dongollo river bed on a succession of six bridges before arriving at Ghinda station, 2,913 ft above sea level. Here the dry, arid scenery has given way to a more temperate scene where vegetation thrives.

From Ghinda to Nefasit, the line climbs through a valley surrounded on both sides by towering hills, twisting and turning as it follows the contours, passing through five tunnels en route. From Nefasit the most dramatic section of this line still lies ahead, with the railway continuing its steep climb up through the mountains on a series of reverse curves and through no less than twenty tunnels – over a distance of 7½ miles it climbs nearly 1,300 ft. The views from the train's windows are stunning, with sheer drops of over a 1,000 ft, and as the train climbs the temperature becomes noticeably cooler. Carved out of rock, Arbaroba is the penultimate station before the railway makes its final and dramatic ascent up to the plateau. On this final 8-mile section there are three spiral loops and a curving stone viaduct before the line levels out for the final approach to Asmara station.

Located on a rocky highland plateau over 7,000 ft above sea level, Asmara features many fine examples of Italian colonial Modernist architecture and is a poignant memorial to Mussolini's ambitious plans for an Italian empire in Africa. To the west of Asmara, the line awaits a possible reopening to meet the Sudanese railway system but in the meantime some of the Italian-built stations in this important agricultural region have found new uses: Keren station is now a bus station and market while the imposing Arabesque-style station at Agordat is an airport terminal.

LEFT: Built by Fiat in the 1930s, Littorina diesel railcar No. 2 emerges from a tunnel at Km106 over 6,500 ft up in the mountains near Arbaroba in November 2004.

OVERLEAF: Passengers on this train, hauled by Ansaldo-built Mallet 0-4-4-0T No. 442.55 at milepost Km111, need a good head for heights on one of the most spectacular railway journeys in the world.

MADAGASCAR'S RAILWAYS
MADAGASCAR

GAUGE: 1,000 MM (3 FT 3⅜IN.) • **LENGTH:** 543 MILES •
ROUTES:
1. ANTANANARIVO TO ANTSIRABE / ANTANANARIVO TO TOAMASINA /
MORAMANGA TO AMBATONDRAZAKA – 442 MILES
2. MANAKARA TO FIANARANTSOA - 101 MILES

Built by the French colonial rulers, a network of metre-gauge railways
was opened in the north of Madagascar in the early twentieth century,
while a completely separate metre-gauge line was built in the southeast
during the 1930s. Although struggling to survive in the twenty-first
century, both railways remain operational today.

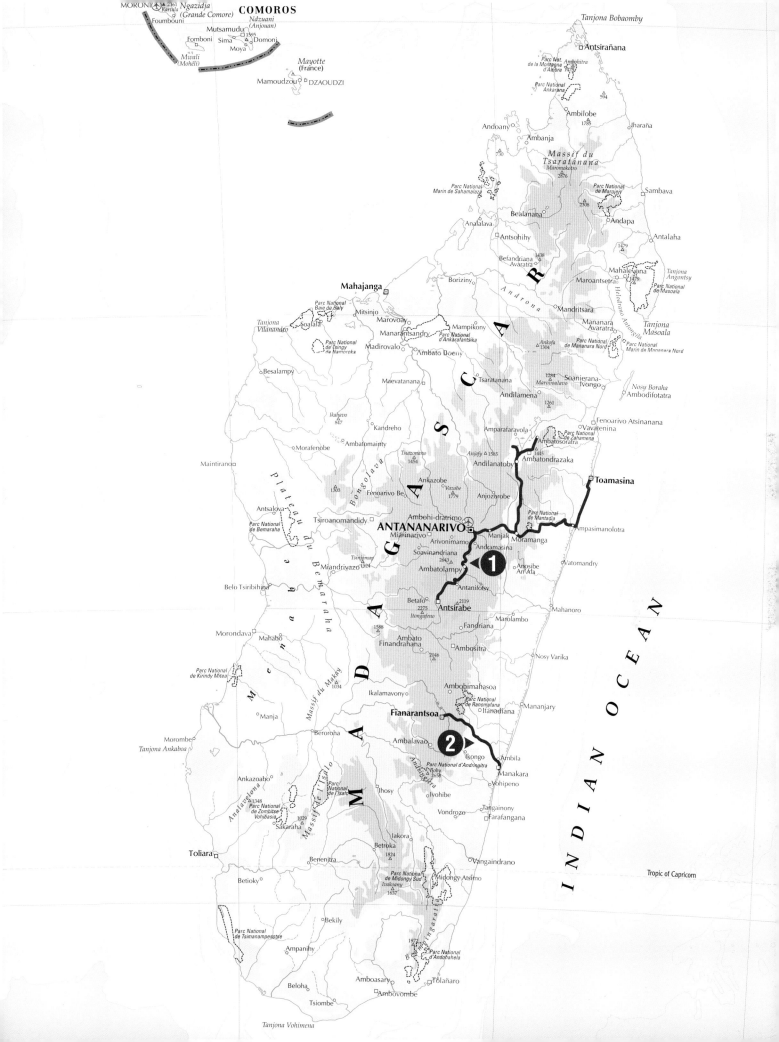

The fourth largest island in the world, Madagascar is located in the Indian Ocean off the southeastern coast of Africa. A steep forested escarpment, carved out by fast-flowing rivers, runs the length of the east coast while to the west lie the central highlands. Rising to a height of nearly 5,000 ft, this plateau, characterized by terraced rice paddy fields, is the island's most densely populated region and the location of its capital, Antananarivo. To the west, increasingly arid terrain slopes gradually down to end as mangrove swamps on the shore of the Mozambique Channel.

By the late nineteenth century the island had been ruled for almost 400 years by a long line of clan chiefs until unified during King Radama I's reign in the early nineteenth century. However, the monarchy ended in 1897 when Madagascar became a French colony. The French were quick to introduce railways with the first, a metre-gauge line between Antananarivo (then named Tananarive) and Ampasimanolotra (then named Brickville) on the east coast, opening in 1909. This railway was then extended northwards up the coast to the port of Toamasina, southwards from the capital to Antsirabe and northwards from Moramanga to Ambatondrazaka. Completed by 1923, this railway system was named the Tananarive-Côte Est Railway

A completely separate railway, isolated from the main network, was built from the port of Manakara, on the southeast coast, inland to Fianarantsoa by the French between 1926 and 1936. Known as the Fianarantsoa-Côte Est Railway, it was built by forced labour using railway equipment seized from the Germans after the First World War. This 101-mile metre-gauge line climbs from sea level at Manakara to a height of 3,900 ft at its inland terminus, traversing remote and difficult terrain up through steep-sided river valleys en route.

Both railways came under French state control during the Second World War and, following Madagascar's independence in 1960, were nationalized in 1974, becoming the Réseau National des Chemins de Fer Malagasy. Over the next two decades the railways were starved of investment and became so run down that they were in danger of abandonment. In 2002 the northern network centred on the capital was privatized and is now

operated by Madarail. Funding for this was provided by the World Bank and the European Investment Bank. The isolated Fianarantsoa-Côte Est Railway is still state owned.

ANTANANARIVO-CÔTE EST RAILWAY (MADARAIL)

Since privatization in 2002, Madarail and its French and Belgian shareholders have invested in modernizing the

PREVIOUS PAGE: Fitted with pneumatic tyres, Michelin 'Viko-Viko' railcar No. ZM516 has stopped to allow passengers to enjoy the view across the valley between Ambatofotsy and Behenjy on the Antananarivo to Antsirabe line.

neglected network. An infrequent service of passenger trains operates on most of the network but the coaches are clean and the fares are very cheap. A 3-coach tourist train, the Trans Lemurie Express, is also available for charter. The novel 1953-built Michelin 'Viko-Viko' railcar which seats nineteen passengers operates weekend excursions from the capital to Andasibe, for the Mantandia National Park, and to Antsirabe. As the railcar runs on flanged pneumatic tyres a couple of spares are also carried in a rear boot.

Freight traffic is the lifeblood of the railway in a country where the roads are either non-existent or, at best, passable – in the rainy season both roads and railways suffer terribly from landslides and floods. On the steeply graded sections of the main line between Antananarivo and the coast, the heavier freight trains are often split

The thrice weekly train pauses at Manampatrana, principal intermediate station on the East Coast Line between Manakara and Fianarantsoa.

into two sections. Chromium and nickel ore, container traffic, petroleum, cement, metal products, rice and flour form the bulk of the freight traffic, which amounted to over 400,000 tons in 2011. Motive power for both freight and passenger trains is provided by Alsthom Bo-Bo single cab diesels built in the 1970s and 1980s, along with a small fleet of more modern Chinese-built Bo-Bo twin cab diesels.

FIANARANTSOA-CÔTE EST RAILWAY

Still state-owned, this railway runs for much of its length through a steeply graded and heavily forested valley that has no road access. One of the steepest adhesion railways in the world, it traverses some of Madagascar's most scenic countryside and passes over sixty-seven bridges and through forty-eight tunnels as it climbs up the escarpment to Fianarantsoa. With seventeen intermediate stops, the mixed train service provided every other day

(except Mondays) in each direction is the only form of transport for local people. Trains consist of a few covered freight wagons, two second-class coaches and a first-class coach for tourists. The highly scenic 101-mile journey takes around ten hours as, at each stop, goods have to be unloaded from or loaded onto the train. The 1952-built Michelin railcar 'Fandrasa' seats nineteen passengers and operates a charter service from Fianarantsoa to Sahambavy, a distance of thirteen miles, where it is turned on a triangle. The railway's workshops are at Fianarantsoa but when heavy repairs are required, locomotives are taken by road northwards to the railway workshops at Antananarivo. Currently only one diesel locomotive is operational and the future of the line is now in doubt unless a foreign saviour – the Chinese are the favourites – steps in soon.

Michelin 'Vito-Vito' railcar No. ZM516 has just crossed the 170-m-long 11-arch viaduct just south of Andriambilany station.

SWAKOPMUND TO WINDHOEK
NAMIBIA

GAUGE: 3 FT 6 IN. • **LENGTH**: 220 MILES •
ROUTE: SWAKOPMUND TO WINDHOEK

Built by the German colonial rulers to link the Atlantic coast port of
Swakopmund to the inland capital, Windhoek, the narrow-gauge railway
across the vast, arid Namib Desert was destroyed during the First World
War. Rebuilt and regauged, the line is still an important freight artery
and is the route for the 'Desert Express' tourist train.

One of the least densely populated countries in the world, Namibia is located in southwest Africa and is bordered to the west by the Atlantic Ocean, to the north by Angola and Zambia, to the east by Botswana and to the south and east by South Africa. Lying between the Namib and Kalahari deserts, it has little rainfall but is rich in mineral deposits.

With the exception of the deepwater port of Walvis Bay, which was annexed by the British, Namibia became a German colony in 1884 following the great carve-up of Africa by the European powers, becoming known as German South-West Africa. Following Germany's defeat in the First World War the country became part of the Union of South Africa in 1920 and remained under its administration until receiving full independence in 1990.

The first railway to be built in Namibia was a short line which opened in 1895 to transport guano to Cape Cross on the Skeleton Coast, around seventy miles north of Swakopmund. It has long since closed. Denied the use of the deepwater port to the south at Walvis Bay, the coastal town of Swakopmund was founded in 1892 as the main harbour for German South-West Africa. Initially transport from here was painfully slow, taking ten days using oxen and carts to travel across the desert then up the Great Escarpment to the Khomas Highland Plateau before arriving at the capital, Windhoek – climbing 5,600 ft over a distance of 220 miles. This slow transport system collapsed in the mid-1890s following an outbreak of rinderpest, or cattle plague, and the Germans hurriedly started building the first major railway route in Namibia, from Swakopmund to Windhoek.

Overseen by the German Colonial Authority, construction started in 1897 using existing German *feldbahn*, or narrow-gauge, equipment with a gauge of 600 mm (1 ft 11 ⅝ in.). The construction team of German army officers and soldiers were joined by 800 locally conscripted workers and the line was opened to the midway point of Karibib on 1 June 1900. With the arrival of the railway, this small settlement soon grew into a railway town where the main workshops were established. Beyond here, construction continued to Windhoek and the entire railway was opened on 19 June 1902.

PREVIOUS PAGE: Built by German soldiers and local labourers the 220-mile single-track railway across the Namib Desert between Swakopmund and Windhoek opened in 1902.

From a junction at Kranzberg, just to the west of Karibib, the Otavi Mining & Railway Company built another 600-mm-gauge line in a northwesterly direction to copper mines at Tsumeb. With railway workshops at Usakos, this 248-mile route opened in 1906 while a 54-mile branch opened from Otavi to zinc and vanadium mines in Grootfontein in 1908. The building of the railway coincided with the Herero and Namaqua Genocide, when around 100,000 people from the Herero and Nama tribes were driven by German soldiers into the desert where they died of thirst.

Despite using primitive equipment – the 0-6-0 tank locomotives used were usually operated back-to-back in pairs – the Swakopmund to Windhoek railway slashed journey times between the coast and the capital. Ox carts had taken ten days but the new railway soon offered a 2-day journey with passengers being accommodated overnight in Karibib. In 1911 the section of line between Windhoek and Karibib was regauged to the Cape gauge of 3 ft 6 in. to bring it into line with the gauge already in use in South Africa. Passengers and freight to or from Swakopmund then had to change trains at Karibib, but despite this the journey time from the coast to the capital was reduced to one day.

In 1914 the railway was extended southwards down the coast to the South African enclave of Walvis Bay but

German forces were quick to move in following the outbreak of the First World War. Their stay was short as South African troops soon retook it, reaching Swakopmund by January 1915. The retreating Germans moved inland, destroying the railway as they did so, before they surrendered at Otavi in July of that year. The damaged narrow-gauge line from Swakopmund to Karibib was then rebuilt by the British to the 3-ft 6-in.-gauge, thus allowing through trains once again along the whole route. The Otavi Railway was also regauged although this was not completed until 1961.

From 1915 to independence in 1990, the railways of Namibia were operated by South Africa. Since then the network has been in the control of the state-run TransNamib which currently operates nearly 2,000 miles of railway throughout the country with a freight link to the South African network in the far southwest. A 160-mile extension northwest from Tsumeb to Ondangwa opened in 2006 and this is currently being extended to the Angolan border.

The 246-mile single-track line from Walvis Bay and Swakopmund to Windhoek is a vital transport artery for Namibia's imports and exports. It is the only route totally within the country that connects the coast to the hinterland and is therefore used by intermodal container trains. TransNamib have also operated a tourist train on the route since 1998. The diesel-hauled 'Desert Express' operates at weekends between Windhoek and Swakopmund. With most of the journey undertaken during daylight hours, this is by far the best way of seeing Namibia's spectacular landscape. The modern train is made up of nine carriages including sleeping cars for forty-eight occupants, the Spitzkoppe Lounge, Welwitschia Restaurant and a car-carrying coach. The train departs from Windhoek on Friday mornings and returns from Swakopmund on Saturday afternoons, with the overnight stop at secure sidings. Excursions to see wildlife and Kalahari sand dunes are included in the package.

In addition to the 'Desert Express', a mixed train (passenger coaches and goods wagons) operates daily except Saturdays along this route. The overnight journey between Walvis Bay and Windhoek takes around twelve hours.

The TransNamib diesel locomotive fleet has been in service since 1968 although four newer locomotives were purchased from China in 2004. The latter have not been a great success due to a high rate of technical problems and unavailability – you get what you pay for.

The railway from Swakopmund to Windhoek is an important transport artery for Namibia's imports and exports. Here a TransNamib diesel-electric locomotive hauls a long freight train across the arid landscape that is a feature along most of the route.

CAPE TOWN TO KIMBERLEY
SOUTH AFRICA

GAUGE: 3 FT 6 IN. • **LENGTH:** 615 MILES •
ROUTE: CAPE TOWN TO KIMBERLEY

Seen as part of a future Cape-to-Cairo railway, the line from Cape Town to Kimberley was built following the discovery of diamonds in the north of the Cape Colony. A feat of late-Victorian engineering, its 615-mile route through the Hex River Mountains and across the flat and arid Karoo Desert can still be enjoyed in the twenty-first century.

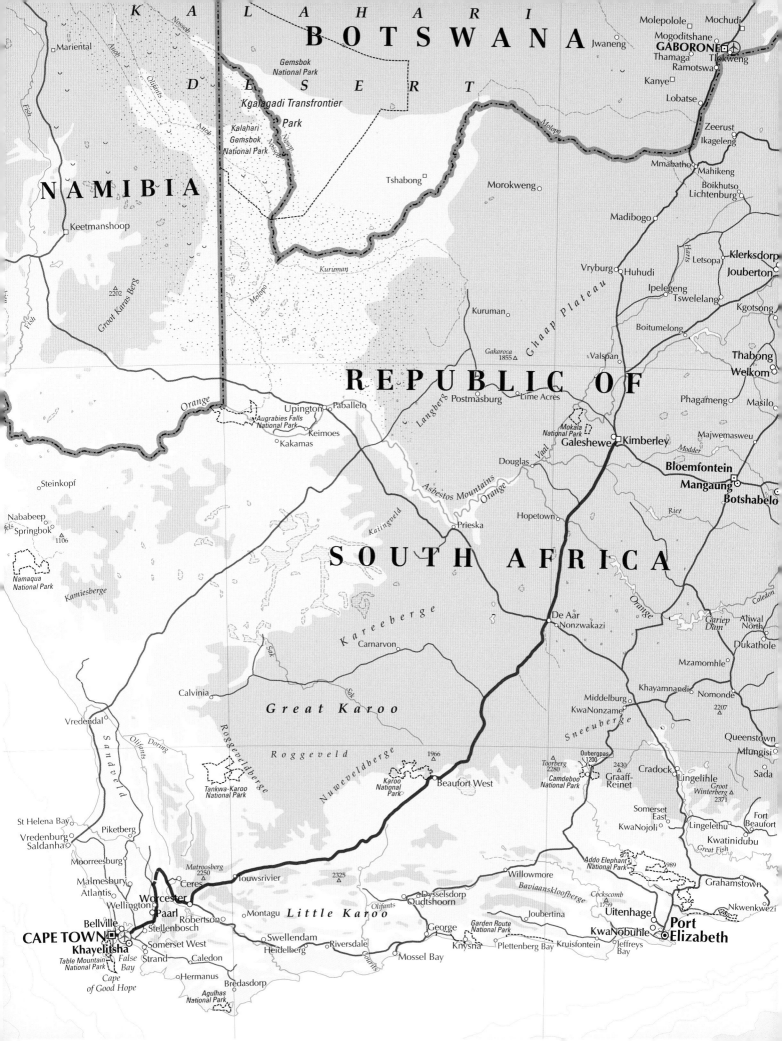

Opening in the early 1860s, the first railways to be built in South Africa were very local affairs around Cape Town. Expansion inland was considered too difficult at that time because of the natural barrier of the Cape Fold Mountains that surrounded the coastal strip around the Cape. However, the discovery of diamonds at Kimberley, 615 miles to the northeast of Cape Town, in 1871 changed all this. The following year the first Prime Minister of the Cape Colony, John Molteno, announced the formation of the Cape Government Railways (CGR) with ambitious plans for an extensive network of railways throughout southern Africa. At the same time the existing privately owned railways were taken over by the CGR, including the short line from Cape Town to Wellington which had opened in 1863.

In 1873 the Cape Colony Government chose a gauge of 3 ft 6 in. for all its proposed lines – known as the 'Cape Gauge', this narrow gauge would make construction through the mountain ranges cheaper and more rapid than standard gauge. Work started on building the railway to Kimberley in the same year, with the existing standard-gauge line from Cape Town to Wellington being regauged and extended northwards to Gouda before looping around the mountains to follow the Breede River Valley southward to the town of Worcester, opening in June 1876.

From Worcester, construction turned eastwards up the Hex River Valley to De Doorns from where the railway climbed up through the Hex River Mountains on gradients as steep as 1-in-40 to the 3,147-ft-summit at Matroosberg on the edge of the Little Karoo Plateau. Descending from here, the railway reached Montagu Road, renamed Touws River in 1883, which soon became an important railway town where banking engines from De Doorns were turned and which, between 1924 and 1981, was the junction for the branch line to Ladismith. Set amidst the flat and arid Karoo region, the small farming community of Matjiesfontein was reached in 1878 – the coming of the railway soon led to it growing into a town and becoming a fashionable Victorian spa and health resort. Continuing across the Karoo, the railway reached Buffelsriver, later renamed Laingsburg, in the same year and Beaufort West in 1880. As the largest town in the Karoo, Beaufort West was already an important sheep-rearing centre and later became the birthplace of Dr Christiaan Barnard who performed the world's first heart transplant in 1967.

PREVIOUS PAGE: A South African Railways 4-8-4 Class 25C condensing locomotive hauls a long passenger train across the vast expanse of the arid Karoo Desert near Riem in June 1971.

From Beaufort West the railway struck out northeastwards across the inhospitable Great Karoo Desert through Three Sisters, so-named after a nearby range of hills, and Hutchinson, which was the junction for the branch line to Calvinia from 1905 to 2001, before reaching De Aar in 1883. De Aar soon became a major railway junction, with main lines opening to Port Elizabeth on the Indian Ocean coastline in the south and Upington on the Orange River in the northwest.

From De Aar, construction of the line continued northwards across the arid landscape before crossing the Orange River to reach Belmont – this small settlement was the site of a battle during the Second Boer War in 1899 between British and Boer forces. The railway to the diamond capital of Kimberley was finally opened in 1885 but this was not the end of the line. The following year gold was discovered in the Transvaal in the Orange Free State to the northeast. Following an agreement with the government of the OFS the Cape Government Railway extended the line to Johannesburg via Bloemfontein in 1892, thus allowing through trains to travel from Cape Town for the first time.

The opening of this important railway route was a link in the English businessman, wealthy mine owner and South African politician Cecil Rhodes' dream to build a railway the length of Africa between Cape Town and Cairo. Although much of it was eventually built there is still a large gap missing between Uganda and northern Sudan. The Cape Government Railway proved its strategic worth carrying British troops and equipment during the Second Boer War between 1899 and 1902. After the end of war in Southern Africa the various British colonies merged to form the Union of South Africa in 1910. At the same time all of the former colonial railways were merged to become the South African Railways (SAR).

Introduced on the route in 1923, the 'Union Express' and 'Union Limited' trains were the forerunners of the famous luxury 'Blue Train' that still operates today. The trains connected with Union Castle Line passenger ships that plied between England and Cape Town until 1977.

In 1954 the section from Cape Town up the steeply graded line through the Hex River Mountains to Touws River was electrified, thus eliminating the use of banking engines for the 1-in-40 climb up from De Doorns. At Touws River new SAR Class 4E electric locomotives were swapped for powerful SAR Class 25 condensing steam locomotives for the rest of the journey northwards across the Karoo to De Aar and Kimberley. Built by the North British Locomotive Company in Glasgow, Scotland, the powerful electric locomotives had been originally ordered to operate on a new electrified line that would have bypassed the steep climb up through the mountains on a newly aligned route through a series of tunnels. This proposal was postponed indefinitely for financial reasons and the existing line was electrified instead with trains being hauled by pairs of Class 4Es.

Introduced between 1953 and 1955, the SAR Class 25 condensing locomotives mentioned above were specially designed to haul heavy trains on the line from Twous River to De Aar and Kimberley. Obtaining sufficient water supplies on this route across the Great Karoo Desert had always been a major problem and extra water supplies needed to be carried in tankers behind the earlier Class 12AR 4-8-2 locomotives. Probably the pinnacle of world steam locomotive design, the first example of the Class 25 4-8-4 was built by Henschel of Germany with a further eighty-nine by the North British Locomotive Company. The two companies shared the construction of the massive condensing tenders, which at 58 ft in length were much longer than the locomotive. These tenders not only carried 5,450 gallons of water and nineteen tons of coal but also eight large radiators on each side which were cooled by steam powered roof fans – in this way spent steam was condensed back to water to be used again. These monster locomotives, with their unique exhaust sound, were put into service hauling freight and passenger trains between Touws Rivers, Beaufort West, De Aar and Kimberley until they were retired following the gradual electrification of the route in the 1980s.

One non-condensing member of the SAR Class 25 was rebuilt between 1979 and 1981 as the prototype Class 26 locomotive. Known as the 'Red Devil' because of the striking colour of its livery, it proved even more powerful than the Class 25 but by this time steam power in South Africa was fast being replaced by diesel and electric traction and this futuristic steam project ground to a halt.

The difficult Hex River Mountain route between De Doorns and Touws River was eventually bypassed by the long-delayed Hex River Tunnel line, which opened after a 45-year delay in 1989. This new 18½-mile route has easier gradients, with a maximum of 1-in-66 on the climb up from De Doorns to the four tunnels through the mountains. The longest of these is 8½ miles long, making it the longest railway tunnel in Africa. Since closure, the original route up through the pass has become a hiking and mountain bike trail.

Formed in 1990, the state-owned Transnet company is now responsible for railway maintenance and rail freight services in South Africa, running intermodal, agricultural and bulk liquid heavy freight trains on the electrified route between Cape Town and Kimberley.

While rail passenger traffic has been declining for some time in South Africa, there are still three ways to enjoy the wonderful scenery of the Cape vineyards, the Hex River Mountains and the Great Karoo Desert along this route.

The cheapest is the Shosholoza Meyl long-distance sleeping and restaurant car train that operates between Cape Town and Johannesburg three times a week. With intermediate stops at Bellville, Wellington, Worcester, Matjiesfontein, Beaufort West and De Aar the journey takes 17¾ hours.

The second option is the more luxurious weekly Premier Classe train that includes lounge, restaurant and sleeping cars, and a car transporter wagon. With intermediate stops at Beaufort West and De Aar the journey takes eighteen hours.

By far the most prestigious and certainly the most expensive way to travel this route is on the 'Blue Train' which operates at least once a week between Cape Town and Pretoria with a journey time of 27½ hours. The northbound train calls at Matjiesfontein for a visit to the restored Victorian colonial village while the southbound service calls at Kimberley for an excursion to the famous open diamond mine.

OVERLEAF: Hauled by two electric locomotives the luxury 'Blue Train' is seen here close to the climb up through the Hex River Mountains on its journey between Cape Town and Pretoria.

SUDAN'S
RAILWAY

SUDAN, AFRICA

GAUGE: 3 FT 6 IN.

Originally built to support British military operations against the Mahdist regime, the railways of Sudan played an important part in the country's economy until the 1970s. Since then civil war, US economic sanctions, labour unrest and a lack of maintenance and investment have brought the country's railways to their knees.

B isected by the meandering River Nile, Sudan was, until 2011, the largest country in Africa. For thousands of years its history has been closely linked with its northern neighbour Egypt but by the late nineteenth century it had virtually become a colony of the British Empire. The turning point came in 1898 when Lord Kitchener's British-led army decisively defeated the Islamist Mahdi army of Abdullah al-Taashi at the Battle of Omdurman. From that date, despite continuing demands from Egypt to unify the two countries, Sudan remained under British rule until 1956 when it gained full independence. In more recent times a long-running civil war in the eastern Darfur region finally ended in 2011, and South Sudan separated into an independent country following a referendum.

The first railways in Sudan were built to support British-led military campaigns against the Mahdist regime. With construction beginning in 1874, the first was built during the reign of Mohammed Ali Basha, then governor of Sudan. The 3-ft 6-in.-gauge line followed the east bank of the River Nile from Wadi Halfa, an important staging post close to the Egyptian border, reaching Saras in 1877 and Ukasha in 1885. Here, work stopped following General Gordon's defeat by Mahdi forces in Khartoum. Construction work resumed in 1896 and the following year had reached its southernmost point at Karma. By that time the railway's *raison d'être* had faded away following the end of war in Dongola Province and it was abandoned in 1905.

The second, more successful, railway to be built in Sudan was opened from Wadi Halfa in a southeasterly direction across the Nubian Desert to Abu Hamad in 1898. Bypassing the enormous S-bend of the Nile, the 3-ft 6-in.-gauge, 217-mile line drastically cut travelling times between the two towns, enabling military forces to strike deep into Mahdi territory. Following the defeat of the Mahdi at the Battle of Omdurman in 1898, the railway was extended along the east bank of the Nile to Atbara and thence to the capital, Khartoum, 563 miles from Wadi Halfa, which was reached at the very end of 1899.

Although the new railway opened up a new trade route from central Sudan to the Mediterranean – using the Nile from Wadi Halfa to Aswan in Egypt and then by Egyptian

railways to Alexandria – the transhipment of goods on and off Nile steamers made it a slow business. To overcome this, a new 294-mile railway was opened between Atbara and a new harbour on the Red Sea coast at Port Sudan in 1906. For twenty-three years this new railway was the country's main rail link with the outside world, allowing the transportation of agricultural goods such as cotton and sorghum from the fertile Nile valley to distant markets.

Railway building continued under British rule with a 138-mile line from Station 10, north of Abu Hamad, westwards to the Nile at Karima, opening in 1905, and a 428-mile line extending south up the Blue Nile from Khartoum to Sennar, thence westwards to Kosti and El Obeid, in 1911. Sennar, the centre of the country's cotton-growing region, became an important junction in 1929 with the completion of the 498-mile line to Gedarif, Kassala and Haiya, where it joined the line to Port Sudan. Serving important cotton and grain-growing regions this new, more direct route took much of the export traffic bound for Port Sudan that formerly used the 1906 route via Khartoum and Atbara. Around the same time a branch line was built from Malawiya across the border to the Eritrean town of Teseney.

From 1929 onwards there were no new 3-ft 6-in.-gauge railways built in Sudan until the 141-mile branch line from Sennar Junction to Ad Damazin opened along the Blue Nile Valley in 1954. Following independence in 1956, a 428-mile westward extension of the El Obeid line from Aradeiba Junction to Babanousa and Nyala in Southern Darfur was completed in 1959 and a 276-mile line from Babanousa southwards to the city of Wau in 1962. Along with an extensive network of cotton plantation lines built between the 1920s and 1960s in the El Gezira region south of Khartoum, the total route length of the rail network in Sudan had reached nearly 3,000 miles by the 1970s. With foreign investment and a thriving agricultural industry, Sudan's railways prospered in the 1960s and 1970s but storm clouds were soon on the horizon.

The 3-ft 6-in.-gauge single-track network remained totally steam operated until the 1950s when British diesel locomotives built by English Electric were first introduced. Despite this, steam locomotives built by the North British Locomotive Company of Glasgow continued in operation, although their numbers started to decline following the introduction of new American General Electric diesels in the late 1970s. By the 1980s the lack of spare parts for the

PREVIOUS PAGE: Back in the good old days of steam when Sudan's railways still worked, 2-8-2 No. 306 heads a Damazeen to Sennar Junction train near Singa on Saturday, 15 January 1983.

diesels, coupled with the country's economic downturn, saw steam operations linger on, albeit on a reduced scale, only ending in 1990.

In more recent years US economic sanctions have blocked the purchase of spare parts for Sudan Railways Corporation's diesels although a few new locomotives have recently been purchased from China.

The sacking of around 20,000 railway workers by the Government in 1992 following years of Communist and union-sponsored labour unrest, US economic sanctions, the civil war in Darfur, poor management, lack of maintenance, neglect, unreliable services and the general stagnation of the Sudanese economy have all conspired to bring the country's extensive rail network to the brink of collapse. Unable to compete with road transport, the railways now only carry around 5 per cent of Sudanese freight traffic and passenger trains run no more – one of the last, the twice-weekly passenger service

from Khartoum to Wadi Halfa, ceased to run in the autumn of 2010. As reported in Al Arabiya News in April 2011, it took one month to transport five tractors by train from Khartoum to Nyala, a journey that once took three days. Those trains that do run cannot travel at more than 25 mph because of the dangerous state of the track.

Having lost its valuable oil industry following the secession of South Sudan in 2011, the Sudanese Government is now looking to China, South Korea and the Ukraine to finance the rebuilding of its neglected railways. A Chinese company is relaying the line from Khartoum to Port Sudan via Atbara using concrete sleepers and, once that is completed, plans to relay the line from Khartoum to Nyala from where there will be a new extension to neighbouring Chad. This line could also be used to transport oil from South Sudan if the two countries can forget their differences. Only time will tell if Sudan's once-great British-built railway system can be rescued from oblivion.

Steam traction continued on Sudan Railways until 1990. Here North British-built 2-8-2 No. 326 passes a termite mound on the Damazeen to Khor Doniya line on Friday, 14 January 1983.

OVERLEAF: A rare sight in a country where railway operations have virtually ceased to exist. A decrepit Sudanese diesel-electric creeps through an unforgiving desert landscape with a ramshackled freight train.

ASIA

QINGHAI-TIBET RAILWAY

QINGHAI REGION AND TIBET AUTONOMOUS REGION, PEOPLE'S REPUBLIC OF CHINA

GAUGE: 4 FT 8½ IN. • **LENGTH:** 1,215 MILES •
ROUTE: XINING TO LHASA

The first railway to be built in remote and mountainous Tibet and opened throughout in 2006, the Qinghai-Tibet Railway is not only the highest railway in the world but it has the highest railway tunnel and highest station. Parts of it are built on permafrost, calling into question its structural stability if world temperatures rise.

When opened in 2006 the Qinghai-Tibet Railway entered the record books as the world's highest railway, taking this title from Peru's Ferrocarril Central Andino (see pages 288-293). A railway from China to Tibet, the world's highest and most remote country, was first proposed in 1950 but the prohibitive cost and lack of technological expertise available at that time halted any progress.

Tibet is called 'the roof of the world' for very good reason as the region includes many of the world's highest mountains, including Mount Everest (29,029 ft), on its southern Himalayan border with Nepal. North of here the Tibetan Plateau, which stretches westwards into India has an average altitude of 14,800 ft above sea level and is roughly four times the size of France. Tibet is bordered to the north by the Kunlun Range of mountains and to the west by the Karakorum Range. Despite its enormous size, Tibet only has a population of around 3 million and is the third least-populated area in the world after northern Greenland and Antarctica. Lhasa, its administrative capital, is located at an altitude of 11,450 ft above sea level in the southeast of the region, on the northern foothills of the Himalayas.

In 1951, and not for the first time, China invaded Tibet but the mainly nomadic scattered people along with an army of Buddhist monks were no match for the invader's modern war machine. Since 1959, when the Tibetan Government was abolished, Tibet has been an Autonomous Region of the People's Republic of China. After being isolated from the rest of the world for centuries, it is worth noting that Tibet's vast untapped mineral wealth was ready to be exploited to fuel China's industrial growth.

Xining, the capital of China's Qinghai Province, was first reached in 1959 when the 117-mile Lanqing Railway from the city of Lanzhou opened. This was the first step in the building of the ambitious Qinzang Railway to Lhasa in Tibet but it took another forty-seven years to complete.

The second stage to be built was the 506-mile westward extension from Xining to Golmud via the north shore of Qinghai Lake. The line opened in 1984 but construction southwards through the Kunlun Pass to Lhasa was held

PREVIOUS PAGE: One of the 675 bridges that were built for the 1,215-mile railway across the high Tibetan Plateau to the capital, Lhasa.

up until 2001 due to the technical difficulties of building a railway on permafrost. The problem was eventually solved by a combination of rock embankments and elevated tracks supported on concrete piers sunk deep into the ground. This system works at the moment but a small rise in temperature brought on by climate change could seriously undermine the railway's infrastructure.

With a workforce of 20,000, construction work progressed from both ends of the line and the railway's highest point at Tanggula Pass was reached in 2005. Reaching an altitude of 16,640 ft this is the highest railway in the world and Tanggula Mountain station (16,627 ft) is also the highest station. The railway was officially opened on 1 July 2006 and its completion was hailed as a major feat by the Chinese Government – the statistics are pretty remarkable: 675 bridges; 340 miles built on permafrost; highest railway in the world; highest railway station in the world; Fenghuoshan Tunnel the highest railway tunnel in the world (16,093 ft); forty-five stations (the majority unstaffed as they are very remote) between Golmud and Lhasa.

Trains on the Qinghai-Tibet Railway are hauled by pairs of Class NJ2 Co-Co 5,100 hp diesel-electric locomotives specially modified to work at high altitudes. A total of seventy-eight of these locomotives were built for the railway by General Electric Transportation Systems in Erie, Pennsylvania, U.S.A. Other GE-designed locomotives have also been assembled under licence at the Qishuyang Locomotive Factory in Changzhou in China. Built by the Bombardier Sifang Corporation, the passenger rolling stock has been specially designed for high-altitude travel with an oxygen supply available at each seat. There is also a doctor on each train.

Since completion of the Qinghai-Tibet Railway in 2006 a 157-mile westward extension to Shigatse, the second largest city in Tibet, has been under construction. Other extensions are also being proposed including connections to Nepal and India.

Current passenger services on the line include daily trains between Beijing and Lhasa and between Shanghai and Lhasa. There are also trains on alternate days to Lhasa from Chengdu, Chongqing, Xining and Lanzhou. The journey time from Xining to Lhasa is just over twenty-four hours while from Golmud it takes around 14½ hours. For intrepid long-distance railway travellers the journeys from Beijing and Shanghai take nearly two days.

Between Xining and Golmud the railway follows the north shore of Qinghai Lake, which is more like a small inland sea. With an area of around 1,700 square miles, this saline lake is located at an altitude of 10,515 ft on the Tibetan Plateau and is an important bird migration crossroads but over the last fifty years many of its tributary rivers have dried up and it has shrunk in size. The city of Golmud is located amidst an area of enormous mineral and natural gas deposits while the nearby Qarham Salt Lake is the largest salt lake in the world.

From Golmud the railway heads south to the Kunlun Pass, 15,656 ft above sea level and site of a bitter battle between Chinese and Japanese troops in 1939. It then heads in a southwesterly direction along the eastern boundary of the Hoh Xil region, a remote and sparsely populated national nature reserve that is home to over 200 species of wild animals including the endangered wild yak and the Tibetan antelope. En route the railway passes through the 4,390-ft-long Fenghuoshan Tunnel, at 16,093 ft the highest railway tunnel in the world.

Continuing in a southwesterly direction across the high Tibetan plateau, the railway crosses the Tuotuo River, the source of the mighty Yangtze River, on a 4,586-ft-long bridge before reaching its highest point at Tanggula Station, at 16,627 ft above sea level the highest railway station in the world. The highest peak in the Tanggula

mountain range is Geladaindong (21,722 ft) where the Yangtze River begins its long journey to the East China Sea. From Tanggula Station the railway descends southwards to the Amdo grasslands, home to Cona Lake, the world's highest freshwater lake that has spiritual significance for Tibetan Buddhists. South of here it crosses the Nyenchen Tanglha Mountains offering passengers fine views of the snow-capped peaks, including more than 240 that are over 19,685 ft, and around 2,900 glaciers.

The final part of this epic journey is through the rich pasturelands of the Damxung region which is home to Lake Namtso, one of the holiest lakes for Tibetan Buddhists and, since the coming of the railway, a popular destination for Chinese tourists. On the final approach to Lhasa the railway loops eastward to cross the Lhasa (or Kyi) River before reaching the city's stark concrete station, 11,450 ft above sea level. This vast building has an overall roof covering four platform faces but there is plenty of room for expansion once the planned extensions to the railway have been built.

The opening of the railway has turned the ancient city of Lhasa into a major tourist destination for Chinese visitors who come to gaze at important Tibetan Buddhist sites such as the lofty Potala Palace, the Jokhand Temple and the extensive gardens at Norbulingka Palace. All three buildings have been awarded UNESCO World Heritage site status.

Sections of the Qinghai-Tibet Railway between the Kunlun Pass and Lhasa are built on elevated tracks supported on massive concrete piers sunk deep into the permafrost.

OVERLEAF: On the high Tibetan plateau the Qinghai-Tibet Railway crosses the Tuotuo River, the source of the Yangtze River, on a 4,586-ft-long bridge before reaching its highest point at Tanggula station.

21ST CENTURY
STEAM IN **NORTHEAST**
CHINA

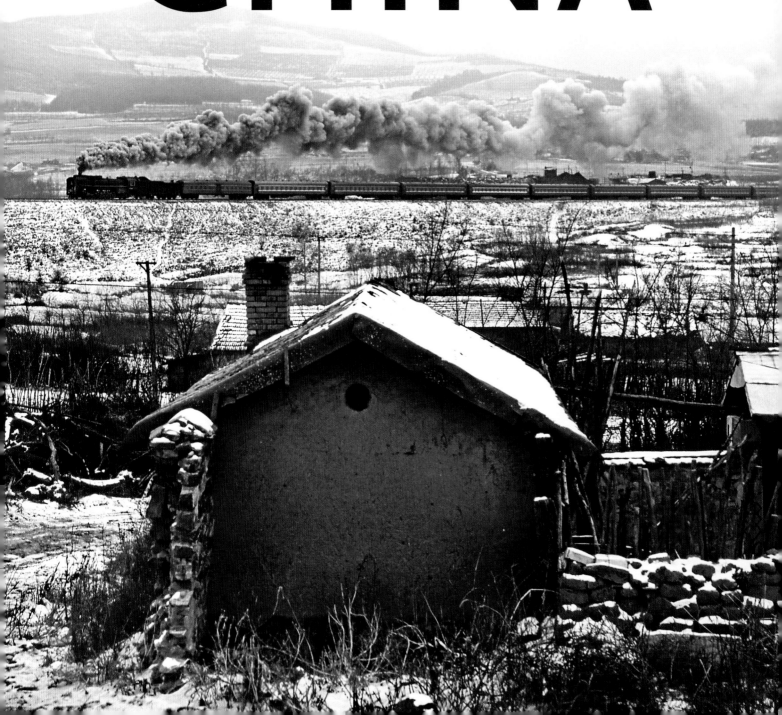

ocated in the far northeast of China, Heilongjiang Province is bordered to the north and east by Russia and to the west by Inner Mongolia. The Heilong Jiang River, scene of many border disputes between Russia and China, marks the division between the two countries in the north while its tributary, the Ussuri River, forms much of the eastern border. The province has a monsoon-influenced, humid continental climate with bitterly cold winters and temperatures plummeting to as low as -40°C. Summers are warm and humid although in the east they can be comparatively cool and refreshing due to the relative proximity to the Sea of Japan.

Much of the province is mountainous and is dominated by the Greater and Lesser Khingan ranges and the Wanda Mountains. The former contains China's largest virgin forest, making it an important area for the forestry industry. The interior is flat and low-lying and is bisected by numerous tributaries of the Amur River. Being rich in minerals such as oil, coal, gold and graphite, the province has long been one of the most important industrial regions in China. The presence of these raw materials proved to be one of the main reasons for the Japanese invasion of northeast China in 1931 which some enlightened historians believe to be the starting point of the Second World War. Under Japanese rule the region became known as Manchukuo, a puppet state under the nominal control of the last Qing emperor, Alsin-Gioro Puyi. Japanese rule ended in 1945 following the invasion of Manchuria by the Soviet Union.

There is today a network of standard-gauge railways in Heilongjiang Province linking the capital, Harbin, with other industrial cities such as Suihua and Yichung in the north and Changchung and Jilin (both in Jilin Province) in the south. The east–west line from Suifenghe on the Russian border north of Vladivostok through Harbin to Manzhouli in Inner Mongolia and thence into Russia, form an important section of the 'Continental Bridge' linking Asia and Europe. With plentiful supplies of locally mined coal and abundant cheap labour, steam locomotives reigned supreme on the Harbin to Changchun mainline well into the 1980s. Until very recently the province also had many steam-operated industrial railways, many of them built as narrow-gauge lines after the Second World War, serving the coal and timber industries. It ought to be remembered that the pollution from the coal-fired power stations of northeast China is reckoned to reduce life expectancies in the region by 5½ years.

PREVIOUS PAGE: As the snow blows in from Siberia, Shuangyashan Coal Railway 'QJ' class 2-10-2 No. 6805 climbs away from Shuangyashan, Heilongjiang Province, at Tudingshan village heading Train 83 to Dianchang on 4 January 2002.

In the grip of an icy cold winter in China's Heilongjiang Province, with a temperature of around -40°C plus wind chill, 762-mm-gauge 'C2' 0-8-0s 041 and 168 of the Huanan Coal Railway struggle to make progress over the plain, with snow drifting across the running line. Shepherds lead their cattle and sheep to shelter in the village of Changlonggang, near Huanan, on 30 December 2009.

Featured on these pages are three industrial lines that remained steam operated in the east of the province into the twenty-first century:

SHUANGYASHAN COAL RAILWAY

A standard-gauge network of lines serving mines around the 'Coal City' of Shuangyashan. Until diesels were introduced in 2002, Class 'QJ' 2-10-2 locomotives were in charge not only of coal trains but also passenger services from Shuangyashan to Dianchang, Fushan and Dongbaowei.

HUANAN FORESTRY RAILWAY

About fifty miles south of Jiamusi this 2-ft 6-in.-gauge line opened in 1952 and originally had a total length of 228 miles. Over the years the forestry operations dwindled

Jixi Mining Bureau 'SY' Class 2-8-2 No.1213 propels a loaded train up the grade from Wanjia Colliery in Sangagli village to Didao Washery, Heilongjiang Province, on 10 January 2010.

until only twenty miles remained open to serve a coal mine. Steam-hauled to the end, it closed in April 2011.

JIXI MINING BUREAU

Located on the Muling River close to the border with Russia, the Jixi Mining Bureau operates standard-gauge lines serving coal mines around the city of Jixi. Despite the introduction of electrification and diesel locomotives on some of the routes, many of the coal trains between collieries and China Rail exchange sidings in Jixi remained steam-hauled using 'SY' Class 2-8-2 locomotives until 2010, finishing completely at the end of 2012.

OVERLEAF: As the mist recedes up the river valley and the ice at the river's edge begins to thaw, 'SY' Class 2-8-2 No. 1417 heads the early morning Sipo to Pindingshan-Bailau mixed service across the Zhanhe River south of Pindingshan city, Henan Province, on 10 January 2003. Operated by the steel company at Wugang, the 20-mile line saw at this time two steam-hauled return passenger workings per day and two diesel-hauled freight workings serving steelworks at Sipo and Wugang and also traffic originating from mineral extraction in the Sipo district.

JITONG RAILWAY
CHINA, JILIN PROVINCE

GAUGE: 4 FT 8½ IN. • LENGTH: 587 MILES •
ROUTE: JINING TO TONGLIAO

Opened across the wilds of remote Inner Mongolia in 1995, this spectacular railway was primarily built to serve the region's vast mineral deposits. With freight and passenger trains hauled by massive 'QJ' locomotives it was also the last steam-operated main line in the world until diesels took over at the end of 2005.

Rampart of
Genghis Khan

Nehe   Bei'an

Choybalsan

Fuyu

Taiping
Ling
1712

Qiqihar

Longjiang   Mingshui

Suihua

Daqing
(Anda)

Zhaodong

MONGOLIA

Öndörhaan

Matad
(Jargalant)

Baruun-
Urt

D O N G   B E I
(M A N C H U R I A)

Harbin

Shangzhi

Ulanhot
(Horqin Youyi Qianqi)

Da'an

Songyuan
(Fuyu)

Fuyu
(Sanchahe)

Saynshand

Baicheng

Taonan

Tongyu
(Kaitong)

Dehui

Jilin
(Kirin)

Changchun

Jiaohe

Dunhua

Tianshan
(Ar Horqin Qi)

Xilinhot

Siping

Liaoyuan

Panshi

Huinan
(Chaoyang)

Fusong

Linxi

Tongliao

Dongbei Pingyuan

Baishan
(Hunjiang)

Da Hinggan Ling

Baochang
(Taibus Qi)

Chifeng
(Ulanhad)

Fuxin

Tieling

Tonghua

Ji'an

Chaoyang

Shenyang

Fushun

Puksubaek-san
252.

Hohhot

Jining
(Tsining)

Chengde

Jinzhou

Liaoyang

Benxi

Baotou

Fengzhen

Zhangjiakou
(Kalgan)

Lianshan

Anshan

NORTH

Huludao

Yingkou

Huich'ŏn

Hamhŭng

Ordos
(Dongsheng)

Huang He
(Yellow River)

Datong

Great Wall

Qinhuangdao

Liaodong
Wan

Dandong
(Andong)

Sinŭiju

Chŏngju

Hŭngnam

C H I N A

BEIJING
(Peking)

Tangshan

Wafangdian

Liaodong Bandao

KOREA

Xinkou
(Xinxian)

Baoding

Tianjin
(Tientsin)

Bo Hai

Dalian
(Lüda)

Korea
Bay

P'YŎNGYANG

Namp'o

Wŏnsan

Anju

MILITARY

Taiyuan

Yangquan

Cangzhou

Sariwŏn

Haeju

Chŏngju

DEMARCATION LINE/1953

SŎUL
(Seoul)

Jinzhong
(Yuci)

Shijiazhuang

Dezhou

Dongying

Laizhou
Wan

Yantai

Weihai

Inch'ŏn

Suide

Xingtai

Jinan

Shandong
Bandao

Suwŏn

SOUTH

Huang He
(Yellow River)

Huang He
(Yellow River)

Jingbang Yunhe

Handan

Zibo

Weifang

Laiyang

Yellow Sea
(Huang Hai)

Taejŏn
(Daejeon)

Lüliang Shan

Changzhi

Anyang (Zhangde)

Tai'an

Kunsan

Linfen

Shancheng
(Hebi)

Puyang

Xintai

Jiaozhou

Zhucheng

Qingdao
(Tsingtao)

KOREA

Houma

Xinxiang

Heze

Jining

Linyi

Rizhao
(Shijiusuo)

Kwangju
(Gwangju)

Yuncheng

Jiaozuo

Kaifeng

Zaozhuang

Mokp'o

Sanmenxia

Zhengzhou

Xuzhou
(Tongshan)

Lianyungang

Luoyang
(Loyang)

Xuchang

Suiyang

Cheju-haehyŏp

Pingdingshan

Zhoukou

Huaibei

Suqian

Huai'an
(Huayin)

Cheju-do

Halla-san
1950

Nanyang

Luohe

Suzhou

Hongze Hu

Yancheng

Shiyan

Danjiangkou

Zhumadian
(Yicheng)

Fuyang

Bengbu

Xinghua

Gaoyou Hu

Taizhou

EAST CHINA SEA
(DONG HAI)

Xiangfan
(Xiangyang)

Suizhou
(Pudu)

Xinyang

Yangzhou
(Hanjiang)

Jingmen

Tianmen

Lu'an

Huainan

Hefei

Nanjing

Wuhu

Ma'anshan

Changzhou (Wujin)

Nantong

Wuxi

Shanghai

ichang

Laohekou

Tai Hu

Suzhou

Pudong

Inner Mongolia has been an Autonomous Region of the People's Republic of China since 1947. Bordered to the north by Mongolia and Russia, by land area it is nearly the size of South Africa and over twice the size of France. Although most of the region is made up of a windswept grassland plateau that experiences temperatures as low as -40°C during winter, it also has enormous reserves of mineral deposits such as coal and iron ore that make it one of the most important mining regions in China.

Railway building in Inner Mongolia is fairly recent. When completed in 1955, the important international Trans-Mongolian Railway provided a rail link between Beijing and Moscow via the Inner Mongolian city of Jining and the Mongolian capital of Ulaanbaatar. By the early 1990s China's growth as an industrial powerhouse was gathering momentum and Inner Mongolia's vast mineral wealth was ready to be exploited. And so the Jitong Railway was born.

Connecting with existing standard-gauge railways at each end, the 587-mile Jitong Railway between Jining and Tonglaio was a joint venture between the state-owned China Railways and the Government of Inner Mongolia. Opened in 1995, it was built to a high engineering standard using modern technology for the infrastructure and track with numerous tunnels, curving viaducts and horseshoe curves incorporated to reduce gradients on the long climb up through the mountains to the Jingpeng Pass. However, with plentiful supplies of coal available in the region coupled with low labour costs, the railway was initially operated using steam locomotives and manually operated semaphore signalling. With the rest of the world's main-line railways having long since eradicated steam power, the Jitong Railway obtained 100 Class 'QJ' 2-10-2 locomotives made redundant by the introduction of diesel and electric haulage elsewhere in China.

Built between 1964 and 1988, the powerful 'QJ' locomotives were the last mainline steam locomotives built for commercial work in the world. Over 4,500 were built at the Datong Locomotive Works and were equipped with 12-wheel tenders, mechanical stokers and electric lights. These latter-day steam-age giants weighed 133 tons, were 96 ft long, had a power output of 2,900 hp and were capable of a top speed of 50 mph.

PREVIOUS PAGE: Two 'QJ' Class 2-10-2s, with No. 7012 leading, cross the viaduct by Erdi village, a place that became termed by photographers as 'Happy Valley', and it is easy to understand why! An eastbound freight for Daban in January 2000.

In remote Inner Mongolian landscape, QJ Class 2-10-2 No. 6811 works a westbound passenger service away from Linxi past Nanawayingzi on 19 April 2004. Diesel locomotives took over this service in 2005.

STEAM SWANSONG 1995–2005

The railway was a complete success, carrying 5 million tons of freight in 1995 and almost double that by 2000. New locomotive servicing and repair facilities were built at Daban, about midway along the route, where locomotives and crews were exchanged for the arduous westbound climb up to 3,222-ft-long Shang Dian Summit Tunnel, around 5,000 ft above sea level. The railway also featured a regular passenger train that took almost a day to cover the entire route – until 2005 it was not only the last steam-operated mainline passenger train in the world, but also the last to convey a dining car and sleeping cars.

As featured on these pages the swansong of steam power on the Jitong Railway lasted ten years and during that period steam enthusiasts from across the world made their pilgrimage to photograph and witness this memorable sight. The 'QJs' were finally retired in December 2005 when they were replaced by Class DF4 3,260-hp diesel-electric locomotives. Despite the official end of steam in 2005 and the withdrawal of locomotive facilities, the Jitong Railway has occasionally operated 'QJ'-hauled steam specials for enthusiasts.

Steam power in the raw! Jitong Railway 'QJ' Class 2-10-2s Nos. 6389 and 7009 emerge from 'Tunnel 3' of the Jingpeng Pass heading an eastbound freight on 25 November 1999.

OVERLEAF: Jitong Railway 'QJ' class 2-10-2s 6996 and 6351 head an eastbound freight through the Jingpeng pass at Xiakengzi village on 29 November 1999.

CHANGBAI MOUNTAIN REGION
JILIN PROVINCE, CHINA

GAUGE: 4 FT 8½ IN. • **LENGTH:** 106 MILES •
ROUTE: TONGHUA-BAISHAN (FORMERLY HUNJIANG)-
SONGSHUZEN-SONGJIANGHE

Located close to the border with North Korea, much of this scenic, steeply graded strategically important route was built by the Japanese during their occupation of Manchuria in the 1930s and remained steam operated until 2002.

The Tonghua-Songjiahne route borders the Changbai Mountains on the southeastern tip of China's Jilin Province, close to the border with North Korea (the Democratic People's Republic of Korea). Under the Japanese occupation of Manchuria, a railway was constructed linking Tonghua, Hunjiang (renamed Baishan in 2006) and Ji'an with the main Manchurian rail network at Meihekou, enabling a connection with the main Shenyang and Jilin line. The railway reached Tonghua in 1937 and the Tonghua-Hunjiang-Ji'an routes were subsequently opened in 1940. The Japanese placed great importance on the line, which was in effect its main wartime strategic supply route for the transport to Japan of the rich deposits of raw materials found in Manchuria and shipped via the Korean ports. The particularly scenic and steeply graded line continuing beyond Hunjiang to Songshuzen and Baihe was not opened until as recently as 1973, its primary purpose being to provide a key transport route to tap the rich timber and coal resources found in the Changbai Mountains region northeast of Hunjiang, where a number of steam-worked narrow-gauge logging railways connected into the standard-gauge network and could be found in operation until the early 1990s.

China Rail 'JS' class 2-8-2 No. 5485 passes Liudaojiang village, heading a Tonghua to Hunjiang freight on 21 November 1999.

The entire route has historically proved troublesome for railway engineers to construct, encountering steep wooded mountains and deep river valleys. Resultantly, the line is rich in engineering structures and has many sharp gradients and curves. It is for this very reason that the smaller and lighter China National Railways (CNR) 'JS' class 2-8-2 was used. It offered greater route availability over the larger and ubiquitous CNR 'QJ' class 2-10-2 and remained in service right up until the official cessation of steam traction on CNR in February 2002. The locomotives were maintained at the Tonghua district depot, coming under the Shenyang Railway Bureau of the CNR. The longevity of mainline steam locomotives, to be found working in extremely arduous conditions along this route, attracted steam railway enthusiasts from around the world anxious to witness this most incredible and historic spectacle into the new millennium.

The 'JS' class 2-8-2 was a product of co-operation between China and the USSR in the 1950s. The class was widely dispersed in China to be used for freight traffic on secondary main lines and for shunting and trip working. A total of 1,135 'JS' were constructed between 1957 and 1965 and a further 781 between 1981 and 1988. Many of

PREVIOUS PAGE: A China Rail 'JS' Class 2-8-2 crosses the Hunjiang River heading Train 4097, the 15.43 Hunjiang to Wangdou passenger service on 20 November 1999.

the 1980s-built locomotives were sold into industrial or local railway service, while other relatively new examples were sold on to industry upon becoming surplus to CNR requirements. A large number were still in service at the turn of the century and several dozen were still in use in early 2014 at the vast opencast coal mine at Sandaoling in Xinjiang Province, on the fringe of the Gobi Desert and the Tian Shan mountain range.

Tonghua is situated to the far southeast of Jilin Province on the Hunjiang, lying in the foothills of the Changbai Mountains. The city is connected by the 80-mile 'Meiji line' with Meihekou, where a connection is made with the main Shenyang-Jilin railway. As well as offering the traditional vital communications route with North Korea, Tonghua is a strategic junction on the new 857-mile Hegang-Dandong railway link, which was completed in September 2012.

This industrial city of Tonghua, rich in natural resources, is the largest steel production base in the Jilin Province and is an important rail hub in this region of China, which traditionally was noted for its trade in ginseng, marten furs and deer antler products. In the 1980s Tonghua had some initial success with the production of sweet red wines, which proved popular for local Chinese consumption but did not attract a viable export market. Tourist attractions in the Tonghua District include the Changbai Mountains Nature Reserve, the Donggou Ancient Tombs and Wandu Mountain Town.

Upon leaving Tonghua to the east, the route to Baishan soon passes a large steelworks that employs in the region of 30,000 workers. In 2012 the complex still utilized a small fleet of the Chinese standard industrial 'SY' class 2-8-2 steam locomotives. The rail route closely follows the course of the Hunjiang River throughout this stretch, crossing it several times as it steadily climbs, initially passing towns established entirely on small coal mining enterprises, before negotiating more consistently rugged terrain. Some twelve miles from Tonghua, at Yayuan, the 59-mile line to Ji'an branches off, one of five border crossings with North Korea.

After 37 miles, and still boasting its 1939-built Manchurian-style station building, Baishan City station is reached, serving the 'International Mineral Water City of China', previously known as Hunjiang, which was literally translated as 'dirty river'. The new city name of Baishan,

meaning 'snowy white mountain', is clearly more befitting of the city renowned for its pure mineral water. From this junction a small branch diverges off the main Tonghua-Baihe route to a further Sino/North Korean border crossing point at Dalizi. One of the established birthplaces of Manchu culture and the city of pilgrimage of the Qing Dynasty, Baishan is located in the southeast corner of Jilin Province on the western fringe of the Changbai Mountain range. It is recognized as one of the top ten ecotourism regions in China, boasting undulating mountains and crisscrossing valleys and rivers. Changbai Mountain is renowned for its snow-capped peak and Tianchi Lake is the largest and deepest volcanic lake in China. It is also the source of the Songhua, Tumen and Yalu rivers, the latter forming the border between China and North Korea. The Baishan area is rich in natural resources and is a major timber-producing area in China, the forests covering approximately 75 per cent of the surrounding district.

Between Baishan and Songjianghe the remaining 68 miles of the line snake through deep wooded valleys skirting the Changbai Mountains Nature Reserve. There are over 100 volcanoes distributed around Mount Changbai and the renowned 43-mile-long Great Canyon is also to be found here. This terrain is really quite distinctive and rarely seen in China.

Motive power on the route today is the standard China Rail 1980s-design 'DF4B' and 'DF4C' class Co-Co diesel electric locomotive, with 1970s-design 'DF5' class Co-Co locomotives based at Tonghua depot working short trip freights and station pilot duties. The opening of a new mountainous rail link between Baihe and Helong in 2012, connecting previously truncated routes close to the North Korean border, now provides direct communication with thirteen key cities in northeast China and forms a direct rail link from the coal-rich Heilongjiang Province, bordering with Russia, to the Yellow Sea Ports of Dandong and Dalian, forming a major rail freight artery through northeast China. The entire journey between Tonghua and Mudanjiang must now rate as one of the most scenic and fascinating of all rail journeys to be experienced in the region.

OVERLEAF: A grandstand view from the apartment blocks! China Rail 'JS' Class 2-8-2 No. 5480 heads Train 8531, the Tonghua to Hunjiang mixed freight, crossing the Hunjiang river bridge at Dong Tonghua in November 1999.

YANGÔN (RANGOON) TO MANDALAY

MYANMAR (BURMA)

GAUGE: 1,000 MM (3 FT 3³/₈ IN.) • **LENGTH:** 388 MILES •
ROUTE: YANGÔN (RANGOON) TO MANDALAY

Built by the British colonial rulers of Burma, the Rangoon to Mandalay railway, along with the rest of the colony's rail network, suffered severe damage following the Japanese invasion of 1942. Although rebuilt, the country's narrow-gauge railways were trapped in a 50-year time warp until the ending of military dictatorship in 2011.

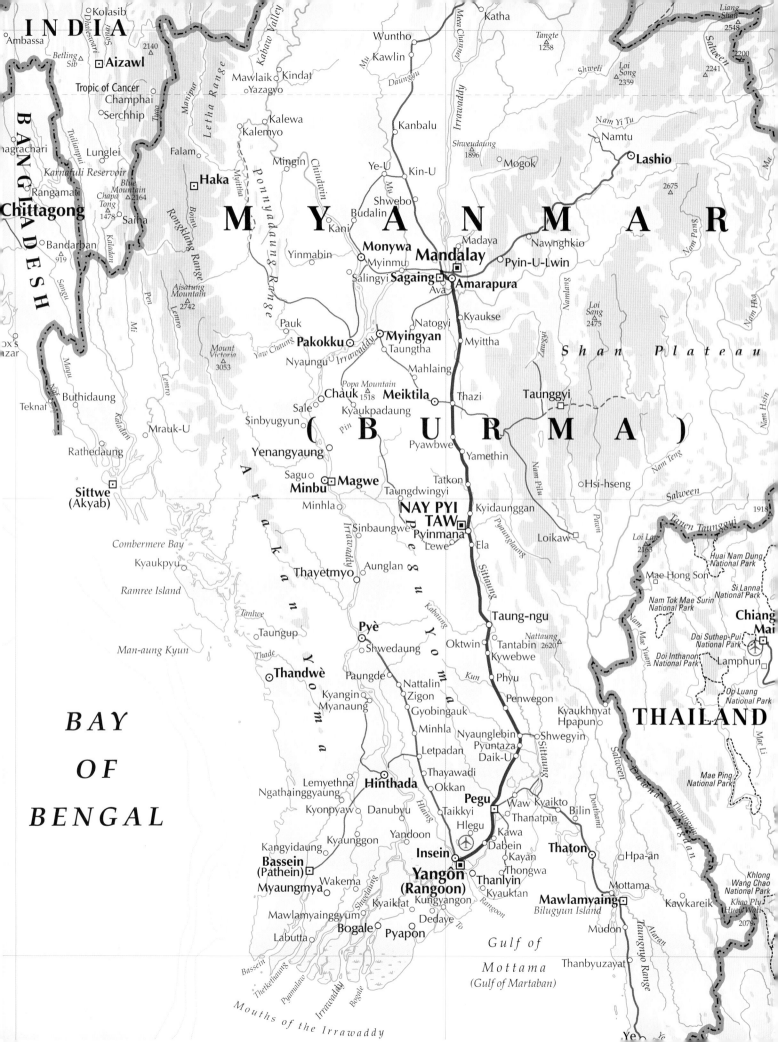

In a series of three wars between 1824 and 1885 the British gradually gained control of the whole of Burma, ruling it as a part of India until 1937 when it became a separate colony. The Second World War saw the colony invaded by the Japanese until they were defeated by General William Slim's British and Indian army in 1945. Burma became independent in 1948 but was ruled by a military dictatorship from 1962 to 2011 when it was replaced by a civilian government.

The first railway to be opened in Burma was the 163-mile line up the Irrawaddy Valley from the then capital, Rangoon, to Prome. Built to transport rice to the port at Rangoon, the narrow-gauge (1,000 mm) Irrawaddy Valley State Railway was constructed by Indian labourers from Bihar State. This was followed by the 166-mile Sittang Valley State Railway (also 1,000 mm gauge) which opened northwards up the Sittang Valley from Rangoon to Taungoo in 1884. The following year, Upper Burma came under British control following the brief Third Anglo-Burmese War, during which the latter railway proved to be of immense strategic value by transporting soldiers and equipment towards the war zone.

Following the end of the war, the Sittang Valley State Railway was extended a further 220 miles north to Pyinmana and Mandalay, the former capital of Upper Burma. A third railway, the Mu Valley State Railway, was opened in stages northwards from Mandalay to Myitkyina, close to the border with China, between 1891 and 1898. Apart from a ferry crossing the Irrawaddy to the west of Mandalay, this new line opened up a continuous 724-mile rail link from Rangoon to the forests of northern Burma, allowing the transportation of valuable hardwood down to the capital for export.

Meanwhile all three railways were merged to become the Burma Railway Company in 1896. Railway building continued in Burma until the end of the First World War including several branches off the Rangoon to Mandalay mainline (from south to north): Pegu to Mulmein and southwards down the coast to Ye; Pegu to Nyuangkashe; Nyaunglebin to Madauk; Pyinmana to Lewe; Thazi eastwards to Kalaw, Heho and Shwenyaung (for Inle Lake); Thazi westwards to Meiktila and Myingyan; and Mandalay to Lashio via the famous Gokteik curving steel viaduct.

Facing increasing competition from road transport the Burma Railway Company was nationalized in 1928. By then the railways had started to lose money on a big scale which was not helped by the fact that coal to fuel locomotives had to be imported from India and railway equipment such as locomotives and rolling stock from Britain. Japan invaded Burma in 1942 and during their occupation the country, its people and its infrastructure suffered terribly. Using forced labour and Allied prisoners of war they built a 258-mile metre-gauge railway from Thanbyuzayat, on the branch line from Pego to Ye, across the border to Thailand via the Three Pagodas Pass. The route included the famous bridge over the River Kwai which was destroyed by RAF bombers in February 1945. The Burmese section of the railway was subsequently abandoned although 81 miles in Thailand is still operational. Under the Japanese occupation Burma's operational metre-gauge rail network shrank from 2,059 route miles in 1942 to 674 route miles at the end of the war.

Following independence from Britain in 1948, the Burmese rail network was slowly restored so that by the early 1960s it had nearly reached its pre-war route mileage. Under the military dictatorship a surge of new railway building and doubling of single-track lines increased the route mileage in the country to its present 3,357 miles. However, until 2011, the railways, like the rest of the country, remained in a time warp, cut off from the rest of the world for fifty years.

The country's metre-gauge railways are now operated by state-owned Myanmar Railways. Most routes are still single-track although the Rangoon to Mandalay mainline is now double-track. Generally the track and infrastructure is in a poor condition with trains being restricted to very low speeds. Worn out German and Japanese diesel locomotives have in recent years been supplemented by more modern examples bought from India and donated by China. As illustrated on these pages, Mynamar Railways also owns a small number of oil-fired steam locomotives, built by Vulcan Foundry of Newton-le-Willows in Lancashire in 1949, some of which have remained in service into the 21st century. Homemade railbuses built from lorry parts and running on rubber tyres are also used on lightly constructed branch lines.

Currently there are three passenger trains a day between Rangoon and Mandalay, one in the daytime and two overnight trains, both with sleeping cars and one with a restaurant car. Journey times are very leisurely and vary between 15½ and 16½ hours for the 388-mile trip.

Chinese-built diesel-hauled trains for Mandalay start from Rangoon Central Railway Station. The original Victorian-period station was built by the British in 1877 but was subject to bombing raids by Japanese aircraft in the Second World War and was then blown up by retreating British forces in 1943. The present building was designed by Burmese architect U Tin in a traditional style with stepped roofs and was completed in 1954. Despite creeping modernization this British-built line still features old-fashioned semaphore signalling operated from Home Counties mock-Tudor-style signal boxes. Much of the line passes through a flat Burmese farming landscape dotted with small villages of thatched huts on stilts and workers tending their land and palm plantations. The gilded conical roofs of stupa-style temples are a frequent sight while at every stop the train is invaded by local vendors.

Heading north up the Sittang Valley, trains call at the ancient cities of Bago (Pegu) and Taungoo, the latter a centre for the forestry industry and home to the Shwesandaw Pagoda which was built near 1,000 years ago. Continuing northwards trains go on to serve Naypyitaw, which has been the country's capital since 2005. With a population of nearly one million, this unfinished modern city is laid out in a grid system and is home to all the government's ministries that were moved lock, stock and barrel from Rangoon, as well as the brand-new 325-ft-tall Uppatasanti Pagoda. Further north, trains call at the small town of Thazi, an important railway crossroads with a line westwards to Meiktila and Myingyan and eastwards to the hill towns of Kalaw, Heho and Shwenyaung. The latter station is the jumping-off point for trips to Inle Lake, Burma's second-biggest lake located at 2,900 ft on the Shan Plateau.

The final leg of the journey takes the railway northwards through Thabyedaung, Myittha and Singaing before trains terminate at Mandalay's new ultra-modern station. From here lines radiate westwards to Monywa, northwards to Myitkyina and eastwards to Lashio. The royal capital of Burma until the invading British arrived in 1885, Mandalay is the second-largest city in the country and is located on the east bank of the Irrawaddy River. The city has a large population of Chinese who have emigrated across the border from Yunnan province over the last twenty-five years. It is also an important centre of the Buddhist faith, home to several monasteries and sacred pagodas, including the Kuthodaw Pagoda which houses the world's largest book of 1460 pages, each 3½ ft by 5 ft, inscribed in stone.

On New-Year's-Day 1999, British-built (Vulcan Foundry 1949) 'YD' Class 2-8-2 No. 962 stands at the head of the daily mixed return service to Bago (Pegu) via Nyaungkhashe at Myutki.

OVERLEAF: On the eve of the Myanmar Independence Day celebrations, 3 January 1999, Myanmar Railways 'YB' class Pacific No. 536 heads a 'passenger' service from Pyinmana to Pyi Win, Ela and Thawatti, the hapless travellers having to ride in cane-carrying wagons well into the night.

'SEVEN STARS' ON KYUSHU
KYUSHU, JAPAN

GAUGE: 3 FT 6 IN. • **LENGTH:** 696 MILES •
ROUTE: FUKUOKA-ÔITA-MIYAZAKI- KAGOSHIMA-ASO-FUKUOKA

Railway building was slow to take off in Japan, lagging behind Europe and North America by four decades. In the southwest, the network of 3-ft 6-in.-gauge lines that were established around the volcanic and mountainous island of Kyushu can be explored today aboard the 'Seven Stars' luxury train.

Chinju
Sach'ŏn
ach'on
'ongyŏng
Namhae-do

Tonghae
Pusan
(Busan)
SOUTH
KOREA

Korea Strait

Higashi-suidō

Tsushima

SEA OF JAPAN
(EAST SEA)

Ōda *Sanbe-san*
△ 1126

Iwami Ginzan Silver Mine
Gōtsu
Gō-gawa
Hamada
Masuda *Garyū-zan*
△1223
Chūgoku-sanchi
Miyoshi

Iki-shima
Genkai-nada
Munakata
Nōgata
Iizuka
Fukuoka
Kasuga
Ōnojō
Chikushino Dazaifu
Tosu

Kita-Kyūshū
Mojikō **Ube**
Nakama
Yukuhashi
Tagawa
Yamada
Buzen
Amagi
Ogōri
△ *Hiko-san*
1200
Kitsuki

Hagi
Nagato
Mine

Shimonoseki
Onoda
Kudamatsu
Hōfu
Tokuyama
Shinnan-yō

Yamaguchi
Iwakuni

Hatsukaichi
Hiroshima
*Itsukushima
Shrine*
Kanmuri-yama
1339 △
1004
△

Higashi-Hiroshima
Kure

Hikari
Yanai
*Seto-naikai
Kokuritsu-kōen*
Hōjō
Matsuyama
Iyo

Suō-nada
Usa
Bungo-Takada
*Futago-
san*
△/21

J A P A N

Yawatahama
Ōzu

Karatsu
Hirado
Matsuura
Taku
Ōkawa
Yanagawa
Kashima
*Ariake-
kai*

Imari
Sasebo
Takeo
Saga

Hita
Kurume
Yame
Chikugo
Ōmuta
Yamaga
Kikuchi

*Aso-Kuju
Kokuritsu-kōen*
*Yufu-
dake*
1584
Beppu
Ōita
Usuki
Tsukumi

Kujū-san
△
1788
Taketa
△1592
Aso-san
*Sobo-
san*
1759

Saiki
Bungo-suidō

Uwajima
△ 1229
Takatsuki-yama

*Ashizuri-
Uwakai
Kokuritsu-
kōen*
Sukumo

S H I K O K U

*Saikai
Kokuritsu-
kōen*
Gotō-rettō

Nishi-
Sonogi-
hantō
Ōmura
Isahaya
Arao
Tamana

Nagasaki
Fukue
*Amakusa-
nada*

Hondo
*Unzen-
Amakusa
Kokuritsu-kōen*
Ushibuka

Kumamoto
△ 1359
Shimabara
*Unzen-
dake*
Uto

Midori-gawa
Kunimi-dake △
1739
Kyūshū-sanchi

Nobeoka

Yatsushiro
Yatsushiro-kai

Minamata
Hitoyoshi
△ *Ichifusa-yama*
1722
Saito
Hyūga

K Y Ū S H Ū

Ōkuchi
Ebino
Kobayashi
*Kirishima-
yama*
△
1700
*Kirishima-Yaku
Kokuritsu-kōen*

Izumi
Akune
Sendai-gawa
Miyanojō
*Koshikijima-
rettō*
Sendai
Kushikino
Kagoshima
Kokubu
Miyakonojō
Nichinan
Kushima

Koshiki-kaikyō
Sakura-jima
△ 1118
*Kirishima-Yaku
Kokuritsu-kōen*
Kagoshima
Tarumizu
Kanoya

Miyazaki

*Satsuma-
hantō*
Kaseda
Makurazaki
Ibusuki
*Ōsumi-
hantō*
Kaimon-dake
924

Ōsumi-kaikyō

E A S T   C H I N A   S E A

(D O N G   H A I)

Kuro-shima
Iō-jima
Take-shima
Mage-shima
Kishika-zaki

Nishino-omote

P A C I F I C

O C E A N

Ōsumi-shotō
*Shin-
dake*
Yaku-shima
Kuchino-Erabu-
shima 649
*Miyanoura-
dake*
△
1935
*Kirishima-Yaku
Kokuritsu-kōen*
Kamiyaku

*Tanega-
shima*

Kyushu is the most southwesterly of Japan's four major islands and, at its closest point, lies only 125 miles from the South Korean mainland. Kyushu has a mountainous interior which is home to Japan's most active volcano, Mount Aso (5,220 ft), and numerous hot mud springs. The majority of the population and the bulk of industry are concentrated in the cities of Kitakyushu, Fukuoka, Sasebo and Nagasaki in the northwest of the island while in the more rural east and south the growing of rice, soy, tobacco and tea supports an agricultural economy.

During the nineteenth century, railway building in Japan was slow to follow the progress made in Europe. Initially the railways were built by foreign engineers, with the first steam locomotive being demonstrated by a Scotsman on an 8-mile track at Nagasaki in 1868. With British funding and engineers, the first public railway to be built was between Shimbashi and Yokohama on Honshu Island which opened in 1872. The gauge chosen was 3 ft 6 in. which remained the standard for Japanese railways until the building of the 4-ft 8½-in.-gauge Shinkansen high-speed lines that first opened in 1964.

Incorporated in 1888, the Kyushu Railway opened the first twenty-two miles of railway on the island between the city of Fukuoka and Chitosegawa in 1889. By 1907, when Japan's railways were nationalized, the company had opened nearly 450 miles of railway mainly in the north of the island. Between 1907 and 1949 the country's railways were operated by the Japanese Government Railways (JGR) but, following Japan's defeat in the Second World War, the JGR was reorganized in 1949 to become a state-owned public corporation known as the Japanese National Railways. With massive post-war aid from the US Marshall Plan, the country's bomb-damaged and rundown railways were rebuilt and in 1964 JNR opened the world's first purpose-built high-speed railway, the Shinkansen or 'Bullet Train', between Tokyo and Osaka. Since then, the high-speed network has expanded with the city of Fukuoka in northern Kyushu being linked to Osaka on the island of Honshu by the Sanyo Shinkansen in 1975.

In 1987 the state-owned Japanese National Railways was privatized. Collectively known as the Japanese Railways Group, the railway system is owned by seven independent companies, three of which are listed on the Tokyo Stock Exchange.

Kyushu's railways are operated by the Kyushu Railway Company. In 2004 the Kyushu Shinkansen opened between Fukuoka and the southern Kyushu city of Kagoshima, while construction of the Nagasaki Shinkansen is expected to be completed by 2023.

In addition to the standard-gauge Kyushu Shinkansen line on the island, the Kyushu Railway Company operates services on the older 3-ft 6-in.-gauge lines. Many of these traverse the highly scenic interior such as the 88-mile Kyudai Main Line that runs along the Chikugo Valley between Kurume and Ōita, and the 92-mile Hohi Main Line between Kumamoto and Ōita. The 205-mile Nippo Main Line hugs the east coast southwards from Ōita to Nobeoka and Miyazaki and thence west inland to Miyakonojo, Hayato and Kagoshima. Probably the most scenic route on the island is the 77-mile Hitatsu Line that runs through the mountains between Hayato in the south and Yatsushiro

PREVIOUS PAGE: Introduced in October 2013, the 'Seven Stars' train takes passengers on a circular tour of the island of Kyushu. It is hauled by a stylish DF200-7000 diesel-electric locomotive sporting an art-deco radiator grill.

on the west coast. To complete a circular tour of the island the 92-mile Hohi Main Line skirts the active volcano of Mount Aso on this highly attractive route through the mountains between Kumamoto and Ōita.

The Kyushu Railway History Museum is located in the former headquarters of the original Kyushu Railway next to the lovingly restored Mojiko station in Kitakyushu. A tourist train operates from the museum along one mile of a former freight line.

'SEVEN STARS'

Introduced in October 2013 the 'Seven Stars' is a luxury train that operates two- and four-day tours around Kyushu. Hauled by a purpose-built DF200-7000 diesel locomotive, the maroon-liveried train consists of seven de luxe coaches that include five sleeping cars, a lounge car and a dining car. The start and finish point of the tours is the modern Hakata station in the northwest city of Fukuoka, southern terminus of the Sanyo Shinkansen from

Osaka. From here the 4-day cruise travels eastwards through Bungomori to Yufuin, where a stop is made to visit hot mud springs, and Lake Kinrin, set below the 5,197-ft peak of Mount Yufudake. From Yufuin the train continues east to Ōita before following the route of the Nippo Main Line overnight down the east coast to Miyazaki.

On the second day the 'Seven Stars' heads westwards from Miyazaki along the Nippo Main Line through Miyakonojo and Hayato before arriving at Kagoshima. Following a visit to a traditional Japanese garden, passengers board the train for the overnight journey back to Hayato and then northwards along the Hitatsu Line to Yatsushiro and Kummamoto. From here it heads east into the mountains on the Hohi Main Line to arrive at Aso in the early morning of the fourth day. After breakfast in the shadow of Mount Aso, the train continues eastwards through the mountains to Ōita from where it retraces its journey back to Fukuoka.

The 'Seven Stars' luxury maroon-liveried train includes sleeping cars, a lounge car, a dining car and an observation car offering a high standard of accommodation for its twenty-eight passengers.

JANAKPUR RAILWAY
INDIA AND NEPAL

GAUGE: 2 FT 6 IN. • **LENGTH:** 31½ MILES (ONLY 18 MILES CURRENTLY OPERATIONAL) •
ROUTE: JAYNAGAR/BIHAR STATE, NORTHEASTERN INDIA TO JANAKPUR/
SOUTHEASTERN NEPAL

The only passenger service still operating in the mountainous country of Nepal, this short narrow-gauge railway has only survived with handouts from the Indian Government. The ramshackled line comes to life during religious celebrations at Janakpur's Hindu temples when trains become hopelessly overcrowded with pilgrims.

Sandwiched between China and India, the country of Nepal contains eight of the world's highest mountains in its northern Himalayan region. Since the end of the Anglo-Nepalese War in 1816 the country has had a long and friendly relationship with Britain: Gurkha soldiers have served continuously with the British Army and in 1924 the two countries signed an agreement of friendship. While its southerly neighbour, India, could boast an extensive network of British-built railways by the beginning of the twentieth century, impoverished Nepal had none. Only two short railways were eventually opened across the border from India and, today, only one and a short stub of the other exists.

Nepal's first railway was the 28-mile-long narrow gauge Nepal Government Railway (NGR) that opened from Raxaul, across the border in Bihar State, to Amlekhganj. Built to a gauge of 2-ft 6-in., it opened in 1927 and not only transported Nepalese timber across the border to India but was the only route connecting the capital Kathmandu with India – the intervening distance between Amlekhganj and Kathmandu had to be undertaken on foot or by lorry along rough tracks until the opening of the Tribhuvan Highway in 1956. The railway closed in 1965 when a highway was built across the border. A 3½-mile section has in more recent years been converted to broad gauge allowing freight trains to cross the border from India to serve an Inland Container Depot at Sirsiya.

Nepal's second railway is the 2-ft 6-in.-gauge line from Jaynagar in Bihar State, India, to Janakpur in southeastern Nepal which opened in 1937. Originally it extended northwards from Janakpur to Bijalpura but that 13½-mile section of line was closed in 2001 following flood damage to two bridges. Named after the Hindu God Vishnu, the first steam locomotive on the line was only retired in 1994 when the Indian government gave four diesel locomotives to the railway. Other vintage steam locomotives lie rotting at Janakpur depot. In 2004 the railway was renamed Nepal Railways Corporation.

A disaster was narrowly averted in 2012 when a diesel locomotive took off from Jaynagar station without its driver (he had gone to get a drink of water) and ran across the border at speeds of up to 30 mph. It was finally brought to a stop when it was diverted into a shunting yard near Janakpur station, fortunately without crashing or causing any casualties.

With a population of around 30,000 the city of Jaynagar in Bihar State, northeast India, is located on the banks of the holy river Kamla. It is well served by broad gauge-trains to and from seven Indian cities including Kolkata, Amritsar and Danapur. At the other end of the line Janakpur, population 61,000, is one of the most important religious cities in Nepal and consequently is an important destination for pilgrims and tourists. The city is the centre of the ancient Maithili culture and both the great saints, Buddha and Mahavira, are said to have lived there. It is also famous for its 200 religious ponds and temples including the impressively ornate Janaki Mandir Temple, one of the largest in Nepal. Each year thousands of pilgrims travel to the city by train to celebrate major Hindu festivals such as Deepawali, Chhath and Vijayadashami.

The line runs across the flat and marshy Nepalese plain, its survival entirely due to the lack of a road between Jaynagar and Janakpur, and has intermediate stations at Grenze, a border post on the India/Nepal border, Khajuri, Mahinathpur, Baidhee and Parhaba. There are normally three return services each day along the ramshackled line but during religious celebrations at Janakpur's Hindu temples there is a constant shuttle service with trains becoming severely overcrowded and passengers even sitting on the carriage roofs. The infrastructure, locomotives, rolling stock and track are in a poor state, derailments are common and 'health and safety' is non-existent. Nevertheless the railway continues to struggle on and there are currently proposals to modernize it, convert it to broad gauge and extend it northwards to Barbidas.

State-of-the-art signalling! With passengers clinging to the sides and roofs of the carriages, the well-loaded Nepal Government Railway Janakpur to Jaynagar morning train gets underway from Khajuri on 12 January 1999.

PREVIOUS PAGE: Passengers aboard a Jaynagar to Janakpur service in January 1999 wait for the departure of their train as Avonside Engine Co. 1926-built 0-6-2 tank 'Gorakhpur', stands in the adjacent platform with a service for Jaynagar.

OVERLEAF: Filled to overflowing! A decrepit Nepal Government Railway No. ZDM535 heading an equally decrepit Jaynagar-Janakpur-Bijalpura service on the Bilaspur branch in 1999. This section of the ramshackled railway is now closed due to flood damage, but its reopening is anticipated.

DARJEELING
HIMALAYAN RAILWAY
INDIA/WEST BENGAL

GAUGE: 2 FT · **LENGTH:** 52 MILES ·
ROUTE: NEW JALPAIGURI TO DARJEELING

Built by the British rulers of India, the Darjeeling Himalayan Railway was declared a World Heritage site by UNESCO in 1999. This steeply graded roadside line climbs into the Himalayan foothills along a series of dramatic zig-zags and loops to the former hill station of Darjeeling. In recent years political unrest, floods and landslides have disrupted the life of this railway gem.

The hill station of Darjeeling was established by the British rulers of India in the mid-nineteenth century to provide an escape from the stress of colonial rule and the hot climate on the plains during the long summer months. Built nearly 7,000 ft up in the foothills of the Himalayas, Darjeeling became a health resort where British civil servants and their families could relax in the temperate climate. A cart road connecting Siliguri, on the plains, with the town was completed in 1842; a military depot for British soldiers and a sanatorium were set up, and commercial tea planting was introduced. Scottish missionaries built schools and health centres for the British residents and Darjeeling became the formal summer capital of the Bengal Presidency in 1864.

The growing importance of Darjeeling as a tea-growing and trading centre and its success as a health resort brought with it ever-increasing congestion on the one and only cart road which snaked its way up through the hills from Siliguri – located on the banks of the Mahananda River, the latter town had been connected to Calcutta by a metre-gauge (converted to broad gauge in 1947) railway in 1878. A proposal to build a steam tramway following the course of the cart road between Siliguri and Darjeeling was given the go-ahead by a committee headed by the Lieutenant Governor of Bengal in 1879. Following the success of narrow-gauge railways – in particular the steam-operated Ffestiniog Railway – in the mountainous region of North Wales in Britain, a gauge of 2 ft was chosen for the new, steeply graded line.

The contract to build the railway was awarded to Gillanders Arbuthnot & Company in 1879 and construction work started immediately. By March 1880 the line had opened as far as Tindharia, where the railway's workshops were established, and by August of that year to Kurseong. Initially the course of the line ran alongside the cart road but as it climbed higher the gradient had to be overcome by building a number of 360° loops and zig-zags. Darjeeling was reached in July 1881, when the railway changed its name from the Darjeeling Steam Tramway Company to the Darjeeling Himalayan Railway Company.

In its early years the railway suffered from several major natural disasters – an earthquake in 1897 and a major cyclone in 1899 caused much disruption – but despite this it continued to grow and new extension lines to Kishanganj and Gielkhola were built in 1914 and 1915 respectively to cope with increasing passenger and goods traffic. New bogie carriages replaced the basic four-wheel versions and, in 1919, the Batasia Loop was constructed to ease the gradient on the climb out of Darjeeling. After suffering from another major earthquake in 1934, the railway recovered and during the Second World War played an important role carrying military supplies and personnel to camps around Ghum and Darjeeling. During this time an ambulance train was built at Tindharia Works to carry wounded soldiers.

Following India's independence in 1948 the railway became part of the Indian Government Railways and came under the management of the Assam Railways division.

PREVIOUS PAGE: Leaving Siliguri Junction for Tindharia on 10 February 2008, Darjeeling Himalaya Railway No. 786 brushes past the many small businesses as the railway runs parallel to Hill Cart Road.

It was extended by nearly four miles from Siliguri to New Jalpaiguri in 1962 to meet a new broad-gauge line there – this new line opened for freight in that year and to passengers in 1964. Mail services were finally lost to road competition in 1984 and, following an 18-month closure in 1988-9 during a period of civil unrest, freight services were also lost to the roads in 1993. In 1999, the Darjeeling Himalayan Railway was declared a World Heritage site by UNESCO, only the second railway in the world to receive this recognition.

Operating the steeply graded line is no mean feat – along its fifty-one miles it climbs from 328 ft above sea level at New Jalpaiguri to the summit at Ghum, 7,407 ft above sea level, before descending to Darjeeling, 6,812 ft above sea level. Until the introduction of modern diesel locomotives in 2000 and 2006, motive power was provided by 'B' Class 0-4-0 saddle tank tender locomotives built by Sharp,

Stewart & Company, and later the North British Company, of Glasgow between 1889 and 1925. Three of these diminutive locomotives were also built by the Baldwin Locomotive Works of Philadelphia, USA, and three in the Darjeeling Himalayan Railway's own workshops at Tindharia. Of the thirty-four built only eleven remain on the railway with many out of use or under repair while one, No. 778, has been repatriated to Britain where it has been restored. An articulated Garratt Class 'D' 0-4-0+0-4-0 was also built for the railway in 1910.

Today, most services on the Darjeeling Himalayan Railway are operated by modern diesel locomotives. The only exceptions are the daily Kurseong to Darjeeling service and the daily tourist trains from Darjeeling to Ghum, the

Darjeeling Himalaya Railway No. 786 prepares for reversal at "Reverse 2" south of Tindharia on 10 February 2008.

highest station on the line, which are still handled by the veteran British-built 'B' Class steam locomotives. In recent years services have not only been severely disrupted by landslides and floods during the monsoon season, effectively cutting the railway in two places, but also by local political unrest and labour strikes (known locally as 'bandhs') called by the Gorkha Janmuti Morcha, the principal political party in Darjeeling. One can only hope that peace will soon be returned and that the Darjeeling Himalayan Railway can return to normal life.

NEW JALPAIGURI TO TINDHARIA

Our journey along the Darjeeling Himalayan Railway starts at New Jalpaiguri station which was opened just over three miles south of Siliguri Town in 1964. An important junction station, New Jalpaiguri, actually in the city of Siliguri, is served by broad-gauge (5-ft 6-in) lines to Howrah, Haldibari, Samuktala Road, Barauni and Kathar as well as the narrow-gauge Darjeeling Himalayan Railway. It handles around 177,000 passengers every day and is served by many prestigious long-distance expresses including the Dibrugarh Town to Kanyakumari Vivek Express which operates along the longest train route in the Indian subcontinent, taking almost four days to cover 2,663 miles.

Diesel-hauled Darjeeling Himalayan Railway trains depart from one of two narrow-gauge platforms at New Jalpaiguri station and rattle northwestwards through the city's suburbs to Siliguri Town station. This was the original northern terminus of the metre-gauge line from Calcutta which opened in 1880 and the southern terminus of the DHR from 1881 – the metre-gauge line was converted to broad gauge in 1947. Since then, Siliguri has expanded greatly, experiencing rapid industrial growth and a population boom to around half a million people. Siliguri Junction station soon follows – this only became a major station after a new metre-gauge line was built to Assam in the early 1950s – and then Sukna station. For much of its route to Darjeeling the railway runs alongside the former cart road and in built-up areas trains rub shoulders with stalls, shops and houses – diesel trains are equipped with loud horns to warn of their approach.

Continuing northwestwards from Sukna, DHR trains leave the flat plains to start their climb into the Darjeeling Hills, passing the site of a loop line that was removed

following flood damage in 1991 before reaching the next stop at Rangong. The gradient of the railway now increases dramatically as it winds its way up through the forested slopes. Beyond Rangtong station trains pass the site of another loop which was removed in 1942 before reaching the first zig-zag on the line – here trains gain height by reversing up the side of the hill before moving forward again at a higher level. After negotiating the first 360° loop on the line, trains call at Chunabhatti before climbing even higher through two more zig-zags to reach the town of Tindharia.

TINDHARIA TO DARJEELING

Tindharia is the major intermediate station on the line where the railway has its workshops, engineers' office, a large locomotive shed and a Railway Hospital. Trains leave Tindharia, continuing their long climb into the hills through Agony Point Loop (so named as it has the tightest curve on the line), Gayabari station, a final zig-zag and Mahanadi station before arriving at Kurseong. Located at an altitude of 4,864 ft above sea level, Kurseong became a rest town during the days of British rule and featured many villas, bungalows and schools along with a TB sanatorium. The station here is a dead-end and trains for Darjeeling have to reverse across a busy road junction before continuing their climb through the bustling bazaar where they rub shoulders with the fronts of colourful shops and market stalls.

From Kurseong the railway heads northwards on its steep climb to the summit of the line at Ghum, en route, calling at Tung, Dilaram, Sonada, Rangbul and Jorebungalow stations. At 7,407 ft above sea level, Ghum station is also home to a railway museum with the larger exhibits displayed in the goods yard. It is also the southern terminus of the steam-hauled tourist trains from Darjeeling. From Ghum, trains start their descent to Darjeeling, negotiating the famous Batasia Loop en route, from where there are superb, far-reaching views across to Darjeeling and the snow-capped Himalayas, with the peak of Kanchenjunga beyond. Here there is also a memorial to Gurkha soldiers of the Indian Army who died during the turmoil of Indian Independence in 1947. The final part of our journey follows the old cart road into Darjeeling where trains run alongside shops, houses and market stalls before ending their long journey at the ugly concrete terminus station, 6,812 ft above sea level.

With a population of around 130,000, this colourful, bustling town still features leftovers from British rule in the shape of several acclaimed public schools. World-famous for its distinctive black tea and once the centre for the Gorkhaland independence movement in the 1980s, the town and the surrounding area suffer from pressure on their fragile ecology due to the growth of population and tourism and the lack of any meaningful planning. Internationally famous for its flora and fauna, the town is home to the Lloyd's Botanical Garden and the Padmaja Naidu Himalayan Zoological Park while the nearby Jaldapara National Park supports forests, rhinoceros, elephant, tiger and leopard.

Darjeeling Himalayan Railway 0-4-0ST No. 785 runs along the Hill Cart Road near Tindharia, with a special to Darjeeling in February 2008. This section of line has just been reopened following a massive landslide in 2011.

THE KALKA TO SHIMLA RAILWAY
NORTHWEST INDIA/ HIMACHAL PRADESH STATE

GAUGE: 2 FT 6 IN. • **LENGTH:** 60 MILES •
ROUTE: KALKA TO SHIMLA

Built by the British colonial rulers of India and granted UNESCO World Heritage site status in 2008, the steeply graded and highly engineered narrow-gauge railway up to the hill town of Shimla is a popular destination with tourists from both home and abroad.

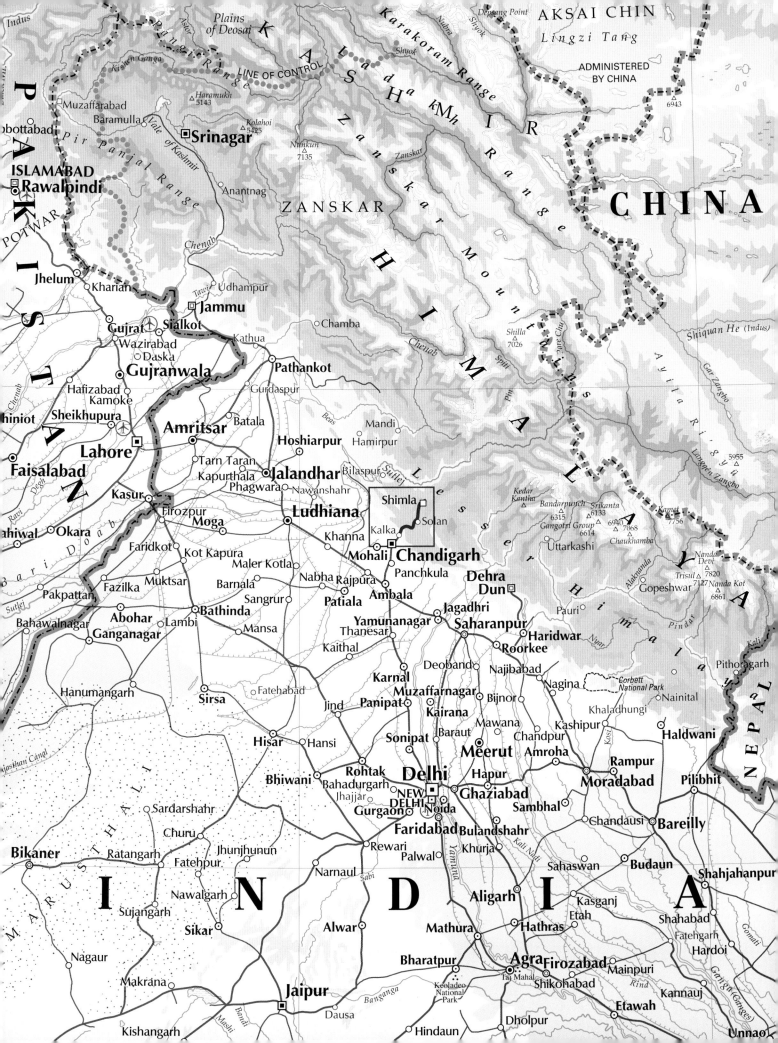

ocated in the Himalayan foothills at an altitude, at its highest point, of 7,234 ft above sea level, the city of Shimla (population 172,000) had its beginnings in the early nineteenth century when British army officers and civil servants, attracted by its mild temperate climate, spent their holidays there during the hot Indian summers. Shimla grew rapidly and by the 1870s had become the summer capital of the British Raj and the summer headquarters of the British-led Indian Army. Many of the finer buildings were designed in Neo-Gothic and English Tudor styles, making Shimla a real home-from-home for the British inhabitants.

Transport along steep, winding tracks to Shimla through the forested foothills was slow, especially during the monsoon season when horse-drawn vehicles would often become mired in mud. Matters improved when the broad-gauge Delhi to Kalka railway opened in 1891 but that still left a journey of around sixty miles to climb the 5,000 ft up to Shimla. To overcome this, a narrow gauge-railway was proposed between Kalka and Shimla. A gauge of 2 ft was chosen as it allowed the railway to negotiate the many sharp bends and steep gradients encountered en route. Started in 1898, construction was slow and involved the building of no less than 107 tunnels, 863 stone viaducts and twenty stations, with the railway having a ruling gradient of 1-in-33. The line was finally completed in

November 1903 but the original cost of building it had doubled by then. Two years later the railway was regauged to 2 ft 6 in. to bring it into line with other narrow-gauge systems in Britain's vast empire.

The cost of working and maintaining the line was high and, despite charging over the odds for fares, the company was soon in financial trouble. At the beginning of 1906 it was purchased by the Indian Government.

Motive power was British and was initially provided by 0-4-2Ts supplied by Sharp, Stewart and Company similar to the locomotives used on the Darjeeling Himalayan Railway (*see* pages 186-191). These were supplemented by more powerful 2-6-2Ts built by Hunslet and the North British Locomotive Company between 1904 and 1910, but two 2-6-2+2-6-2 articulated locomotives supplied in 1928 were soon deemed too large for the line and sent to pastures new. Diesels were first introduced in 1955 and by 1971 had replaced steam workings.

In 2008 the railway was honoured by being granted World Heritage site status by UNESCO as part of their Mountain Railways of India – the other two railways also awarded this status were the Darjeeling Himalayan Railway (*see* pages 186-191) and the Nilgiri Mountain Railway (*see* pages 198-203).

PREVIOUS PAGE: Railbus No. 3 of the Kalka to Shimla Railway crosses one of the many galleried viaducts on the 60-mile long line on the approach to Dharampur on 8 April 2013.

Shades of a Beyer-Peacock Hymek at Shimla station as diesel locomotive ZDM3 Class No. 701 shunts carriages before departing with the the 14.25 departure to Kalka on 9 April 2013.

The Kalka to Shimla Railway's only working steam locomotive is British-built 'KC' Class 2-6-2T No. 520 dating from the first decade of the twentieth century, seen emerging from a tunnel between Taradevi and Shoghi on 9 April 2013.

Today, Shimla is one of the most popular tourist destinations in India, and the Kalka to Shimla Railway still plays an important part in supporting the local economy. The city's temperate climate, its historic links with the days of the British Raj personified by the 'English Home Counties' architecture and the growth of the hotel industry and health tourism are all key factors in attracting visitors from home and abroad.

The 60-mile journey up through the foothills to Shimla starts at Kalka station, which is also served by broad-gauge electric trains that terminate here from Delhi. Affording passengers panoramic views of the distant Himalayas, diesel-hauled trains head off from Kalka in a northeasterly direction and soon reach the picturesque village of Taksal. Continually climbing around sharp curves, through tunnels and over bridges, trains call at Gumman, Koti and Sonwara before arriving at Dharampur, home to the first TB sanatorium in India. Built of local stone, many of the railway viaducts on this route have multi-arched galleries similar to the aqueducts built by the Romans in Europe – one of the highest, between Sonwara and Dharampur, has no fewer than five arched, tiered galleries to carry the railway over a deep ravine.

From Dharampur trains call at Kumarhatti before arriving at Barog, named after the engineer who built a nearby tunnel, the longest on the line. Poor Barog got his calculations wrong and committed suicide after the two ends of the tunnel failed to meet in the middle. The small town is 5,120 ft above sea level and is a popular tourist destination. A further 2½ miles brings the railway to the large town of Solan, midway point between Kalka and Shimla, and home to India's oldest distillery.

Continuing their climb, trains call at Salogra, Kandaghat (jumping-off point for visitors to the Maharaja of Patiala's summer palace at Chail), Kanoh and Kathleeghat before arriving at Shoghi, forty-seven miles from Kalka. Shoghi is characterized by pastel-coloured, modern houses that were built on the hillsides as a Housing Board Colony in 2001. Now reaching the end of their journey, diesel trains continue the climb through Taradevi, Totu and Summer Hill before terminating at Shimla station.

There are currently five trains running daily on the railway. Four are made up of diesel-hauled trains taking between 4¾ hours and 5 hours 50 minutes. The other train and also the fastest is the Deluxe Rail Motor Car, a 1940s-vintage railbus that seats only fourteen passengers. On some journeys a meal is served at picturesque Barog station while certain trains have their own on-board catering facilities and even beds. However you may wish to travel on this fascinating railway, the journey will always be memorable.

OVERLEAF: A diesel train on the steeply graded 2-ft 6-in.-gauge Kalka to Shimla Railway crosses the 5-tiered, multi-arched, curving viaduct between Sonwara and Dharampur.

NILGIRI MOUNTAIN RAILWAY
SOUTHERN INDIA/TAMIL NADU STATE

GAUGE: 1,000 MM (3 FT 3⅜ IN.) • **LENGTH:** 26 MILES •
ROUTE: METTUPALAYAM TO UDHAGAMANDALAM (OOTY)

Built by the British rulers of India to serve the hill station of Ooty, the heavily engineered Nilgiri Mountain Railway uses the Swiss Abt system to conquer gradients as steep as 1-in-12. Still partly steam-operated and a UNESCO World Heritage site, it is a popular destination with Indian tourists wishing to escape the searing summer heat of the plains.

Udhagamandalam, or Ooty for short, is a picturesque hill station located at an altitude of 7,350 ft in the Nilgiri Hills in the state of Tamil Nadu in southern India. Set on the eastern slopes of the Western Ghats, the Nilgiri region was ceded to the British East India Company at the end of the eighteenth century by the Treaty of Srirangapatnam. By 1830 Ooty had become a popular summer and weekend resort for the British wishing to escape from the searing heat in Madras. From May to October each year the entire Madras Government including the Governor and his family would decamp to Ooty where its temperate climate, lush green valleys, lakes and superb scenery earned it the title of 'Queen of the Hill Stations'. The British made Ooty a real home-from-home with summer bungalows, churches and inns and enjoyed hunting with hounds, riding, golf, cricket, snooker, swimming and tennis.

Ooty was reached along a steep and winding road which was completed in 1832 up through the foothills from Mettupalayam – the latter was reached by the Madras Railway in the 1870s but the slow journey from there by horse and cart up into the Nilgiris soon led to demands for a narrow-gauge railway. The first attempt to build the line came in 1882, when a Swiss engineer surveyed a route, and a local company was formed with the Madras Government offering free land for the line. Nothing came of this and in 1885 another company was formed which proposed using the Swiss Abt system to overcome the steepest gradients. This ingenious system features two solid racks with vertical teeth mounted centrally between the rails, which are engaged by pinion wheels driven separately on the locomotive. With the Abt system steep gradients can be negotiated by a steam or diesel-hauled train – in Britain it is still used on the Snowdon Mountain Railway.

Construction work for the railway started in 1891 and the Abt section from Mettupalayam to Coonoor was opened in 1899. The Madras Government bought the unfinished line in 1903 and continued with construction, opening from Coonoor to Ooty in October 1908. Featuring gradients as steep as 1-in-12, sixteen tunnels and 250 bridges, the 26-mile line was operated by the Madras Railway until 1908 when it was merged with the Southern Mahratta Railway to form the Madras & Southern Mahratta Railway,

which in turn was nationalized by the Indian Government in 1944. Motive power was provided by steam locomotives built by the Swiss Locomotive & Machine Works at Winterthur in Switzerland until they were gradually replaced in more recent years by Indian-built diesels. However, due to popular demand, some of the surviving twelve steam locomotives have been reintroduced on certain services on the Abt section between Mettupalayam and Coonoor. In 2005 the railway was granted World Heritage site status by UNESCO as part of their Mountain Railways of India – the other two railways also awarded this status are the Darjeeling Himalayan Railway (see pages 186-191) and the Kalka to Shimla Railway (see pages 192-197). The railway still issues old style Edmondson manual tickets to keep it in line with its historic status.

Located 1,070 ft above sea level in the foothills of the Nilgiris, or Blue Mountains, the town of Mettupalayam (population 66,000) is the starting point for the Nilgiri Mountain Railway's line to Ooty. Here the railway has its carriage workshops and a locomotive shed. The town can be reached by the Nilgiri Express on the broad-gauge railway from Chennai (formerly known as Madras) via Coimbatore. Although the Nilgiri Mountain Railway climbs 6,280 ft on its 26-mile route up into the Nilgiris, the first five miles to Kallar is not steep and is worked by adhesion. At Kallar the Abt rack rail begins and steam engines work hard on the 1-in-12 gradient out of the station before halting to take on water at Adderley. Continuing the steep climb up through the forested hills, trains call at Hillgrove and Runnymede stations for more water before arriving at Coonoor, seventeen miles from Mettupalayam and the main intermediate station on the line where the rack rail ends and the railway has its locomotive workshops. Water is not a problem here as the area receives fifty-five inches of rainfall a year, most of it during the monsoon season.

The town of Coonoor (population 50,000) is located 6,070 ft above sea level and is an important centre of the Nilgiri tea industry. It is also a popular tourist destination and the starting point for several trekking trails into the hills. The steam locomotive is taken off at Coonoor and replaced by a diesel which then has to reverse its train out of the station before continuing to Ooty. The steepest gradient on this section is 1-in-23 and the first stop is at Wellington where the Indian Armed Forces have their Defence Services Staff College. This is followed by Aruvankadu where there is a cordite factory, established by the British in 1903, that supplies the Indian armed forces.

PREVIOUS PAGE: Climbing continuously on the Abt rack section between Kallar and Coonoor, a steam-hauled train on the Nilgiri Mountain Railway crosses a precarious viaduct near Hillgove.

Continuing to climb towards Ooty, trains reach the village of Ketti, home to a tea factory and a factory that makes needles for hand sewing machines, knitting pins and other haberdashery products. The latter was established by the British in 1949, originally to make simple gramophone needles. After leaving Ketti trains soon reach the penultimate station at Lovedale, home to the Lawrence School, an educational establishment founded by Sir Henry Montgomery Lawrence in 1858. Before he was killed in the Indian Mutiny, Lawrence had come up with an idea for special schools that would educate children whose fathers had been killed while serving in the Indian Army – the school's motto is 'Never Give In'.

After following the shore of Ooty Lake, the Nilgiri Mountain Railway terminates at Ooty station. The 26-mile journey takes 4¼ hours at an average speed of just over 6 mph, making it one of the slowest train journeys in the world. A popular tourist destination set deep in the Nilgiri hills, the town has a population of 94,000 which depends not only on tourism for its livelihood but also on agriculture, notably the cultivation of English summer vegetables and fruits. It is surrounded by mountains, lakes, forests, grasslands, several national parks and tea plantations. Ooty is also home to Government rose and botanical gardens, a 65-acre lake and deer park and nineteenth-century British buildings such as St Stephen's Church, colonial bungalows and Fernhills Palace. Golf and cricket are still popular pastimes – the town was the birthplace of English cricket captain Colin Cowdray in 1932 when his father ran a tea plantation there.

A steam-hauled train bound for Udhagamandalam (Ooty for short) crosses the Bhavani River soon after leaving the lower terminus of the Nilgiri Mountain Railway at Mettupalayam.

OVERLEAF: The hillside towns and villages and the lush scenery of the Nilgiri Mountains make the Nilgiri Mountain Railway a popular destination for visitors from both home and abroad.

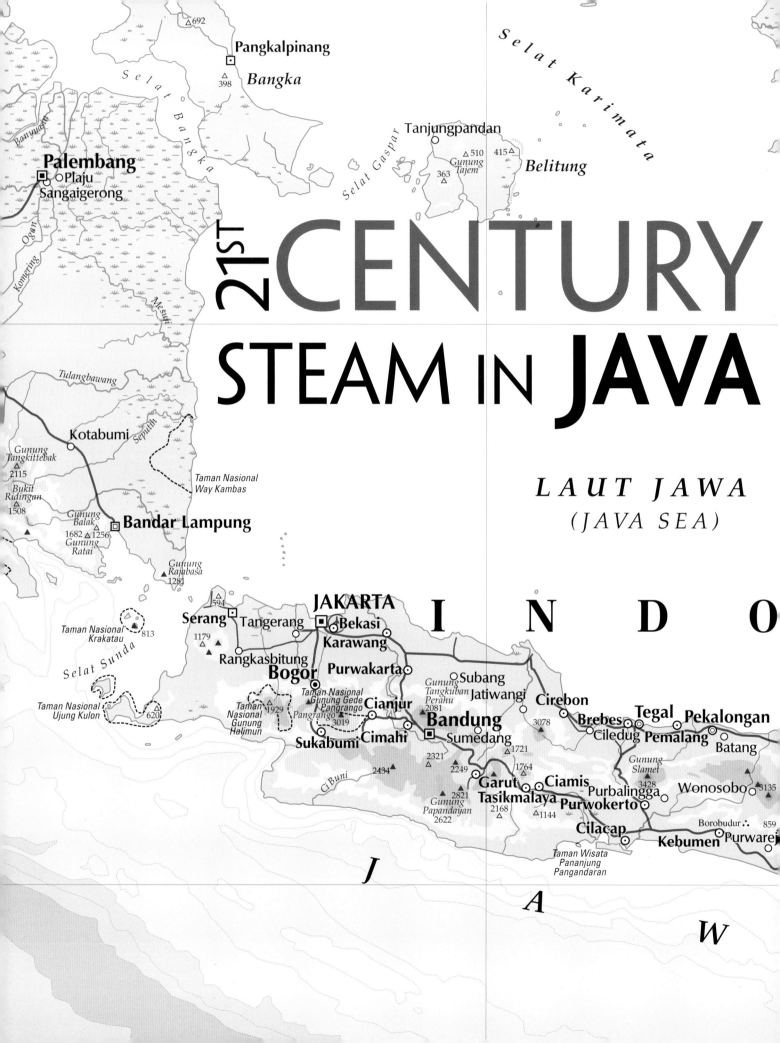

Pulau-pulau
Karimunjawa

Bawean Gunung Besar
                △695

N E S I A

Madura

*Kepulauan
Kangean*

Kudus Gunung
          Muria
          △
          1602

          ⊙ **Pati**
      Blora   **Tuban**   *Solo*
ndal   **Bangkalan**   △   **Sumenep**
⊡ **Semarang** *Lusi* **Bojonegoro** **Lamongan** **Gresik**   471
Purwodadi   **Cepu**   ⊙ **Pamekasan**
Salatiga   *Solo*   **Surabaya** ⊡
      Sragen   **Mojokerto** **Sidoarjo**   *Selat Madura*   **LAUT BALI**
emanggung Sangiran **Ngawi** **Jombang**   **Bangil**   (*BALI SEA*)
Magelang ⊙ **Surakarta** **Madiun** **Kertosono**   **Pasuruan**
△2911   *Taman*   **Probolinggo** **Situbondo** ⊙
Gunung **Nganjuk Pare**   2198 3343 *Nasional Bromo*   △
Merapi ▲3265   *Tengger Semeru*   **Bondowoso** ⊙   1247 *Taman Nasional*
Klaten *Gunung*   △   *Gunung* *Baluran*
Yogyakarta *Lawu* **Ponorogo** 1731 ▲ 2874 ⊙ **Malang**   △3089 *Merapi* ▲2800 **Banyuwangi** **Singaraja**
⊡   △   *G. Semeru*   3332 ▲   ⊙
Bantul   **Tulungagung** **Blitar**   △3676 **Jember** ⊙   2276 ▲ 1717
              Ngunut *Brantas*   **Lumajang**   *Gunung Taman Nasional Bali Barat* ▲3142 1174
                                              ⊙   △1386
                                    Gunung   *Betiri* *Taman Nasional Bali Barat*
A (J A V A)   ▲*Betiri* *Taman Nasional*   **Bali** **Denpasar** ⊡
                                        1223 *Meru Betiri*   359   △529 *Selat Lombok*
                                      Taman Nasional Alas Purwo △   **Lombok**

Forming part of the Republic of Indonesia, the volcanic island of Java is the most heavily populated island in the world. From the early seventeenth century the island, along with much of the vast Indonesian archipelago, came under the control of the Dutch, firstly by the Dutch East India Company and then, from 1800, as a colony. In 1867 the first railway, from Semarang to Yogyakarta in Central Java, was opened by the Dutch colonial government. Although this was constructed to the standard gauge of 4 ft 8½ in., all later railways were built to a gauge of 3 ft 6 in. and by the late nineteenth century a network of these lines had opened between the capital Jakarta in the west and the city of Surabaya in the east. By the early twentieth century most towns and cities on the island were rail-connected, and a network of narrow-gauge lines and street tramways had also been constructed to connect sugar cane plantations with sugar mills and logging operations with timber mills.

Java's sugar industry dates back to the time of the Dutch East India Company in the seventeenth century. The introduction of steam power in the mills and the building of steam-operated narrow-gauge feeder railways in the late nineteenth century greatly increased production, which by the 1930s had reached a peak when 179 factories produced nearly three million tons of sugar. The invasion of the Dutch East Indies by the Japanese in 1942 was a major catastrophe not only for the sugar industry, which by 1945 had been reduced to just thirty operating factories, but also for the railways on Java, which were plundered by the invaders with equipment being sent to other parts of the short-lived Japanese empire.

The Japanese were defeated in 1945 and Indonesia was granted independence from the Dutch in 1949. Both the sugar cane industry and the railways slowly recovered, with the former being nationalized in 1957 and the latter in 1958.

Built to a bewildering array of narrow gauges ranging from 600 mm and 700 mm to 720 mm and 750 mm, a small number of the sugar-cane railways of Java remained steam-operated into the early twenty-first century.

The veteran steam locomotives, some nearly ninety years old, built by various European manufacturers, were kept busy during the harvest season hauling trainloads of sugar cane along roadside tramways to the mills for refinement – the harvested sugar cane was initially hauled to the 'main line' by teams of buffalo along temporary tracks laid in the fields. Both the locomotives and the steam-operated mill machinery burn mainly 'bagasse', the waste product from the milling process, or occasionally wood. Sadly, in recent years, many of these operations have been taken over either by diesel locomotives or by lorries, with the railways between the fields and mills being ripped up. However, at a few locations steam locomotives are still used to carry out shunting operations in the mill yards.

While many of Java's sugar mills have been modernized, probably the most famous of the steam-operated mills still in operation is Olean Mill near Situbondo in East Java, which in 2013 still used steam traction to haul the sugar cane from the fields. The mill itself has a magnificent collection of vintage Dutch- and British-built stationary steam engines that power the crushing and milling processes and, along with its steam-operated railway, is a possible candidate for UNESCO World Heritage site status.

Of the logging railways on Java only the Cepu Forest Railway on the border between Central and East Java remains steam operated. Built during the First World War, the 3-ft 6-in.-gauge railway network once extended nearly 200 miles into the teak plantations of the Perhutani Forest. The railway remained operational until the last decade of the twentieth century but since then it has been reduced to around twenty miles in length and now functions as a steam-operated tourist line.

PREVIOUS PAGE: Cane cutters return home from the fields as Jung 1961-built 0-6-0 tank '29' returns a load of cane to the Semboro mill in east Java just before sunset on 15 August 2004.

The procession of three loaded cane trains from the fields to Olean Mill just before sunset is a daily spectacle for the locals during the cane harvesting season in eastern Java. 700-mm gauge 1920-built Orenstein & Koppel, No. 5 'Bromo', hauls loaded cane wagons through the streets of Olean in 2004.

KHYBER PASS RAILWAY

NORTHERN PAKISTAN/ KHYBER PAKHTUNKHWA PROVINCE

GAUGE: 5 FT 6 IN. • **LENGTH:** 32 MILES •
ROUTE: PESHAWAR TO LANDI KOTAL

Built by the British rulers of India, the heavily engineered broad-gauge railway up to the strategically important Khyber Pass, on the border with Afghanistan, opened in 1926. Never seriously fulfilling its military role, it mainly carried non-fare-paying local tribesmen until its closure, steam-operated to the end, following floods in 2006.

Reaching an altitude of 3,510 ft above sea level the Khyber Pass connects the tribal areas of northern Pakistan and eastern Afghanistan through the Spin Ghar Mountains. For thousands of years it has provided a vital trade and militarily strategic route between the Indian subcontinent and Central Asia.

Russian influence in Afghanistan during the mid-nineteenth century led the British rulers of India to fear an invasion through the Khyber Pass. A strategic railway was first mooted at this time as a way of quickly bringing troops for its defence but it was not until 1879, halfway through the Second Anglo-Afghan War, that a survey was carried out. Many more years lapsed until construction of a metre-gauge railway following the River Kabul was started in 1905. By 1907, with only nineteen miles of track laid westwards from Kacha Garhi (west of Peshawar), the international climate had changed and Russia was no longer considered a threat to India. Two years later the unfinished railway was dismantled to be used elsewhere in the country.

Meanwhile, railway building by the British – primarily for strategic reasons – in what is now Pakistan had started in 1861 with the opening of a line between Karachi, on the Arabian Sea coast, inland to Kotri. Over the next forty years the rail network was slowly expanded and by the end of the nineteenth century the broad-gauge (5-ft 6-in.) main line up the Indus Valley to the city of Peshawar had opened.

To the west of Peshawar lies the strategically important fortress town of Jamrud from where the British Indian Army mounted operations into the Khyber Pass and where the Khyber Rifles had its headquarters. A broad-gauge railway linking Peshawar and Jamrud was opened in 1901.

By 1919, at the time of the Third Anglo-Afghan War, international tensions once more raised the prospect of an invasion of India through the Khyber Pass and Colonel Sir Gordon Hearn was given the task of surveying the best route for a railway through it. Hearn proposed a broad-gauge line between Jamrud and the Afghan border near Landi Kana with a ruling gradient of 1-in-33 – between Jamrud and the summit at Landi Kotal in the Pass the railway would climb 2,000 ft in just over twenty-one miles. Beyond here the line would drop 872 ft in five miles with some gradients as steep as 1-in-25.

Construction of the new line started in 1920 and involved excavating cuttings out of solid rock and building ninety-two bridges and thirty-four tunnels. Four reversing stations allowed trains to gain or lose height by zigzagging backwards and forwards uphill or downhill – to halt runaway trains, steep catch sidings were placed at strategic points on the route. The section from Jamrud to the summit at Landi Kotal finally opened in November 1925, with the remaining five miles down to Landi Kana opening in April 1926. Although track was actually laid a further two miles to the Afghan border at Torkham this section was never used. Despite the vast amounts of money lavished on the line traffic was never heavy, seeing only one or two trains per week. Most of the passengers carried were local tribesmen who were allowed to travel free in exchange for the railway being built through their lands. The Landi Kotal to Landi Kana section was closed in December 1932 following pressure from the Afghan Government which saw it as a potential threat to their country's sovereignty.

The Second World War brought concerns of a German invasion of India through the Khyber Pass and concrete tank obstacles were built along the valley floor. Following the partition of India in 1947, Pakistan's railways came under the new Government's control and the newly formed Pakistan Railways continued to operate a weekly passenger service, mainly used by tribesmen, to the Khyber Pass. Although this service ceased in 1982, a tourist train called the Khyber Steam Safari was introduced between Peshawar and Landi Kotal in the mid-1990s using three vintage British-built oil-fired 2-8-0 steam locomotives maintained at Peshawar locomotive shed. Sadly, this service ceased in 2006 after floods washed away track and major bridges. It can only be hoped that the line will be repaired in the future but this may be some time coming due to the continuing threat of terrorist activity in this dangerously volatile region.

Until 2006 steam trains for the Khyber Pass departed from Peshawar Cantt station on the first Sunday of each month. Consisting of a parlour car, two second-class coaches and two water tankers, trains were topped and tailed by a steam locomotive at each end to allow them to reverse direction up the zigzag sections beyond Jamrud. On leaving the station the train gingerly made its way through Peshawar's suburbs of Notia Gate, Swati Gate and Bara Gate where vehicles were often parked rather close to the little-used line, in some cases having to be bumped out of the way before the train could continue.

After Bara Gate the train approached the main 9,000-ft runway of Peshawar International Airport where it came to a halt before receiving clearance from the control tower to move on – this is the only international airport in the world to be crossed by a railway. After rumbling diagonally across the runway the train picked up speed through Kacha Garhi and Hayatabad before paralleling the N5 highway to Jamrud, less than one hour and just over ten miles from Peshawar.

From Jamrud station (1,496 ft above sea level) the train embarked on its slow three-hour, 21-mile journey up to Landi Kotal in the Khyber Pass. With a steam locomotive at the front and rear, trains would leave Jamrud in a westerly direction and start the steep continuous climb

through Bagiari before reaching the first reversing station at Medanak (2,086 ft above sea level). After zigzagging uphill the train continued to the second reversing station at Chagai (2,270 ft above sea level) where the process was repeated. Continuing to climb through this wild and remote landscape where old forts occasionally brought back reminders of its turbulent past, the train continued westward through Kata Kushta, Zintara and Sultan Khel before finally arriving at Landi Khotal (3,494 ft above sea level). Here the journey ended, with the 5-mile section down to Landi Khana and its two reversing stations having closed in 1932. Reflecting its military origins, the station building at Landi Kotal is built like a fortress and has no windows or doors facing the platform. Until 2006, the arrival of the monthly steam tourist train brought crowds of local tribesmen to Landi Khotal but since its closure the eerily deserted station and rusting tracks await their future with some uncertainty.

Topped and tailed by 'SGS' Class 0-6-0s the weekly passenger train for Landi Kotal arrives at Chagai reversing station in January 1981. Note the ancient British semaphore signals and the steep runaway siding in the foreground!

OVERLEAF: Bandit country! Vulcan Foundry 'SGS' Class 0-6-0s top and tail the weekly passenger train from Peshawar to Landi Kotal across Bagiari bridge over the N5 road, in March 1980.

HEDJAZ RAILWAY
SYRIA AND JORDAN
GAUGE: 3 FT 5¹¹/₃₂ IN. • LENGTH: 138 MILES •
ROUTE: DAMASCUS (SYRIA) TO AMMAN (JORDAN)

Opened in 1908, the Hedjaz Railway was built by the Turks to carry pilgrims from Syria and Jordan on their journey to the Holy City of Mecca. It had a short life, being destroyed at its southern end by guerrillas led by Lawrence of Arabia during the First World War. The remaining northern section has been closed since 2011 following the outbreak of the Syrian Civil War.

The 138-mile line between Damascus, the capital of Syria, and Amman, the capital of Jordan, is all that remains of an 820-mile railway that once stretched from Damascus to Medina in Saudi Arabia. Known as the Hedjaz Railway, it was built to transport Muslim pilgrims to Mecca, the birthplace of Muhammed and the holiest city in Islam, but the railway never got beyond Medina.

A pilgrimage to Mecca during Hajj is obligatory for all Muslims at least once in their lifetime and before the railway was built pilgrims had to endure a 2-month journey by camel caravan through hostile country. Hajj occurs in the twelfth and last month of the Muslim lunar calendar and therefore its date on the Western Gregorian calendar changes from season to season. During winter the pilgrims endured torrential rain and freezing temperatures while in the summer they had to cross hot, scorching deserts, guided by local tribesmen who earned their living from leading them.

By the beginning of the twentieth century the once all-powerful Ottoman Empire was in terminal decline but, despite this, Istanbul still controlled the populations not only of Turkey, but also Syria, Lebanon, Palestine, Jordan, Iraq and much of the Arabian Peninsula. Railways had slowly spread their tentacles out from the centre of power in Istanbul and by 1903 had reached Damascus.

The first proposal for a railway from Damascus to Mecca was mooted in 1864 but it took another forty years before construction began. Finance for the building of the railway came from the Turkish Sultan Abdul Hamid, the Turkish Government, the Shah of Iran and the Khedive of Egypt, and while the railway's *raison d'être* was to carry pilgrims, there were also serious strategic military implications that were not lost on the British Government. With German engineers in charge, construction was carried out by around 5,000 Turkish soldiers who faced major physical obstacles such as the rugged Naqab Escarpment in southern Jordan and the soft sands of the northern Arabian Desert. They also faced attack from tribesmen and camel caravan operators, angry at seeing their livelihood being stolen from them.

Using German-built locomotives and rolling stock, the railway finally opened to Medina on 1 September 1908 and was an instant success, carrying 30,000 pilgrims by 1912 and ten times that number by 1914. The previous 2-month journey by camel caravan had been slashed to four days by train, although the planned extension from Medina to Mecca never materialized due to the onset of the First World War. Unfortunately the Turkish army also used the railway to carry troops and equipment to garrisons along the route and after Turkey joined the Central Powers in 1914 it became a legitimate target for guerrilla attacks by dissident Arabs led by Emir Faisal and T.E. Lawrence (Lawrence of Arabia). Prior to the war, Lawrence had been gathering important military information in the Middle East for the British Government under the cover of archaeological expeditions and on the outbreak of war he was posted to Cairo as an intelligence officer.

In 1916, Lawrence was sent to work with Arab forces in the kingdom of Hedjaz, which today forms the western part of Saudi Arabia. The Hedjaz Railway ran through the kingdom to Medina where there was a large Turkish garrison. With large numbers of Turkish troops holed up in their garrison, Lawrence and his band of guerrillas set to work destroying the railway, and as soon as the Turks repaired the damage it was attacked again. Their first attack on the railway inside Saudi Arabia was at Abu Na'am, where the track was mined on either side of the station and a train destroyed by artillery, killing around seventy Turkish troops.

Following Turkey's defeat at the end of the First World War and despite several later attempts to rebuild it, the southern section of the short-lived Hedjaz Railway and its wrecked trains and stations were soon abandoned in the Arabian Desert. Preserved by the dry desert air, some of them are still there today. The section south from Ma'an to Mudawwara, near the Saudi Arabian border, was rebuilt in the late 1960s and part of this is now used by phosphate trains to the port of Aqaba on a line that was completed in 1975. The northern section from Damascus to Ma'an in southern Jordan via Amman continued in operation for many years, although the 147-mile section from Amman to Ma'an has since closed.

PREVIOUS PAGE: Nippon 4-6-2 No. 82 runs across the main road in Qasir with a special working for Amman, Jordan, in October 2001.

Hopefully the inhabitants of this suburb in Amman, Jordan, don't have any washing hanging out as 2-8-2 No. 71 climbs away from the capital with a freight train for Qasir in 2001.

Two branch lines of the Hedjaz Railway were also built from the junction at Deraa, just north of the Syria/Jordan border. One line went westwards to serve the port of Haifa and the other eastwards to Busra. The former is now closed while the latter is still survives.

Pilgrims bound for Mecca now travel by road or by air. All that remains of the Hedjaz Railway is the 138 miles of line between Damascus and Amman, currently closed due to the continuing Syrian Civil War. Prior to this an infrequent service of passenger trains operated between the two capitals until 2006. Then, in 2010, the Hedjaz Jordan Railway resumed a weekly service between Amman and the city of Deraa but this ceased the following year. The railway's future is very uncertain.

Prior to the railway's enforced closure, workers had restored sixteen of the original steam locomotives to working order. Until 2006 these locomotives were used to haul the tourist trains that feature on these pages. The main workshop of the Hedjaz Railway is at Cadem in Damascus and was still in use restoring steam locomotives and rolling stock until the onset of the war. The yard here is a veritable graveyard of Hedjaz Railway steam locomotives, all in varying degrees of decomposition, while the adjacent railway museum contains artefacts and models of the railway. Further south down the single-track line, the intermediate stops all feature 2-storey stone station buildings, many of them now roofless, a passing loop and an occasional round water tower. At Deraa, the junction for the branch line to Busra, there is a more substantial station, freight yard and 2-road engine shed. The next derelict station is at Neesib, before the railway crosses into Jordan and heads through Mafraq, Samra and Zarqa to terminate in Amman. On the approach to the city's Mahattah station,

trains cross a spectacular 2-tiered 10-arch viaduct that resembles a Roman aqueduct.

South of Amman the railway to Ma'an has been closed for many years although a few of the station buildings, Turkish blockhouses and forts still linger on alongside rusting track in this arid semi-desert landscape. At Ma'an the railway comes back to life, as it is now used by long diesel-hauled freight trains carrying phosphate from local mines down to the port of Aqaba. Thirty-three miles south of Ma'an lies the deserted Batn al-Ghul station where the railway once descended to the desert, turning almost back on itself on a looping route through spectacular rock cuttings.

The final section of the Hedjaz Railway from the Jordan/ Saudi border at Khalat Ammar to Medina is a railway graveyard. Amidst the arid desert landscape of this inhospitable region lie stations, Turkish blockhouses, engine sheds, water wells and occasional lengths of track partly hidden by shifting sand. At several locations, in particular at Hadiyah and Bwaira stations, steam locomotives and the skeletal remains of rolling stock, derailed by Lawrence of Arabia and his bands of guerrillas nearly 100 years ago, still lie at grotesque angles in their final death throes. A railway museum located in the former locomotive shed at Medain Saleh station contains several unrestored Hedjaz Railway locomotives. At Medina, once the southern terminus of the railway, the station and engine shed were reopened as a museum in 2006 and contain several steam locomotives and rolling stock on a length of track.

Shepherds try to control their flock of nervous sheep as Hartmann 2-8-2 No. 262 approaches Izra, Syria, with a northbound passenger charter train on 29 April 2004.

AUSTRALASIA

THE GHAN
AUSTRALIA

GAUGE: 4 FT 8½ IN. · **LENGTH:** 1,851 MILES ·
ROUTE: ADELAIDE (SOUTH AUSTRALIA) TO DARWIN (NORTHERN TERRITORY)

The 3-ft 6-in.-gauge railway from Port Augusta to Alice Springs was completed across the Australian outback in 1929. In 1980 it was rerouted to the west as a standard-gauge line with a northerly extension to Darwin opening in 2004. Today, 'The Ghan' passenger train covers the entire route in just over two days.

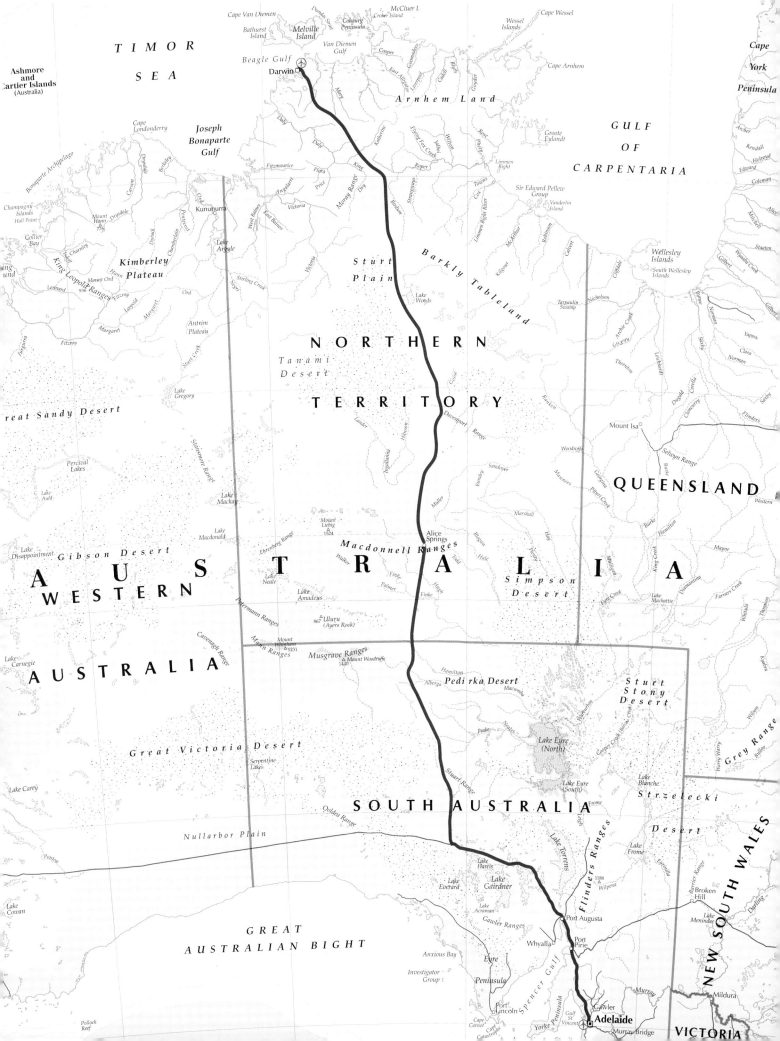

Even in the mid-nineteenth century most of Australia's vast inland wilderness was totally unknown to the continent's European settlers. The first-ever crossing from south to north was undertaken by Robert Burke and William Wills in 1860 but on their return journey from the Gulf of Carpentaria to Melbourne they both lost their lives.

Australia's first railways were initially confined to the southeast, in the colonies of New South Wales, Victoria and South Australia. However, there was little joined-up thinking when the network started to expand in the 1860s as there was no uniformity of gauge. Three different gauges were used – the narrow gauge of 3 ft 6 in., the standard gauge of 4 ft 8½ in. and the Irish broad gauge of 5 ft 3 in. – which in later years, as the network expanded and lines of different gauges met, caused many operational difficulties.

Only one year after Burke and Wills' ill-fated expedition, the Scottish explorer, John McDouall Stuart, went on to successfully map a south–north route for an overland telegraph connection linking South Australia with Britain. A telegraph line was established between Adelaide and Port Augusta in 1865 and in 1872 it was extended northwards across the vast wilderness to Darwin. From here it was linked by submarine cable to Java and then westwards to Britain. The building of this line not only opened up the Northern Territory for colonial settlers but also, with the discovery of gold, indirectly led to a gold rush.

Meanwhile, a proposal to build a transcontinental railway northwards from Port Augusta to Darwin had led to the formation of the Great Northern Railway Company of South Australia in 1869. Nothing came of this, however, until the South Australian Government started construction of the 3-ft 6-in.-gauge Port Augusta & Government Gums Railway in 1878. Its southern terminus was at Port Augusta, at the head of Spencer Gulf, which had already been reached by railway from Adelaide, some 175 miles to the south. Closely following the route of the overland telegraph, construction proceeded northwards through the Pichi Richi Pass to the west of the Flinders Ranges via Hawker and Beltana before reaching Marree in 1883. It was later extended to the south of Lake Eyre and northwards to Oodnadatta in 1891 and

there it stopped. Passengers wishing to travel further north had to ride on Afghan camels!

Up in the Northern Territory the 3-ft 6-in.-gauge Palmerston & Pine Creek Railway was opened in 1889. Built by thousands of Chinese labourers, it was planned to extend the 146-mile line southwards across the Sturt Plain and the Macdonnell Ranges to Alice Springs and thence to link up with the line from Port Augusta at Oodnadatta but this never materialized. In 1926 the Commonwealth Government took control of the two railways, extending the southern section from Oodnadatta to Alice Springs and the northern section from Pine Creek to Birdum (316 miles from Darwin). Both lines opened in 1929 but the 600-mile missing link between Birdum and Alice Springs was cancelled for lack of funds.

The opening of the line from Port Augusta to Alice Springs saw the introduction of a passenger train that became affectionately known as 'The Afghan Express'. Abbreviated to 'The Ghan', it received its name in memory of the Afghan camel drivers who accompanied Australia's pioneer colonial explorers in the nineteenth century. The railway was prone to washouts during periods of heavy rain when previously dry riverbeds would suddenly become roaring torrents, causing considerable damage to the infrastructure. Trains always carried spare sleepers and equipment so that the crew could repair the line. Water supply for steam locomotives was a constant problem in this arid landscape so each train conveyed water tankers behind the locomotive. Water towers supplied by bore water from artesian wells were also built at strategic locations along the route. One of the key watering points was at Alice Springs, so named after the wife of the overland telegraph's engineer, Charles Todd, who discovered the source in 1871.

In 1957 the railway from Port Augusta to Marree was realigned on a new route to the west of the Pichi Richi Pass and built to the standard gauge to allow heavier freight traffic to be transported from coalfields at Leigh Creek down to Port Augusta Power Station. From that date there was a break of gauge at Marree, which became the new starting point for 'The Ghan' to Alice Springs. By that date steam had been replaced by diesel traction.

In the north, the narrow-gauge North Australia Railway was kept busy during the Second World War when a new railhead was opened alongside the Stuart Highway at Larrimah, north of Birdum. The line continued to transport iron ore from Frances Creek down to the harbour at Darwin until 1976 when it closed.

The original route from Port Augusta to Alice Springs was replaced by a brand-new standard-gauge railway that opened further west in October 1980. From that date the narrow-gauge line from Marree to Alice Springs was closed. The new line heads north from a junction on the Trans-Australian Railway to Perth (see pages 228-233) at the near-deserted township of Tarcoola (population thirty-eight), 230 miles northwest of Port Augusta. Skirting the Woomera Prohibited Area, once home to the Anglo-Australian rocket testing range during the Cold War, it heads north through Carnes and Manguri before paralleling the trans-continental Stuart Highway for over 100 miles. Leaving the highway behind, the railway continues northwards for another 250 miles into the wilderness lands of the Northern Territory before arriving at Alice Springs. On the original route, the standard-gauge section from Leigh Creek to Marree closed in 1986, while the 24-mile section between Port Augusta and Quorn has reopened as a heritage railway known as the Pichi Richi Railway (see box feature below).

The missing link between Alice Springs and Darwin was finally given the green light in 2000, when the governments of South Australia and the Northern Territory awarded the contract to build the 882-mile railway to Asia Pacific Transport Consortium. Construction work northwards from Alice Springs started in 2001 and by 2003 Darwin had been reached. With its route never far from the Stuart Highway, this major engineering project involved bridging six major rivers and was opened for freight and passenger trains in 2004.

Freight services between Adelaide and Darwin are operated by Genesee & Wyoming Inc. With six services per week, the company carries around 800,000 tons of intermodal freight and 70,000 tons of bulk liquids on the route each year. Intermodal trains can operate up to 2,000 yds in length (over one mile) and weigh around 4,500 tons. In the north the company also operates twenty-four bulk trains per week carrying manganese, iron and copper ores between mine sites and the Port of Darwin.

Great Southern Rail operates 'The Ghan' passenger and motorail train on the route. Apart from December–January when it is fortnightly, 'The Ghan' operates once a week all year round with an extra weekly service between June and September. The journey time northbound is 53 hours 10 minutes/54 hours 10 minutes while southbound it is 50 hours 30 minutes/51 hours 30 minutes. En route, the train calls at Alice Springs and Katherine where passengers alight for sightseeing tours. The train is made up of between sixteen and twenty air-conditioned coaches including restaurant, club and sleeping cars, and is hauled by a pair of Australian-built Class 'NR' Co-Co 4,000 hp diesel-electric locomotives.

Sections of the original narrow-gauge route through Oodnadatta to Alice Springs that was closed in 1980 are now a heritage trail. Bridges, closed stations, water towers and even diesel locomotives abandoned in the desert are a memorial to this pioneering railway.

OVERLEAF: Made up of between sixteen and twenty stainless-steel air-conditioned coaches 'The Ghan', seen here on its long journey through the vast Australian outback, also conveys passengers' vehicles in two 'Motorail' wagons.

PICHI RICHI RAILWAY

Opened in stages between 1974 and 2001, the 3-ft 6-in.-gauge Pichi Richi Railway follows the route of the original line to Alice Springs for twenty-four miles between Port Augusta and Quorn. The railway is named after the Pichi Richi Pass that it travels through. 'The Afghan Express' is made up of restored 1920s 'Ghan' coaches hauled by the only original surviving steam locomotive, 1925-built 4-8-0 NM25, that once hauled trains to Alice Springs.

The 'Pichi Richi Explorer', which operates through the pass between Quorn and Woolshed Flat, consists of steam-hauled early nineteenth-century South Australian Railway coaches or an early diesel railcar. The railway is also restoring an historic coach that was used by General Douglas MacArthur during the Second World War when he visited Alice Springs after he fled the Japanese invasion of the Philippines.

TRANS-AUSTRALIAN RAILWAY
AUSTRALIA

GAUGE: 4 FT 8½ IN. • **LENGTH:** 1,652 MILES •
ROUTE: ADELAIDE (SOUTH AUSTRALIA) TO PERTH (WESTERN AUSTRALIA)

Linking Western Australia with the country's eastern cities, the standard-gauge Trans-Australian Railway opened for business in 1917. Featuring the world's longest stretch of dead-straight track across the arid Nullarbor Plain, the route and its remote settlements are today served by the 'Indian Pacific' train.

Perth, the capital of Western Australia, remained isolated from Australia's eastern states until the early twentieth century when the Trans-Australian Railway was built across a thousand miles of inhospitable desert known as the Nullarbor (No Trees) Plain. Before the railway was built the only form of transport between the west coast and the eastern cities was a long and often rough sea voyage across the Great Australian Bight, while the first east-west crossing of the Nullarbor Plain was achieved by English explorer Edward Eyre and his aboriginal guide, Wylie, in 1841. In 1877 a telegraph line was built across the desert and it was this man-made structure that Arthur Richardson followed on his bicycle in 1896.

To the east, the Port Augusta to Alice Springs railway (*see* pages 222-227) had opened as far as Oodnadatta by 1891. To the west, the first railway in Western Australia had opened in 1871 and by 1896 the Eastern Goldfields Railway had opened a 313-mile line eastwards through an inhospitable landscape from Northam to Kalgoorlie – Northam was already connected to Perth by the Eastern Railway. The Northam to Kalgoorlie line followed the route of the Goldfields Water Supply Scheme, a pipeline carrying drinking water to the arid goldfields around Kalgoorlie and Coolgardie – the pipeline is still in use

---

PREVIOUS PAGE: Topped and tailed by Class 'NR' diesel-electric locomotives, the 25-coach 'Indian Pacific' air conditioned train glides across the waterless and inhospitable Nullarbor Plain on its 2,704-mile journey between Sydney and Perth.

today. It is worth noting here that all these railways to the east and west were built to the narrow gauge of 3ft 6in.

The Australian self-governing colonies of Queensland, New South Wales, Victoria, Tasmania, South Australia and Western Australia federated in 1901 to form the Commonwealth of Australia. One of the incentives held out to Western Australia to join the federation was the promise of a trans-continental railway linking Perth, the capital, with the eastern cities. Surveying of the route across the featureless Nullarbor Plain between Port Augusta and Kalgoorlie was completed in 1909 and construction started from both ends in 1912. Despite the onset of the First World War, work progressed until the two lines met in the desert in 1917. The railway's claim to fame is that its route includes the longest stretch of straight track in the world – 297 miles across the Nullarbor Plain. Although the existing railways at each end were built to the 3-ft 6-in. gauge, the new 1,052-mile railway was built to the standard gauge of 4 ft 8½ in. and these two breaks of gauge would deny a true trans-continental service until 1970.

Water supplies for steam locomotives on the route were non-existent, as the railway did not cross a permanent watercourse along its entire length. To overcome this, the line's original chief engineer requested diesel locomotives but this was to no avail, so steam haulage had to be supported by extra water tankers carried on each train. Australian-built Class 'GM' diesel-electric locomotives replaced steam haulage in 1951.

As well as being an important freight route, the new line saw the introduction of the 'Trans-Australian Express', which commenced running between Port Augusta and Kalgoorlie in 1917. For much of its long life the twice-weekly train conveyed sleeping cars, with seating accommodation only included from 1981 until the train's demise in 1991. The route of the train was extended to Port Pirie in the east in 1937 and to Perth in the west in 1969 following the conversion to standard gauge of these narrow-gauge lines. The Port Pirie to Adelaide section was also converted in 1982, further extending the train's route but, facing increased competition from air travel, it last ran in June 1991.

One long-lived curiosity of this railway was the 'Tea and Sugar Train', which started running in 1917 to supply isolated communities and settlements along its route. The train not only brought the necessities for everyday life but also a butcher's shop, a bank, medical facilities, a cinema and even Father Christmas in his grotto at Christmas. It last ran in 1996.

Despite the withdrawal of the 'Trans-Australian Express' between Adelaide and Perth in 1991, the 'Indian Pacific' has operated between Sydney and Perth since 1970, the year that this trans-continental route was completely converted to standard gauge. The train is operated by Great Southern Rail who also run 'The Ghan' from Adelaide to Darwin (*see* pages 222-227). From Sydney the route of the 'Indian Pacific' takes it via Bathurst, Broken Hill, Adelaide and Port Augusta, before crossing the Nullarbor Plain to Kalgoorlie and East

Perth. The train runs twice a week between Adelaide and Perth and once a week between Sydney and Perth – journey time for the 2,704-mile journey is 66¼ hours westbound and 71¼ hours eastbound.

On its journey between Port Augusta and Kalgoorlie the train calls at the isolated outback railway settlements (by request) of Pimba (population fifty), Kingoonya (deserted apart from a hotel), Tarcoola (population thirty-eight and junction for the line to Darwin used by 'The Ghan' (see pages 222-227), Cook (population four and a scheduled stop for trains that cross here) before crossing the Nullarbor Desert in a dead straight line for 297 miles to Loongana (population zero and a request stop) and Rawlinna (also a request stop serving Australia's largest sheep station, slightly smaller than the island of Cyprus). Civilization is eventually reached at Kalgoorlie before the last leg of the journey westwards to East Perth station. The train has four classes, sleeping cars, a restaurant car and Motorail wagons conveying passengers' motor cars. As with 'The Ghan', motive power is provided by a pair of Class 'NR' diesels.

OVERLEAF: The outback in bloom. The Class 'NR' 4,000-hp diesel-electric locomotives that haul the Indian Pacific train across southern Australia were built by A. Goninan & Co., founded in Australia in 1899 by two brothers from Cornwall, England.

The iconic image of Australia. A red kangaroo watches the progress of the double-headed 'Indian Pacific' train as it makes its way across an arid landscape in South Australia.

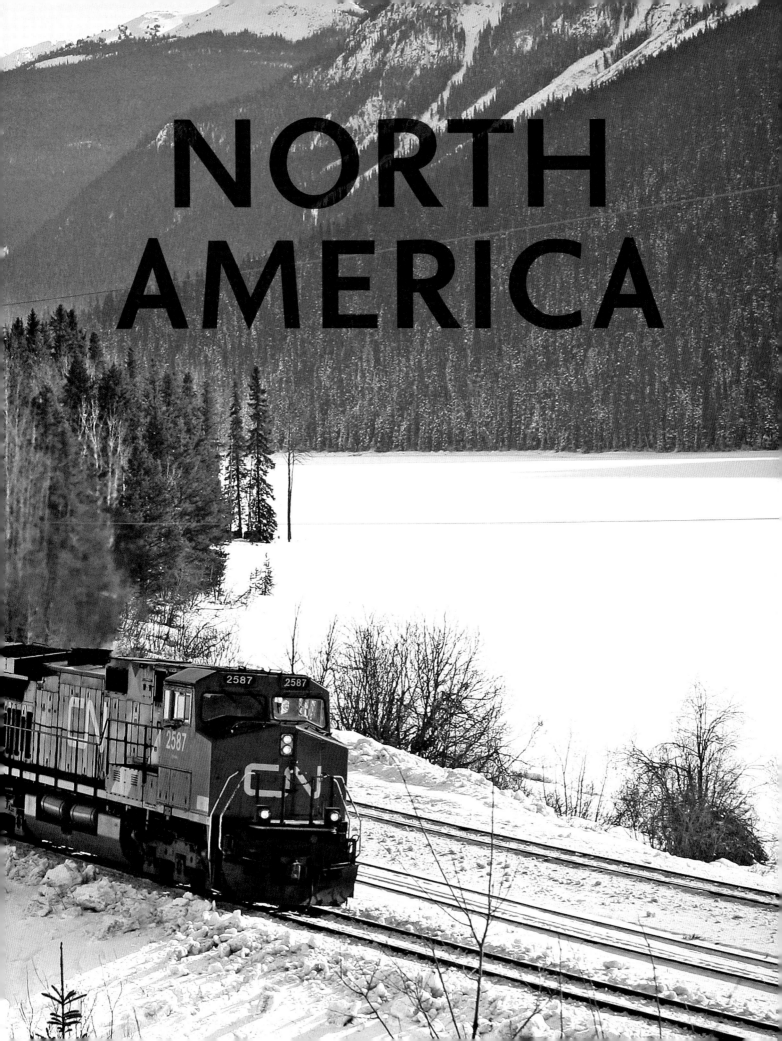

NORTH AMERICA

CUMBRES & TOLTEC SCENIC RAILROAD

USA/COLORADO AND NEW MEXICO

GAUGE: 3 FT · **LENGTH:** 64 MILES ·
ROUTE: CHAMA (NEW MEXICO) TO ANTONITO (COLORADO)

Once part of an extensive network of narrow-gauge railroads operated by the Denver & Rio Grande Railroad, this authentic and historic steam-operated line takes passengers on a truly awe-inspiring scenic 64-mile journey through the Rocky Mountains along the Colorado-New Mexico border.

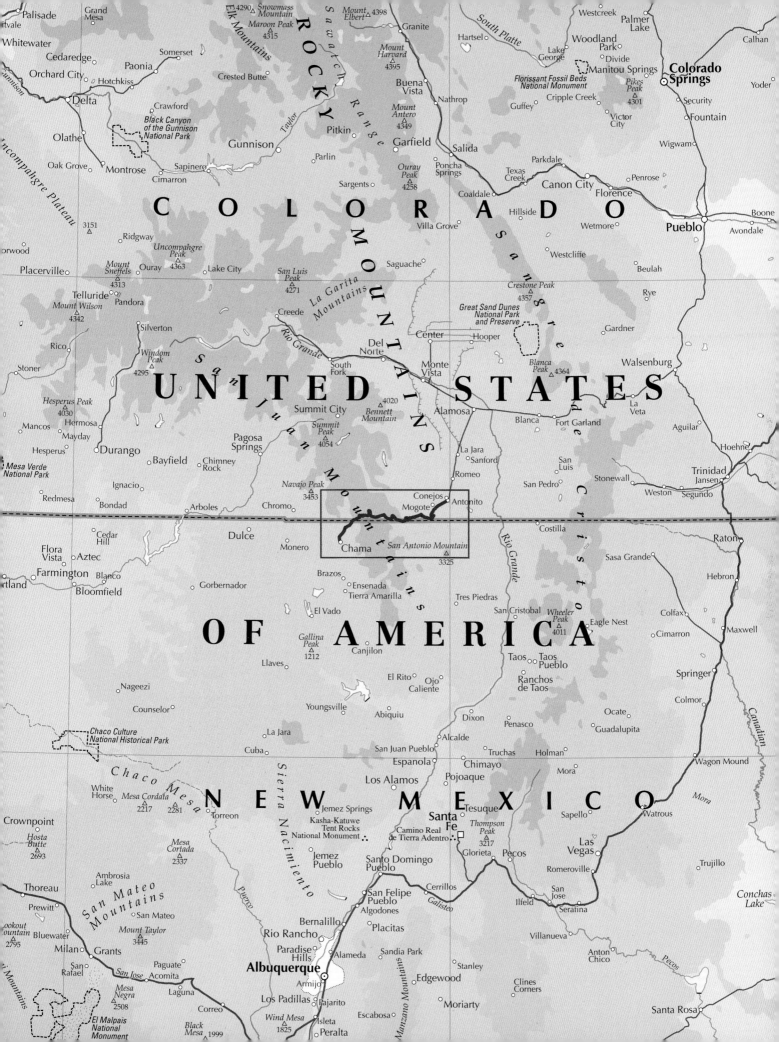

The Cumbres & Toltec Scenic Railroad had its beginnings in 1870 when the Denver & Rio Grande Railway was incorporated by its two co-founders, General William Palmer, a soldier, civil engineer and industrialist, and William Bell, a British physician and photographer of the American West. The new railway was designed to tap into the rich mineral deposits that abounded in the Rocky Mountains to the west and southwest of the growing city of Denver in Colorado. Unusually for an American railroad, a narrow gauge of 3 ft was chosen along with the burning of coal instead of wood to fuel the steam locomotives. Palmer had personally witnessed the fuel efficiency of coal-burning and the cost-effectiveness of narrow-gauge railways on his honeymoon to Britain in 1870 when Scottish engineer Robert Fairlie successfully demonstrated his coal-burning articulated locomotives on the narrow-gauge Ffestiniog Railway in North Wales. After his visit, Palmer had no doubt that narrow gauge also lent

PREVIOUS PAGE: Working hard, Class 'K36' 2-8-2 Nos. 488 and 484 on the climb out of Chama, approaching Lobato Trestle, with the 10.00 Chama to Antonito service on 14 October 2007.

Autumn colours on the Cumbres & Toltec Scenic Railroad – Class 'K36' 2-8-2 Nos. 488 and 484 climbing towards Windy Point, near the summit at Cumbres with the 10.00 Chama to Antonito service in October 2007.

itself to the mountainous terrain of Colorado – its ability to operate with sharper curves and steeper gradients coupled with lower construction costs were the deciding factors along with the large deposits of high-quality coal that had by then been found in Colorado and Utah.

Construction southwards from Denver started in 1871 but Palmer's ultimate goal of reaching El Paso in Texas was thwarted by the rival Atchison, Topeka & Santa Fe Railroad which reached the strategic Raton Pass along the Colorado-New Mexico border first. The battle for this pass and the Royal Gorge route in Colorado led to a two-year Railroad War which was only resolved when the two companies came to an agreement in 1880 and the Denver & Rio Grande (D&RG) instead set its sights on reaching Salt Lake City in Utah via the Royal Gorge.

Meanwhile, the company had extended its line from Cuchara Junction and Walsenburg westwards to Alamosa via the 9,500-ft Veta Pass in 1878 and then pushed southwards to Antonito and into New Mexico to eventually reach Sante Fe. From Antonito the D&RG built a line westwards along the Colorado-New Mexico border over the 10,015-ft Cumbres Pass to Chama and Durango, which it reached in 1881 – the section from Antonito to Chama today operates as the Cumbres & Toltec Scenic Railroad. A year later the line was extended northwards from Durango, deep into the Rockies, to the rich mining region around Silverton – this section of line is now operated by the Durango & Silverton Railroad (*see* pages 242-247).

By the end of the nineteenth century much of the extensive D&RG system in Colorado and Utah had been converted to standard-gauge but what remained still constituted the largest narrow-gauge network in the USA.

The beginning of the twentieth century saw the D&RG merge with the Rio Grande Western Railroad but this enlarged railway empire fell foul of speculators and it was taken over by the US Railroad Administration during the First World War. At the end of the war the company fell into receivership but was reincorporated as the Denver & Rio Grande Western Railroad in 1920. Bankruptcy reared its ugly head again in 1935 but the company kept operating through the Second World War and in 1947 merged with the Denver & Salt Lake Railroad. The latter had opened a much more direct route between Denver and Salt Lake City in 1928; known as the 'Moffat Road', it considerably reduced journey

times between the two cities. The route's principle engineering feature is the 6.2-mile Moffat Tunnel, which cuts through the Continental Divide at a height of 9,239 ft above sea level.

The 1950s saw the mass introduction of diesel locomotives on the D&RGW and by 1956 all its standard-gauge steam locomotives had gone to the scrapyard. Steam still reigned supreme on the company's extensive narrow-gauge network, although by the 1950s many of these routes had been abandoned. Fortunately two of the most scenic routes – Chama to Antonito and Durango to Silverton – survived in operation until they were sold to tourist railway operators. By the late 1950s freight traffic from mining operations in the area had been drastically reduced and closure seemed inevitable but an oil boom near Farmington, New Mexico kept the lines busy for another ten years. By the late 1960s even this traffic had dried up and abandonment was applied for. The section between Durango and Chama saw its last train in 1968. However, the 64-mile line from Chama to Antonito was jointly purchased by the States of Colorado and New Mexico in 1970 and operates today as the Cumbres & Toltec Scenic Railroad. The 45-mile line from Durango to Silverton continued in operation until 1980 and the following year was reopened as the Durango & Silverton Narrow Gauge Railroad – for full details *see* pages 242-247.

Since 1970 the Cumbres & Toltec has been owned by a bi-state entity known as the Cumbres & Toltec Scenic Railroad Commission, with day-to-day operations being undertaken by a number of contracted operators. In 1973 the railway was listed on the National Register of Historic Places and has featured in several films including '*Indiana Jones and the Last Crusade*'.

Apart from occasional appearances of the 1930s Galloping Goose No. 5 railcar, all trains are steam hauled using locomotives that were built and operated their entire life for the Denver & Rio Grande Western. All are 2-8-2 'Mikados' including the large K-37 Class which were originally built as standard-gauge locomotives. Those in most regular use are the veteran K-36 locos which were built by the Baldwin Locomotive Works in 1925. Along with these original steam locomotives, the railroad yard at Chama and the line's infrastructure and rolling stock make this one of the most popular destinations for aficionados of pre-1960 steam operations in the United States.

During the peak season, trains on the Cumbres & Toltec Scenic Railroad operate each morning from both ends of the line – Chama and Antonito – and meet midway at Osier where lunch is provided for passengers. Locomotives are turned at Osier on a reversing loop before heading back with their respective trains to their original departure stations. Passengers wishing to travel along the entire length of the line on the same day change trains at Osier and, after completing their journey, are bussed back to their original departure stations. All seats are reserved and advance booking for this ride of a lifetime is essential.

Original D&RG mileposts are located along the line and date from the original network of tracks that operated throughout this part of the country. Distances are measured from Denver; the terminus milepost at Chama is numbered 344.1 and that at Antonito is 280.7.

At the western end of the line Chama, in Rio Arriba County, New Mexico, is but a small village with a population of around 1,200, set at an altitude of 7,871 ft above sea level. From here, double-headed steam trains set off on their strenuous and spectacular climb to the summit of the line at Cumbres Pass – at 10,015 ft above sea level it is the highest railway line in the USA, with trains climbing 2,144 ft over a distance of 13½ miles.

Soon after Cumbres comes Tanglefoot Curve, a loop so tight that the engine at the front almost seems to meet the caboose at the rear. Continuing its meandering journey through the mountains trains cross Cascade Creek on a 137-ft-high trestle bridge, the highest on the line, before pulling into Osier, a rustic railroad settlement that is the midway point and lunch stop.

At the eastern end of the line, Antonito, in Conejos County, was once on the route of an old Spanish trail. As well as being the eastern terminus of the Cumbres & Toltec Scenic Railroad, it is also the southern terminus of the standard-gauge San Luis & Rio Grande Railway which operates excursion trains from Alamosa. A former sheep-herding camp known as San Antonio Junction, this railroad town was also the birthplace of award-winning Chicago poet Aaaron A. Abeyta and today has a population of around 900.

RIGHT: Class 'K36' 2-8-2 No. 487 crosses the state border into Colorado with the 10.00 train from Chama to Antonito in October 2007.

DURANGO & SILVERTON NARROW GAUGE RAILROAD

USA/COLORADO

GAUGE: 3 FT • **LENGTH:** 45 MILES •
ROUTE: DURANGO TO SILVERTON

World famous for its appearances in Hollywood's Wild West movies and still operating 100 per cent coal-fired steam locomotives, the Durango & Silverton Narrow Gauge Railroad takes visitors on a dramatic trip up into the mountains via the Animas Canyon to the old silver-mining town of Silverton.

Like the Cumbres & Toltec Scenic Railroad (*see* pages 236-241), the Durango & Silverton Railroad had its beginnings in 1870 when the Denver & Rio Grande Railway (D&RGR) was incorporated by its two co-founders, General William Palmer, a soldier, civil engineer and industrialist, and William Bell, a British physician and photographer of the American West. The new railway was designed to tap into the rich mineral deposits that abounded in the Rocky Mountains to the west and southwest of the booming city of Denver in Colorado. Unusually for an early American railroad, a narrow gauge of 3 ft was chosen along with the burning of coal instead of logs to fuel the steam locomotives.

The D&RGR reached the new railroad town of Durango via the Cumbres Pass (10,015 ft above sea level) in August 1881. Construction of the line up the valley of the River Animas to Silverton started almost immediately and involved crossing the Animas and its tributary mountain creeks on no less than twelve bridges. Despite these physical obstacles progress was swift and the line opened to passengers and freight on 10 July 1882, with locally mined silver ore transported down the line to a smelter in Durango. With the coming of the railway Silverton, at 9,308 ft above sea level, became a boom mining town for a short while until the economic depression, or 'Panic', of 1893, when the railroad building bubble burst. The price of silver plummeted and over 15,000 American companies, including several major railroads and 600 banks failed, many of them in the West. Unemployment and homelessness soared and many people faced starvation. The Silverton line struggled on into the twentieth century and managed to survive despite enormous odds such as the decline of mining in the area, competition from road haulage, dwindling passenger numbers, floods and heavy winter snowfalls.

During the Second World War the old silver smelter in Durango was brought back to life to process locally mined uranium for the Manhattan Project, continuing in operation into the late 1940s during the Cold War. Following the end of the war the railway was thrown a lifeline by the growth in domestic tourism. Interest was no doubt fuelled by the railway's appearance in several Hollywood movies of the 1950s including '*Ticket to*

Tomahawk', which included a brief appearance by Marilyn Monroe, '*Around the World in Eighty Days*' and '*Night Passage*', starring James Stewart. Yet more movie stardom came with appearances in '*Butch Cassidy and the Sundance Kid*' in 1969 and '*Support Your Local Gunfighter*' in 1971.

By the early 1950s freight traffic had dwindled to a trickle and was handled on the mixed trains that by then only ran, mainly for tourists, during the summer months. Despite the D&RGR replacing its fleet of standard-gauge steam locomotives by 1956, the Silverton branch continued to use 2-8-2 'Mikado' locomotives built by the Schenectady Locomotive Works and the Baldwin Locomotive Works in the 1920s – the present owners of the line still use these and can rightly claim that it operates 100 per cent coal-fired locomotives.

By the 1960s the D&RGR regarded its remaining narrow-gauge lines as an anachronism and made efforts to abandon them. However, the company's application to close the Silverton line was turned down by the Interstate Commerce Commission because of its growing tourist patronage. The line between Antonito and Durango via the Cumbres Pass had a brief reprieve when an oil boom kept it busy carrying construction materials. The last train to operate into Durango from the east ran in 1968 and the section from Antonito to Chama was purchased as a tourist railway by the States of Colorado and New Mexico two years later (*see* pages 236-241).

Following its abortive attempt at abandoning the Silverton line, the D&RGR reluctantly agreed not only to invest in improvements to the infrastructure and rolling stock but also to make its Durango terminus and surroundings more amenable to tourists. Despite these improvements, increasing passenger numbers and the railway's registration as a National Historic Landmark, the company still set its sights on ridding itself of the isolated and archaic line. Then, in 1979, along came millionaire Florida citrus grower Charles Bradshaw who made an offer that the D&RGR could not refuse and in 1981 he bought the 45-mile railway lock, stock and barrel.

Under new ownership the scenic Durango & Silverton Narrow Gauge Railroad soon became a highly successful tourist attraction. Old steam locomotives and rolling stock were lovingly restored, new rolling stock was built, track and infrastructure were upgraded and double-headed trains

PREVIOUS PAGE: Class K36 2-8-2 No. 486 returning to Durango alongside the Animas River with the 14.30 to Durango on 15 October 2007.

were introduced. Passenger numbers continued to grow and so did the workforce, and the railway's success brought in visitors from around the world. Extra trains were introduced and by 1986 there were four return services each day along the entire route. Bradshaw sold the railway in 1997 and it was sold again in 1998 to American Heritage Railways who own and operate it today. There are two museums operated by the railways: the D&SNG Museum is located in the roundhouse in Durango while the Freight Yard Museum is located at Silverton Depot.

The headquarters of the Durango & Silverton Narrow Gauge Railway is in the former railway town of Durango in Colorado. With a population of around 17,000 and located at an altitude of 6,512 ft above sea level, the town was developed by the Denver & Rio Grande Railroad in the early 1880s when it opened its narrow-gauge railways to serve mineral mining operations in the area. The original railway hotel, named after the line's founder General Palmer, is still open for business next to the terminus station. Operating year-round (in winter, trains only travel to Cascade Canyon), steam-hauled trains take 3½ hours to make the 45-mile journey up the Animas Valley to Silverton, where a 2¼-hour stopover allows passengers to look around the Freight Yard Museum and take lunch before returning back down to Durango.

From Durango to Silverton the railway climbs 2,796 ft around tortuous curves, along mountainside ledges and

Baldwin 'K28' Class No. 473 runs alongside Highway 550 north of Durango, Colorado, approaching Trimble with the first train of the day to Silverton on 8 September 2008.

through the spectacular Animas Canyon. As the Animas River has not been dammed to generate hydroelectric power it is one of the last free-flowing rivers in the USA and is at its height during the period of snowmelt runoff in June. Steam trains depart from Durango station and make their way slowly through the town, gingerly crossing several highway intersections before heading up the valley to the first stop at Hermosa where water is taken on. From here they climb out of the valley with the locomotives working hard around curved rock faces on sharp bends as they make the half-hour climb up to Rockwood, making the first crossing of the Animas River en route.

From Rockwood, trains enter the dramatic Animas Canyon where they make their way slowly onto the 'highline', a section where they crawl along high cliffs to Tacoma, followed by Tank Creek where locomotives take on water. Still following a narrow rock ledge, trains soon reach Tall Timber Resort followed by Cascade Canyon where winter trains are turned on a wye – the risk of avalanches further up the valley makes this the limit of operations between November and early May.

Crossing the Animas for the third time, trains continue to climb up through sharp reverse curves to Needleton where more water is taken on. From here the climbing continues and the gradients get steeper up to Elk Park where the railway crosses the Colorado Trail. One of the worst locations for avalanches during the winter, Elk Park is also a popular hunting camp in season and is surrounded by peaks reaching over 14,000 ft. Beyond here the climb becomes more gradual before trains reach the sharp curve at Cataract where the Animas Canyon is at its narrowest point. After crossing the Animas for the final time trains slow down for the approach into Silverton where they are turned on a wye for the return journey back down to Durango.

With a population of just over 600, the former silver-mining town of Silverton is set in a secluded mountain valley, 9,318 ft above sea level, in a designated National Historic Landmark District. There is now no mining and the town relies mainly on tourism for its survival – the late nineteenth-century architecture, museum, jail, tours of the Old Hundred Gold Mine and visits to the ghost town at Animas Fork all lend a Wild West flavour.

RIGHT: Class K36 2-8-2 No. 488 eases its way along the 'highline' above the Animas River with the 08.45 Durango to Silverton train on 15 October 2007.

'EMPIRE BUILDER'
UNITED STATES OF AMERICA

GAUGE: 4 FT 8½ IN. • LENGTH: 2,206 MILES/2,257 MILES • ROUTE: CHICAGO TO SEATTLE/PORTLAND

One of America's most long-lived and famously named trains, the 'Empire Builder' takes the northerly route across the prairies and the Continental Divide that was opened by the Great Northern Railway in 1893. The route not only features the awe-inspiring scenery of the Rockies but also passes through two of the longest railway tunnels in the USA.

Introduced by the Great Northern Railway (GNR) in 1929, the 'Empire Builder' is one of the most famous and long-lived named trains in the world. Its route from Chicago to Seattle and Portland takes it along the USA's most northerly transcontinental railroad that was opened across the prairies and the Continental Divide to the Pacific coast in the late nineteenth century.

Much of the route follows in the footsteps of the explorers Meriwether Lewis and William Clark who were the first Americans to cross the western half of what is now the USA. Commissioned by President Thomas Jefferson, their two-year expedition between 1804 and 1806 trailblazed a route westwards along the Missouri River before crossing the continental divide and following the Columbia River to the Pacific coast.

The Great Northern Railway was led by the successful businessman and entrepreneur James J. Hill, who during the 1870s and 1880s became a multi-millionaire by buying bankrupt businesses and reselling them at a profit. Following the international financial crisis of 1873 many American railroads went to the wall – one of these was the St Paul & Pacific Railroad which Hill bought in 1878. Hill then formed the St Paul, Minneapolis & Manitoba Railway in 1879, gradually extending it to Grand Forks and westwards to Devils Lake in North Dakota in 1885. By 1889 the railway had penetrated as far west as Fort Assiniboine (near today's town of Havre) in northern Montana. In 1890 Hill's railroad empire, which by then included the Montana Central Railway, became known as the Great Northern Railway.

Construction of the line westwards from Fort Assiniboine into the mountains started in 1890, taking it through the Lewis Range via the 5,213-ft Marias Pass that had been discovered by the railroad's surveyor John Stevens the previous year – in 1910 the GNR was responsible for establishing the Glacier National Park in which the pass is located. West of here the route of the line followed the Middle Fork of the Flathead River before reaching the Cascade Range of mountains in Washington State. The mountain range was initially crossed by a temporary, steeply graded switchback route over the 4,061-ft Stevens

Pass, named after the railway's surveyor, and thence down to Seattle. The line, built entirely with private funds, opened throughout from St Paul to Seattle in 1893, bringing in its wake thousands of Northern European settlers attracted by the low price of land sold to them by the railway.

Hill's empire continued to expand, with the purchase of the Chicago, Burlington & Quincy Railroad in 1901 providing the missing link between St Paul and Chicago. Portland in Oregon State was reached through the Columbia River Gorge by the Spokane, Portland & Oregon Railway, a joint venture between the GNR and its arch rival the Northern Pacific Railway, in 1909.

Often blocked by heavy snowfall, the notorious, steeply graded switchback route over the Stevens Pass was replaced by a tunnel in 1900. This, the first Cascade Tunnel, was just over 2½ miles long but steam locomotive drivers and passengers were often choked by fumes on the uphill eastbound grade. To overcome this problem the line through the tunnel was electrified in 1909, with heavy trains being hauled along a 4-mile section by up to four electric locomotives. Despite the eradication of the fumes the tunnel's approaches still suffered from heavy snowfall during the winter: the worst incident came in 1910 when an avalanche struck a train, killing nearly 100 people.

Replacing the first tunnel a second, lower, Cascade Tunnel was opened in 1929 and, at 7¾ miles in length, it is the longest railway tunnel in the USA. Drastically reducing journey times it was also electrified and remained so until 1956 when a powerful ventilation system was installed to allow the passage of diesel locomotives.

In 1970 the second longest railway tunnel in the USA was opened on the GNR route to the west of Whitefish in Montana. The 7-mile Flathead Tunnel was built as part of a 60-mile deviation of the railway caused by the building of the Libby Dam which flooded the Kootenai River to form the 90-mile-long Lake Koocanusa, half of which extends across the US/Canada border into British Columbia.

Introduced in 1905, the GNR's 'Oriental Limited' originally ran between St Paul and Seattle where it connected with the railway's steamship service across the Pacific Ocean to the Far East. In 1909 the train's route was extended to Chicago and remained the company's premier trans-continental train until 1929 when the 'Empire

Builder' was introduced. This train was used heavily by armed forces personnel during the Second World War, often necessitating the running of two portions, after which steam haulage was replaced by streamlined diesel-electric locomotives in 1947. Calling at more stations and on a slightly longer route, the 'Oriental Limited' was replaced by the 'Western Star' in 1951, although the journey time was a much slower fifty-eight hours compared to the forty-five hours taken by the 'Empire Builder'. Facing ever-increasing competition from cheap air travel, the 'Western Star' was withdrawn in 1971.

Much of the former GNR route from Chicago to Seattle and Portland is now operated by the BNSF Railway which was formed in 1996 following decades of mergers between the Great Northern, Northern Pacific, Burlington Northern and the Atchison, Topeka & Sante Fe railways. The only sections that are not operated by BNSF are those between Chicago and Minneapolis.

With a route mileage of around 32,000 miles, BNSF is the second largest freight railway network in North America. Its Northern Transcon section includes the country's most northerly transcontinental route between Chicago and Seattle, which is used heavily by long intermodal trains as well as being the route of the 'Empire Builder'.

Named in honour of the GNR's founder, the 'Empire Builder' is today operated by Amtrak, the publicly funded National Railroad Passenger Corporation that was formed in 1971 to save the country's remaining, but unprofitable, passenger routes from closure.

The 'Empire Builder' is Amtrak's busiest long-distance train, taking forty-five hours to travel the 2,206 miles from Chicago to Seattle. Hauled by two General Electric 'P42' Genesis diesel locomotives the 12-coach train includes coaches for Portland in Oregon that are detached or attached at Spokane. Passengers are accommodated in double-deck Superliner coaches which include baggage cars, sleeping cars, a dining car and a lounge car.

The 'Empire Builder' starts its long journey at Chicago's iconic Union Street station, which was built in 1925 and is now the third busiest station in the USA, also served by fifteen other of Amtrak's named trains. Heading off in a northerly direction along the west shore of Lake Michigan, the train calls at Glenview then crosses into Wisconsin where it makes a stop at Milwaukee before heading northwestwards to Columbus, Portage, Wisconsin Dells, Tomah and La Crosse, where it crosses the Mississippi River. Now in Minnesota, the 'Empire Builder' continues through a forested landscape to St Paul's restored Midway Station before heading off into the vast prairies to Detroit Lakes, where it crosses the Red River to enter North Dakota and reach Fargo station.

From the important junction at Fargo the train heads north to Grand Forks before turning west across a flat prairie landscape to Devils Lake. Here the railway's route has often been flooded by rising waters but this problem has recently been solved by raising the track by ten feet. Beyond Devils Lake the train continues its westerly course, crossing into Montana near the confluence of the Yellowstone and Missouri rivers just west of Williston.

Leaving the prairies behind, the train starts its long climb up into the Glacier National Park, first calling at Malta, Havre and Shelby before crossing the Lewis Range at Marias Pass. En route, trains also cross the iconic Two Medicine Trestle Bridge and make seasonal stops at ski resorts before arriving at Whitefish's mock-Tudor style station, one of the busiest on the line. From here trains soon enter the 7-mile-long Flathead Tunnel before briefly entering Idaho and then crossing into Washington State to Spokane, where the Portland portion is detached for its journey down through the Columbia River Gorge.

The Seattle portion of the train sets off from Spokane on its route through the Cascade Mountains via the 7¾-mile Cascade Tunnel before reaching the city of Everett and its impressive new station. The next stop is Edmonds station before the train ends its long journey from Chicago at King Street Station in Seattle. Opened in 1906, this station along with its impressive clock tower was built jointly by the Great Northern and Northern Pacific railways and has recently been the subject of extensive restoration.

OVERLEAF: Class P42 diesel-electric locomotives Nos. 19 and 85 cross Two Medicine Hat Bridge as they leave Glacier National Park, Montana, with the eastbound 'Empire Builder' in September 2010.

WHITE PASS & YUKON RAILROAD

USA/ALASKA AND CANADA/YUKON

GAUGE: 3 FT · **LENGTH:** 67½ MILES ·
ROUTE: SKAGWAY (ALASKA) TO CARCROSS (YUKON)

Built in the wake of the Klondike Gold Rush, the narrow-gauge White
Pass & Yukon Railroad led a profitable existence transporting minerals
from the remote Yukon Territory in northern Canada down to the
Alaskan port of Skagway. Despite closure in 1982 it has since partially
reopened as a tourist railway connecting with cruise liners at Skagway.

GULF

OF

ALASKA

ALASKA
U.S.A.

YUKON

CANADA

BRITISH COLUMBIA

Boundary
Mount Fairplay 1989
Divided Mountain 1562
Sixtymile
Dawson
Rock Creek
Flat Creek
Mount Patterson
2088
Stewart
Bear Creek
Indian
Barlow
Elsa
Keno Hill
Mount Joy 2235
Horn Peak 2515
Keele Peak 2972
Tiritya 2383
Natla
etlin Junction
Northway Junction
Nabesna Village
Northway
White
Thistle Creek
Stewart
Mayo
Stewart Crossing
Flat Top 1636
Grey Hunter Peak 2214
Mount Armstrong 2159
Mount Selous 2176
Backbone Ranges 2353
2667
Chisana
Mount Allen 2890
Beaver Creek
1600
Coffee Creek
Yukon
Pelly
Pelly Crossing
Hess
Mountains
2353
utzotin Mountains
1876
Koidern Mountain 1656
Dawson Range
Apex Mountain 2022
Glenlyon Peak 2190
Mount Connolly 2139
Tay
Mount Hogg 2065
Traffic Mountain 2054
2572
isana
Mt Bona 5029
Mount Natazhat 4095
Burwash Landing
Destruction Bay
2305
Red Granite Mountain 2006
Carmacks
Lower Laberge
Faro
Fox Mountain 2404
Ross River
Anvil Range
Pelly
Mountains
Cassiar
Tuchitua
Mount Murray 2162
White
Wrangell-St Elias National Park and Preserve
Mount Wood 4842
5226 Mount Lucania
Kluane
Kluane Lake
Aishihik
YUKON
Liard
Mount Queen Mary 3886
Kluane National Park
Haines Junction
Champagne
Takhini Hotspring
Whitehorse
Marsh Lake
Johnson's Crossing
Brooks Brook
2079
Rancheria
Meister
Watson Lake
Mount Logan 5959
Mount Vancouver 4785
Mount Hubbard 4577
Beloud Post
Mount Arkell 2209
Yukon
Jakes Corner
Tagish
Teslin Lake
Teslin
Rancheria
Upper Liard
Mount St Elias 5489
Mount Cook 4194
Mount Seattle 3069
Robinson
Mount Skukum 2382
Carcross
Mt Draper 1728
Mount Foster 2173
Bennett
Surprise
Atlin
Stikine
Mountains
Yakutat
Alsek
Klondike Gold Rush National Historical Park
Chilkoot Trail National Historic Site
Atlin Lake
McDame
Mount Bigger 2514
Klukwan
Skagway
Mount Nesselrode 2470
Cassiar
ALASKA
U.S.A.
Mount Lodge 3210
Mt Barnard 2504
Chilkat
Haines
Devils Paw 2616
Tulsequah
Porter Landing
Mount Fairweather 4670
Glacier Bay National Park and Preserve
Mount Crillon 3871
Excursion Inlet
St Terese
Auke Bay
Mount Ogden 2268
Stikine Plateau
Dease Lake
Gustavus
Funter
Juneau
Douglas
Sheslay
Elfin Cove
Hoonah
Hawk Inlet
BRITISH COLUMBIA
Telegraph Creek
Tahltan
Stikine
Pelican
Tenakee Springs
Chichagof Island
Admiralty Island Nat. Monument-Kootznoowoo Wilderness
Mount Sumdum 2032
Windham
Mount Ratz 3136
Mount Ambition 2328
Mount Edziza 2787
Glenora
Chichagof
Chatham
Admiralty Island
Sumdum
Skeena Mountains
Cobol
Angoon
Hood Bay
Cape Fanshaw
Mount Ratz 3136
Sitka National Historical Park
Baranof
Sitka
Kake
Kupreanof Island
Kupreanof
Devil's Thumb 2767
Kate's Needle 3049
Mount Ambition 2328
Baranof Island
Goddard
Mount Yanovski 1080
Kuiu Island
Petersburg
Stikine
Stikine
Mount Cote 1323
Mount Lewis Cass 2092
Mount John Jay 2286
Mount Pattullo 2729
1064
Point Baker
Whale Pass
Bell Island Hot Springs
Wrangell
Stewart
Big Port Walter
Port Alexander
Edna Bay
Coffman Cove
Meyers Chuck
Adams Mountain 2316
Hyder
Prince of Wales Island
Thorne Bay
Revillagigedo Island
Misty Fiords National Monument Wilderness
Klawock
Kasaan

The story of this remote railway starts in 1896 with the famous Klondike Gold Rush. In that year gold was discovered in the Klondike region of the Yukon in northwest Canada. Between 1897 and 1899 around 100,000 prospectors descended on the region in anticipation of striking it rich. However, reaching the goldfields in this inhospitable and inaccessible region was no mean feat as there were no roads or railways. The only routes were through the ports of Dyea and Skagway in southeast Alaska and from there the Klondikers, as they became known, had to follow either the White Pass or Chilkoot trails into Canada and down to the Yukon River, then make their way by boat to the Klondike. The mountainous terrain and harsh winters coupled with the demands of the Canadian government that each prospector had to carry a year's supply of food saw many fall by the way – only 30,000 reached the Klondike and, of these, only 4,000 found gold. Boom towns, such as Dawson City, sprang up along the route to accommodate prospectors but by 1899 many had left to discover pastures new in western Alaska. Gold mining continued with more sophisticated equipment into the early twentieth century but by 1903 production had peaked. As the gold rush died down, companies mining other valuable minerals such as silver, copper and lead took its place.

Seeing an opportunity to open up this vast mineral-rich region, three companies started to build a 325-mile railway in 1897 from the Alaskan port of Skagway across the mountains to Fort Selkirk in the Canadian territory of Yukon. A gauge of 3 ft was selected which allowed the railway to have sharper curves by following the contours, thus reducing construction costs. Construction started in May 1898 but soon ran into problems with Skagway's local mafia and in July the fledgling project was taken over by the White Pass & Yukon Railway Company (WP&YR) with its headquarters in London.

With the new owners in the driving seat, construction pushed on at a rapid pace with the 2,885 ft summit at White Pass being reached in February 1899. Bennett, at the southern tip of Lake Bennett, was reached in July and the entire 110 miles of railway from Skagway to Whitehorse opened in August 1900. Unfortunately, by then, the Klondike Gold Rush had petered out and the planned 215-mile extension to Fort Selkirk was replaced by railway-owned riverboats plying along the Yukon River between Whitehorse and Dawson City.

By 1900 most of the gold prospectors had left the Yukon but they were soon replaced by commercial mining of other minerals – the only way out for these valuable ores was along the WP&YR to Skagway from where they were shipped out. The railway remained profitable through the First World War and managed to survive the Great Depression of the 1930s but by the outbreak of the Second World War it was in a run-down state and closure was a serious threat. However, the Japanese attack on Pearl Harbour on 7 December 1941 threw the railway a lifeline: fearing a Japanese invasion of Alaska, the US Government decided to construct the strategic 1,700-mile Alaska Highway and Whitehorse was directly on the planned route. In order to move the enormous amounts of equipment and men needed for the construction of the highway, the run-down railway was taken over by the US Army which introduced additional steam locomotives and rolling stock commandeered from other 3-ft-gauge systems, such as the Denver & Rio Grande Western Railroad (*see* pages 236-241) in the USA. Despite severe winter weather, the increase in traffic was dramatic and by 1943 it had risen by a remarkable 1,000 per cent – on one day alone in August there were nearly forty train movements along the line.

While other narrow-gauge railways in the USA were on their last legs, the 1950s saw the WP&YR at the forefront of modernization with the introduction of diesels and container trains. Another lifeline for the railway came in 1969 when the world's largest zinc mine opened at Faro in the Yukon – the ore was transported by road to Whitehorse for onward shipment along the railway to Skagway. Passenger traffic was also increasing thanks to cruise liners calling at Skagway, where tourists could (and still do) transfer directly from their ship on to the train for the scenic journey through the White Pass.

The railway's luck finally ran out in the summer of 1982 when rapidly falling metal prices on the world markets led to the closure of the zinc mine. With its major source of income gone the railway staggered on with passenger traffic until October when it was forced to close.

Fortunately this was not the end of the line for the WP&YR. The scenic qualities of the railway were not lost on the operators of cruise ships that called at Skagway. Their encouragement and support eventually led to its partial reopening as a summer-only tourist railway, firstly to Fraser in 1989, to Bennett in 1992 and finally to Carcross in 2007. The remaining closed section from there to Whitehorse may be reopened in the future.

White Pass & Yukon Railroad trains depart from the dockside at Skagway alongside huge visiting cruise liners, allowing direct access onto the train for cruise-ship passengers. To cater for this influx of visitors up to four trains are sometimes required, each following the other up to White Pass. Motive power is normally provided by 1950s and 1960s Alco and General Electric diesels but the railway also operates restored steam locomotives in the shape of a 1908-built 2-8-0 and a 1947-built 2-8-2 (both built by the Baldwin Locomotive Works).

A lawless town during the Klondike Gold Rush when its population grew to 10,000, Skagway (population today 920)

A diesel-hauled Summit Excursion train on the White Pass & Yukon Railroad has just left 15-mile Tunnel and crossed over the wooden trestle bridge near to the station known as Slippery Rock.

comes alive during the summer months with the arrival of numerous cruise ships. From sea level at the dockside, the WP&YR climbs for twenty miles up to White Pass, 2,865 ft above sea level. The first two miles through the town are fairly level but after passing the railway's maintenance shops the line starts to climb, following the east shore of the Skagway River before looping eastwards to cross the East Fork. Here there is an old caboose wagon which can be hired from the US Forest Service as accommodation. Still climbing, the railway regains the east bank of the river from where there are fine views of Mount Harding and the Harding Glacier. At Heney Station it heads east to cross the river near Glacier Station then loops westwards before crossing Glacier Gorge to disappear into Tunnel Mountain. Now heading north, the railway passes Inspiration Point and Dead Horse Gulch before reaching a tunnel that was opened in 1969 to replace the adjacent Steel Bridge – with the opening of the zinc mine near Whitehorse in that year the bridge was considered unsafe for the heavy mineral trains that were being introduced. White Pass Summit and the US/Canadian border is soon reached and from here the railway levels out, picking its way between clear mountain lakes to reach Fraser in British Columbia, where the Canadian customs officials check passengers' passports.

From Fraser the railway heads northeastwards alongside a string of lakes before looping westwards around the mountains to Bennett at the southern tip of Lake Bennett. Here, the Chilkoot Trail joins from Dyea in Alaska. Bennett was once an important staging post for gold prospectors from where they travelled by raft or boat along the lake to Carcross – the coming of the railway in 1900 led to the town's demise. From Bennett the railway hugs the shore of the lake, crossing into Yukon to its present terminus at Carcross. Once named Caribou Crossing, this small town has a population of less than 300 and depends more or less entirely, during the summer months, on the visitors who arrive here by train.

The remaining forty-five miles of railway to Whitehorse have been closed since 1982. However, the track is in place and there are currently proposals to reopen it. A tourist tram operates along a mile of the track in Whitehorse, the capital of Yukon and the largest city (population 23,000) in northern Canada.

RIGHT: With its train of clerestory coaches Baldwin-built 2-8-2 No. 73 exits 15-mile Tunnel to cross the wooden trestle bridge on a section of the railroad that was carved out during the extremely harsh winter of 1898–99.

ACROSS THE CANADIAN ROCKIES
CANADA

GAUGE: 4 FT 8½ IN. •
LENGTH: 1,474 MILES VIA CALGARY/1,555 MILES VIA EDMONTON •
ROUTE: WINNIPEG TO VANCOUVER

While the Dominion of Canada was formed from three British colonies in 1867, the western province of British Columbia remained isolated until it was enticed to join in 1871 by promises made by the Canadian government to build a railway within ten years across the Rockies.

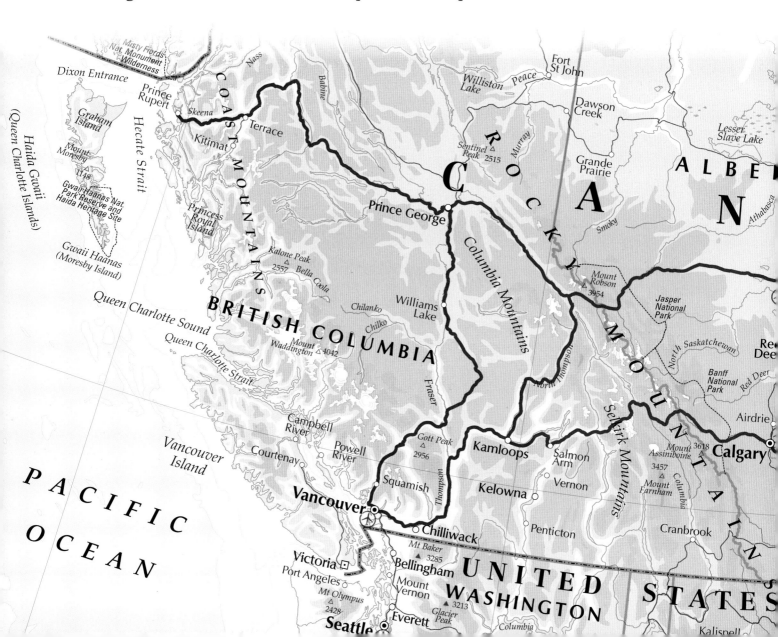

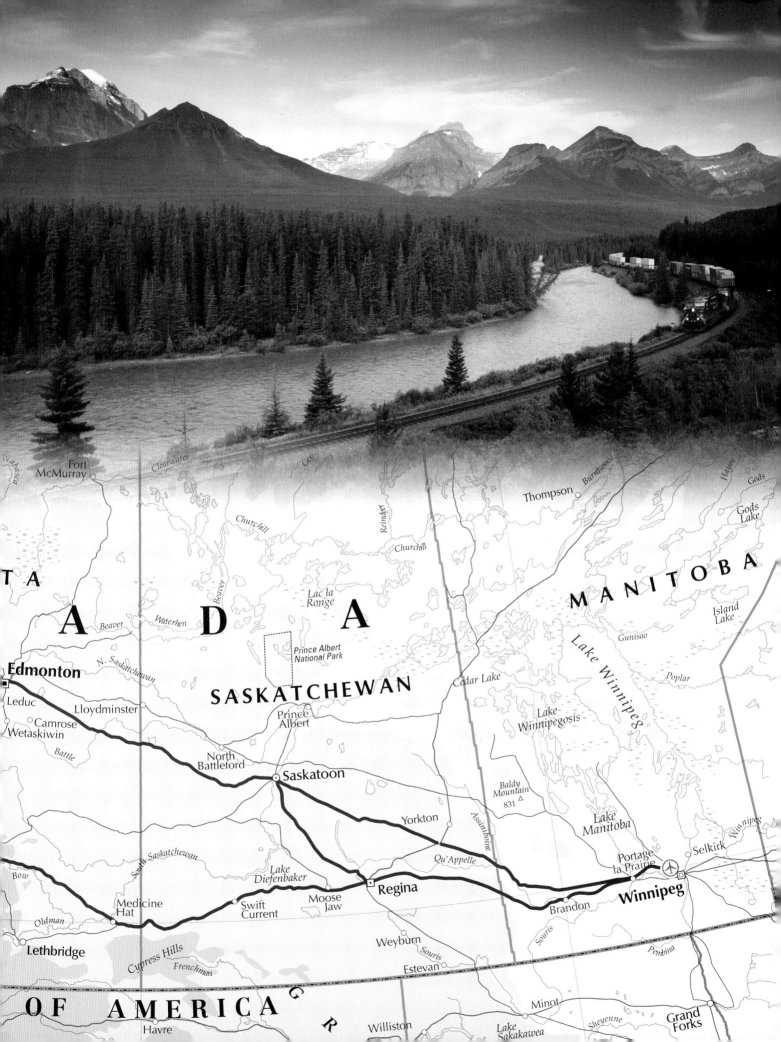

T A

A D A

Fort
McMurray

Wabasca

Clearwater

Churchill

Geike

Reindeer

Thompson

Burntwood

Hayes

Gods

M A N I T O B A

Gods
Lake

Churchill

Lac la
Ronge

Island
Lake

Edmonton

Leduc

Camrose

Wetaskiwin

Beaver

Beaver

Waterhen

N. Saskatchewan

Battle

Lloydminster

D

A

Prince Albert
National Park

SASKATCHEWAN

Cedar Lake

Gunisao

*Lake
Winnipeg*

Poplar

Lake
Winnipegosis

North
Battleford

Prince
Albert

Baldy
Mountain
831 △

Lake
Manitoba

Saskatoon

South Saskatchewan

Yorkton

Assiniboine

Winnipeg

Lake
Diefenbaker

Qu'Appelle

Portage
la Prairie

Selkirk

Bow

Medicine
Hat

Swift
Current

Moose
Jaw

Regina

Brandon

Winnipeg

Oldman

Lethbridge

Cypress Hills

Frenchman

Weyburn

Souris

Souris

Pembina

O F   A M E R I C A

Estevan

Havre

Williston

Minot

Sheyenne

Lake
Sakakawea

Grand
Forks

G

R

CANADIAN PACIFIC RAILWAY

While the Dominion of Canada was formed from three British colonies in 1867, the western province of British Columbia remained isolated until it was enticed to join in 1871 by promises made by the Canadian government to build a railway within ten years across the Rockies.

However, progress was initially slow under government ownership with only 300 miles of railway having been opened by 1880. In that year a group of Scottish Canadian businessmen formed a syndicate to complete the transcontinental railway and thus, with financial support and land given by the government, the Canadian Pacific Railway (CPR) was incorporated in 1881. Also included in the deal were the sections of railway already built or in the process of being built by the government, including the route along the eastern banks of the Fraser and Thompson rivers from Port Moody to Kamloops in British Columbia and, in the east, a branch from Thunder Bay, on the north shore of Lake Superior, to Winnipeg.

In the east, construction of the railway westwards across the barren and lake-littered landscape of the Canadian Shield started from Bonfield, Ontario – eastwards from here the CPR leased the Canadian Central Railway and Ontario & Quebec Railway in 1884 to gain access to Toronto, Ottawa and Montreal. The route of the CPR took it through Winnipeg in Manitoba then across the Prairies on a southerly route to Regina in Saskatchewan and Calgary in Alberta. To the west of Calgary the railway engineers were faced with surmounting the Rocky Mountains, taking a steeply graded route, mainly built by poorly-paid and overworked Chinese coolies, up through Kicking Horse Pass, 5,390 ft above sea level, which was reached in 1884. To the west of the pass the railway then made a steep descent down Big Hill on a gradient of 1-in-23 before climbing up Field Hill to cross the Selkirk Mountains at Rogers Pass, 4,360 ft above sea level.

Meanwhile construction of the line had also been continuing eastwards from Kamloops up through Eagle Pass in the Monashee Mountains. This was the last section of the CPR to be completed, with the ceremonial last spike being driven at Craigellachie on 7 November 1885. By then the CPR was in dire financial straits and, not for the first time, had to be bailed out by the government.

The first transcontinental train ran between Montreal and Port Moody in July 1886, taking five days and sixteen hours for the journey, but less than a year later the western terminus had been changed to Gastown, which by then had become known as Vancouver.

The most difficult stretch of line to operate on the entire CPR, if not in North America, was the steep gradient of Big Hill, which was eventually bypassed by the Spiral Tunnels which opened in 1909, and the climb up to Rogers Pass was eased by the opening of the 5-mile Connaught Tunnel in 1916. The latter was supplemented by the 9-mile Mount Macdonald Tunnel which opened in 1988 and is the longest railway tunnel in the Americas.

Also operating steamer services on the Great Lakes and a large international shipping company, the CPR went on to transport vast numbers of European immigrants setting out for a new life on the Prairies. The company actively supported the Allied war effort in both World Wars as well as weathering the Great Depression of the 1930s. Despite continuing to operate a thriving freight business CPR struggled to compete with passenger road transport and airline travel following the end of the Second World War. In one sense it joined in the competition by operating its own national and international airline from 1942 to 1987, but by then the much-reduced passenger rail services on the network had been taken over by Via Rail.

Introduced in 1955, the most famous passenger train operated by CPR was 'The Canadian' which ran between Toronto and Vancouver with a separate section from Montreal joining at Sudbury. Made up of new stainless-steel rolling stock, including 'vista dome' cars hauled by streamlined diesel locomotives, the train was transferred to the new Via Rail operation in 1978. In early 1990 it was rerouted to run over the Canadian National Railway's more northerly route via Edmonton (*see* right), replacing its flagship 'Super Continental' train and ending over 100 years of regular passenger services along the CPR route via Calgary, although the eastbound train still uses the CPR's line along the Thompson and Fraser rivers between Vancouver and Kamloops.

PREVIOUS PAGE: A CPR freight train heads alongside the Bow River in the Banff National Park.

RIGHT: Deep in the Thompson River Gorge a long Canadian National diesel-hauled coal train winds its way through a series of rock shelters.

CANADIAN NATIONAL RAILWAYS

The second transcontinental railway to open across the Canadian Rockies was the Grand Trunk Pacific Railway (GTPR). The company was the western division of the National Transcontinental Railway, of which the 1,790-mile eastern division between New Brunswick, Quebec, northern Ontario and Winnipeg was built by the federal government. Instead of terminating at Vancouver, the 1,740-mile western division from Winnipeg was designed to serve a new deepwater port at Prince Rupert, close to the Canada/Alaska border. Construction work started from Winnipeg in 1905, reaching Saskatoon in 1907 and Edmonton in 1909 before crossing the Continental Divide at Yellowhead Pass, 3,711 ft above sea level, in 1911. From here construction continued in a northwesterly direction along the Fraser River to Prince George and then westwards across difficult terrain, finally opening to Prince Rupert in 1914.

The third transcontinental railway across the Rockies began life in 1899 with the incorporation of the Canadian Northern Railway (CNoR). This new company was formed by the amalgamation of a network of railways that had been opened across the Prairies connecting Winnipeg with Ontario and North Dakota in the USA. As a direct competitor of the established CPR the new company not only expanded eastwards but also set its sights on reaching Vancouver by a more northerly route via Saskatoon in Saskatchewan and Edmonton in Alberta, paralleling the GTPR. By 1905 the new railway had opened between Winnipeg and Edmonton but here further construction westwards across the Rockies had to wait for five years until funding was provided by the government

of British Columbia. Started in 1910, the route taken through the mountains paralleled the Grand Trunk Pacific Railway via the Yellowhead Pass before heading off south down the North Thompson River to Kamloops where the CPR came in from its route via Kicking Horse Pass. Here the railway engineers were faced with taking the difficult west banks of the Thompson and Frazer rivers to Vancouver as the rival CPR had already taken the easier east side of the rivers for its own route. The line eventually opened in 1915 but by then the CNoR, with its network stretching from Nova Scotia in the east to Vancouver Island in the west, was in such a dire financial position that it was nationalized in 1918, becoming part of the newly formed Canadian National Railways (CNR).

Although the GTPR had opened to Prince Rupert in 1914 it also faced severe financial difficulties and its operations were handed over to the Canadian Government Railways in 1919, eventually becoming part of the CNR in 1923.

Operating between Montreal and Vancouver the CNR's flagship transcontinental train, the 'Super Continental', was introduced in 1955. Although in direct competition with the CPR's modern 'The Canadian', this new train used refurbished coaching stock without any dome cars, although the latter were belatedly added in 1964. The train was taken over by Via Rail in 1978 but was withdrawn in 1981, only to be reintroduced in 1985 between Winnipeg and Vancouver. The end came in 1990 when it was replaced by the CPR's 'The Canadian' which still operates over the CNR route between Toronto and Vancouver.

Via Rail's westbound 'Canadian' passes Henry House as it approaches Jasper, Alberta on the northerly CNR route in February 2005.

Canadian National Railways was privatized in 1995 and now owns 20,400 miles of railways in Canada and the USA while the Canadian Pacific Railway owns 14,000 miles of track in both countries. What remains of passenger services in Canada is mainly operated by Via Rail, which was formed as an independent federal Crown corporation in 1978. It does not own any track and has to pay user fees to either CPR or CNR. In Western Canada it operates only two passenger services: the thrice-weekly (May to October)/twice-weekly (October to April) 'The Canadian' between Toronto and Vancouver along the CNR route via Yellowhead Pass and Jasper; and the thrice-weekly tourist train between Jasper and Prince Rupert with an overnight layover in Prince George, which operates between June and September.

In addition to the two Via Rail services the Rocky Mountaineer rail touring company operates tourist trains on three routes in Western Canada between May and September: on the CPR route from Vancouver to Banff or Calgary; on the CNR route from Vancouver to Jasper; and over the CN-operated section from North Vancouver via Whistler and Quesnel to Prince George and Jasper.

Both CNR and CPR routes across the Rocky Mountains to Vancouver are vital freight arteries carrying not only trans-continental traffic but also locally generated traffic such as coal and timber. Vancouver docks, the nearby port of Robert Banks and Prince Rupert further north all handle import and export containers and the railway companies are trying hard to convince shipping lines to use these places as the first ports of call in North America to reduce shipping times from Asia and because the distance to Chicago is comparable with the distance from Seattle or Long Beach. Long eastbound trains hauled by up to four diesel-electric locomotives heading for northeastern USA carry imported automobiles on autoracks and intermodal containers in unit trains while general merchandise is carried in mixed trains. Enormously long westbound unit trains of up to 150 cars (about 1¾ miles long) carry coal, sulphur, potash and grain for export – wheat is collected from all over the Prairies and transported westwards for export with each train carrying upwards of 12,000 tons of grain.

Canadian National diesel-electrics Nos. 5710, 5435 and 2555 stop at Swan Landing and prepare to set back to detach wagons in the yard for transfer to the Grand Prairie, June 2001.

SUGAR CANE STEAM IN CUBA

U.S.A.

Port Charlotte
Stuart
Hobe Sound
Riviera Beach
Fort
Myers
Caloosahatchee
Lake
Okeechobee
Pahokee
Belle
Glade
West
Palm Beach
La Belle
Clewiston
Cape Coral
Bonita Springs
Everglades
Lake
Worth
Boca Raton
Naples
Fort Lauderdale
Marco
Big Cypress
Nat. Preserve
Plantation
Carol City
Hollywood
Hialeah
Miami Beach
Alice
Tow
Cutler
Ridge
Miami
South Miami
Everglades
Nat. Park
Homestead
Biscayne
Nat. Park

Florida Bay
Key
Largo
Florida Keys
Islamorada
Pine
Islands
Key
West
Marathon

Straits of Florida

Cay Sal
Bank

Tropic of Cancer

Nicholas Channel

LA HABANA
(Havana)
Guanabacoa
Varadero
Archipiélago de Sabana
Marianao
2
Cotorro
Matanzas
Cárdenas
Corralilla
Guanajay
San José
de las
3
La Isabela
Artemisa
1
Lajas
Madruga
Rancho
Veloz
Sagua la Grand
La Esperanza
Güira
Güines
Jovellanos
Unión
Los Arabos
Sto
Caibarién
Viñales
de Melena
Surgidero
de Batabanó
de Reyes
Colón
Domingo
Camajuan
Minas
Los
Palacios
Jagüey
Grande
Hanábana
Santa Clara
de Matahambre
Consolación del Sur
Cruces
Placetas
Mantua
Golfo
Península
Antón Recio
Palmira
Cabaiguá
Pinar
del Río
de Batabanó
de Zapata
Cienfuegos
San
Juan 1156
Fomento
Guane
San Juan
y Martínez
Nueva
Sancti Spíritus
Península
Gerona
Santa
Archipiélago
Trinidad
Casilda
de Guanahacabibes
Lafé
La Demajagua
Fé
de los
Canarreos
Tunas
de Zaza
Jíbaro

Isla
de la Juventud

CUBA

Yucatan Channel

G R E A T E R

Archipiélago
de los Jardines
de la Reina

C A R I B B E A N

S E A

Cayman Islands
(U.K.)

Spot Bay

Grand
Cayman
West Bay
GEORGE
TOWN
Bodden
Town

Great Exuma
Long Island
Deadman's Cay
Clarence Town
Mortimer's

THE
BAHAMAS

Crooked Island
Crooked I. Passage
Colonel Hill
Albert Town
Snug Corner
Betsy Bay
Mayaguana
Abraham's Bay

Acklins Island

Duncan Town

Columbus Bank

Caicos Passage

Blue Hills
Little Inagua I.
Turks and Caicos Islands
(U.K.)

Great Inagua

Bahamas National Trust Park

Matthew Town
Clarion Bank

Great Bahama Bank

Old Bahama Channel
Archipiélago de Camagüey
Cayo Romano

Chambas
Morón
Bolivia
Ciego de Ávila
Primero de Enero
Esmeralda
Jaronú
Gaspar
Sola
úcaro
Florida
Caunao
Minas
Nuevitas
Lugareño
Puerto Manatí
Jesús Menéndez
Samá
Vertientes
Sibanicú
Hatuey
Martí
Camagüey
Puerto Padre
Gibara
Rafael Freyre
Banes
San Pedro
Guáimaro
Las Tunas
Holguín
Antilla
Guatemala
Moa
Francisco
Jobabo
Omaja
Cueto
Nicaro
Sagua de Tánamo
Santa Cruz del Sur
Guayabal
Guamo
Salado
Cauto
Mayarí
Alto Cedro
Parque Nacional Alejandro de Humboldt
589
Baracoa
Golfo de Guacanayabo
Jiguaní
Jamaica
Toa
Maisí
Manzanillo
Bayamo
San Luis
Campechuela
Yara
Palma Soriano
La Maya
Jauco
Niquero
Pico Turquino
Caimanera
Guantánamo
Boquerón
Sierra Maestra 1994
Santiago de Cuba
Siboney
Daiquiri
Guantánamo Bay Naval Base (U.S.A.)
Port-de-Paix
St-Louis du Nord
Jean-Rabel
Le Môle St-Nicolas
Gros Morne
Parque Nacional Desembarco del Granma
Pilón
Portillo
Baie de Henne
Plaisance
Ennery
Windward Passage

A N T I L L E S

HAITI
St-Marc
Île de la Gonâve
Verrettes
Gonaïves
Anse-à-Galets

Nearly 800 miles in length, Cuba is the largest island in the Caribbean and at its nearest point is only ninety miles from Florida, USA. After being discovered by Christopher Columbus in 1492 the island was ruled for over 400 years by Spain during which time the indigenous population was virtually wiped out by imported disease. The short Spanish-American War in 1898 ended Spanish rule with Cuba gaining independence in 1902. Despite this, the country came firmly under US influence until Fidel Castro's socialist government replaced the corrupt Batista regime following the Cuban Revolution in 1959. Since 1965 the country has been governed as a one-party Communist state which, until the collapse of the Soviet Union in 1989, was totally dependent for its survival on support from Moscow. The United States embargo against Cuba, which was introduced during the Cold War in 1960 and is still in place today, has severely restricted economic growth in the country where food and fuel rationing continues to this day.

Cuba is not only famous for its tobacco and cigar industry but also for its sugar production, being the world's biggest exporter of sugar until the introduction of the US embargo. From then on the Soviet Union subsidized the Cuban sugar industry by paying grossly inflated prices until the bottom fell out of the market in the 1990s. French immigrants introduced the growing of sugar cane into eastern Cuba in the late eighteenth century and by the nineteenth century, with the aid of slave labour, the island had become the most important producer of sugar in the world. The fertile soil, low-lying lush hills and perfect climate were ideal for growing sugar cane. The boom continued through the nineteenth century, aided by the introduction of new steam-powered technology for processing sugar in the mills and more efficient means of transport in the form of steam railways.

Railways came early to Cuba with the first being opened from Havana to Bejucal in 1837 – not only was this the first steam railway in Latin America but it also preceded the first railway to be built in Spain. The network, most of it built to the standard gauge of 4 ft 8½ in., was greatly expanded, particularly in the east of the island, in the early twentieth century by the American railway executive, William Van Horne, following his success in building

Canada's first trans-continental railway, the Canadian Pacific, which had opened in 1886 (*see* pages 260-267). Cuba's booming sugar cane industry was also opening hundreds of miles of railways – mainly standard gauge but also some with narrower gauges such as 2 ft 6 in. – to carry the perishable raw sugar cane from plantations to mills and the refined sugar to ports for export. Until the 1959 revolution, when foreign-owned businesses were nationalized, many of these mills were American-owned and consequently the majority of steam locomotives used on their lines were built by US companies such as Baldwin, Vulcan Iron Works and Alco.

PREVIOUS PAGE: PREVIOUS PAGE: With the home steam fleet in poor health, 2-8-0 No. 1518 was drafted in from Reynold Garcia Mill and is seen here crossing the 'motorway' with a train of loaded sugar cane for Australia Mill in March 2002.

Cuba's foreign-owned sugar-cane industry and its railway network was nationalized following the Revolution, coming under the control of MINAZ (the Ministry of Sugar Production). Apart from a few exceptions such as in China, steam had been replaced by diesel and electric traction on most of the world's railways by the 1970s but in economically isolated Cuba the picture was very different. Unable to buy new equipment and fuel, the sugar-cane railways were stuck in a time warp, continuing to rely on vintage steam haulage until the end of the twentieth century, coming to life each year – as illustrated on these pages – during the sugar cane harvest, or 'Zafra',

between early January and the end of May. The early years of the twenty-first century saw the demand for and price of sugar fall worldwide, leading to the closure of many of the mills on the island along with their steam operations. By 2005 they had virtually disappeared leaving just a couple of steam-operated tourist lines in operation today such as the one at Australia Mill in the Matanzas Region to the east of Havana.

Rafael Freyre's fine-looking Baldwin 2-8-0 No. 1388 (works No. 31375 built in 1907) passing through the outskirts of Barjay village, Holguin, with a long, heavily loaded train of sugar cane for the mill on 12 April 1998.

SOUTH
AMERICA

LA TROCHITA
ARGENTINA/PATAGONIA
GAUGE: 750 MM (2 FT 5½ IN.) • **LENGTH**: 250 MILES •
ROUTE: ESQUEL (CHUBUT PROVINCE) TO INGENIERO JACOBACCI
(RIO NEGRO PROVINCE)

Only completed in 1945, this narrow-gauge railway crosses Argentina's 'Wild West' in the shadow of the Andes Mountains. Threatened with total closure in the 1990s, the southern section still clings to life with tourist trains operated by original oil-fired steam locomotives.

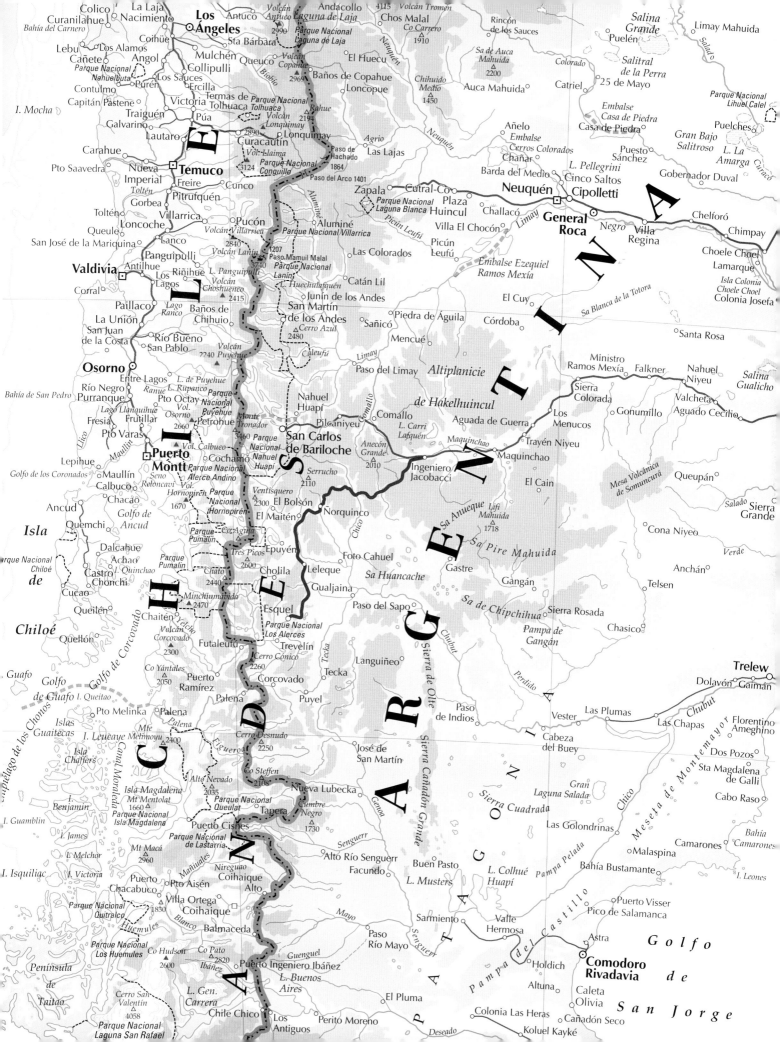

The region known as Patagonia lies at the southern end of South America and is shared by Argentina and Chile, split by the southern end of the Andes mountains in the west. Argentine Patagonia is mainly characterized by windswept steppe-like plains with little vegetation, dotted with lakes and intersected by rivers, such as the Río Negro, that flow west-east from the Andes down to the Atlantic. Closer to the Andean foothills, vegetation becomes more abundant and the lakes are significantly larger.

During the early twentieth century the Argentine Government planned to build a network of railways across Patagonia to serve oil, mining, agricultural and energy industries and provide an outlet for them through the Atlantic ports of San Antonio Oeste and Puerto Deseado. In the event many of these lines were never built due to the impact of the First World War on the country's economy and those that were built in the south were never connected with each other or with the main northern network that connected them to the capital, Buenos Aires.

Despite the country's ailing economy the broad-gauge main line from San Antonio Oeste, on the Atlantic coast, to Ingeniero Jacobacci was completed in 1916 – this remote outpost was named in honour of the railway's director, Guido Jacobacci. It took another eighteen years before the line was extended westwards to San Carlos de Bariloche, situated in the foothills of the Andes on the southern shores of Nahuel Huapi Lake – the coming of the railway in 1934 saw the town become a major tourist centre offering skiing, trekking and mountaineering. Now a city with a population of 130,000, Bariloche is served by a thrice-weekly train service from San Antonio Oeste that originates in the city of Viedma.

Meanwhile, back at Ingeniero Jacobacci, work started on building a 250-mile narrow-gauge railway in a southwesterly direction to Esquel, in the Andean foothills, in 1922. The plan was to link up with a metre-gauge line that was being built up the Chubut Valley from the Atlantic port of Rawson and thus create a network of light railways serving Patagonia. However, the line from Ingeniero Jacobacci to Esquel was to be built using

PREVIOUS PAGE: 'La Trochita' is the world's most southerly railway to operate a steam-hauled passenger service. Built by Henschel in 1922, 2-8-2 No. 135 is seen here hauling a mixed train between Esquel and Nahuel Pan in 1990.

redundant 750-mm-gauge track formerly used on military railways on the Western Front in France and Belgium during the First World War, so if the two railways had been joined then mixed-gauge track would have needed to be laid – in the end the two railways were never connected and the Chubut Valley line closed in 1961. Rolling stock was ordered from Belgium along with 50 2-8-2 'Mikado' oil-fired steam locomotives from the German company of Henschel and, later, twenty-five from the Baldwin Locomotive Works in the USA.

Progress was painfully slow across the inhospitable terrain, with much of the line destroyed by floods in the early 1930s. The winding, switchback route included two summits, both exceeding 4,000 ft above sea level, and it wasn't until 1941 that it had opened as far as El Maitén, 149 miles from Ingeniero Jacobacci, where the railway established its maintenance depot. Esquel was finally reached in 1945 but until 1950, when passenger services were introduced, it offered a freight-only service carrying large amounts of wool north for shipment to the coast. Passenger comforts were basic to say the least, with a wood-burning stove supplied in carriages to keep them warm on the 20-hour journey across Argentina's Wild West – in the bleak Patagonian winter, journeys could often take several days due to snowdrifts. Nicknamed 'La Trochita' ('The Little Narrow Gauge'), the railway was a major freight-carrying line and was instrumental in the development of the area in the 1960s and early 1970s. By then, new road-building and increasing competition from road transport soon led to the railway's gradual decline, although the growth of backpacker tourism in Patagonia during the late 1970s injected a new lease of life – the publication of Paul Theroux's 'The Old Patagonian Express' in 1979 introduced 'La Trochita' to the world stage.

In the run-up to the splitting up and privatization of Argentina's state railways, Ferrocarriles Argentinos, in 1993 the loss-making, worn-out, archaic and remote, La Trochita, was deemed unworthy of saving and closure was announced. However, the outcry both nationally and internationally was enormous and the line was saved in 1994 by the two provincial governments, Río Negro and Chubut. In 1995 the Río Negro provincial government closed the section from Ingeniero Jacobacci to Esquel and, although it was partly reopened in 2003, it still remains closed. 'La Trochita' was declared a National Historic Monument by the Argentine Government in 1997.

At the southern end of the line the town of Esquel (population 32,000) was founded by Welsh immigrants in 1865 and is close to the Los Alerces National Park and the ski resort of La Hoya. Unsurprisingly it is twinned with Aberystwyth in Wales! At its current northern outpost the smaller town of El Maitén (population 3,700) owes its existence to the coming of the railway during the Second World War.

The railway currently has six operational steam locomotives – three German Henschels and three American Baldwins, all of which are oil-fired and have worked on the railway since it opened – they are maintained at its El Maitén headquarters where there is also a small railway museum. Sixteen other locomotives are used for spare parts to keep these six operational. The original 1922-built Belgian carriages complete with wood-burning stoves are supplemented by more modern examples built in the 1950s.

Until recently a weekly passenger service operated in the high season between El Maitén and Esquel, a journey of nine hours, but this service has been suspended. Currently, two tourist trains run along this highly scenic southern section – one southwards from the railway's headquarters at El Maitén to Desvio Thomae and the other northwards from Esquel to Nahuel Pan. Occasionally special trains chartered by enthusiasts will venture further afield and the Río Negro Government (in the past), also operated an intermittent service from Ingeniero Jacobacci to Ojos de Agua.

The economic challenges facing this fascinating railway are enormous and its continued survival amidst Argentina's economic woes cannot be taken for granted.

OVERLEAF: Built by the Baldwin Locomotive Works in 1922, oil-burning 2-8-2 No. 16 is seen here between La Cancha and Nahuel Pan on a southbound working from El Maiten to Esquel.

Made famous by Paul Theroux in his book 'The Old Patagonian Express', the steam-hauled trains of 'La Trochita' still cling to life in the shadow of the Andes. Here a Baldwin-built 2-8-2 works a short passenger train between Norquinco and El Maiten in April 1996.

GUAYAQUIL & QUITO RAILWAY

ECUADOR, SOUTH AMERICA

GAUGE: 3 FT 6 IN. • **LENGTH:** 277 MILES •
ROUTE: GUAYAQUIL TO QUITO

Constructed by thousands of Jamaican labourers, the Guayaquil & Quito Railway was a truly American affair using US engineering know-how, finance and equipment. Climbing high into the Ecuadorian Andes, the railway was virtually destroyed by floods and landslides in the late twentieth century but its reopening in 2013 restores it as one of the most spectacular train journeys in the world.

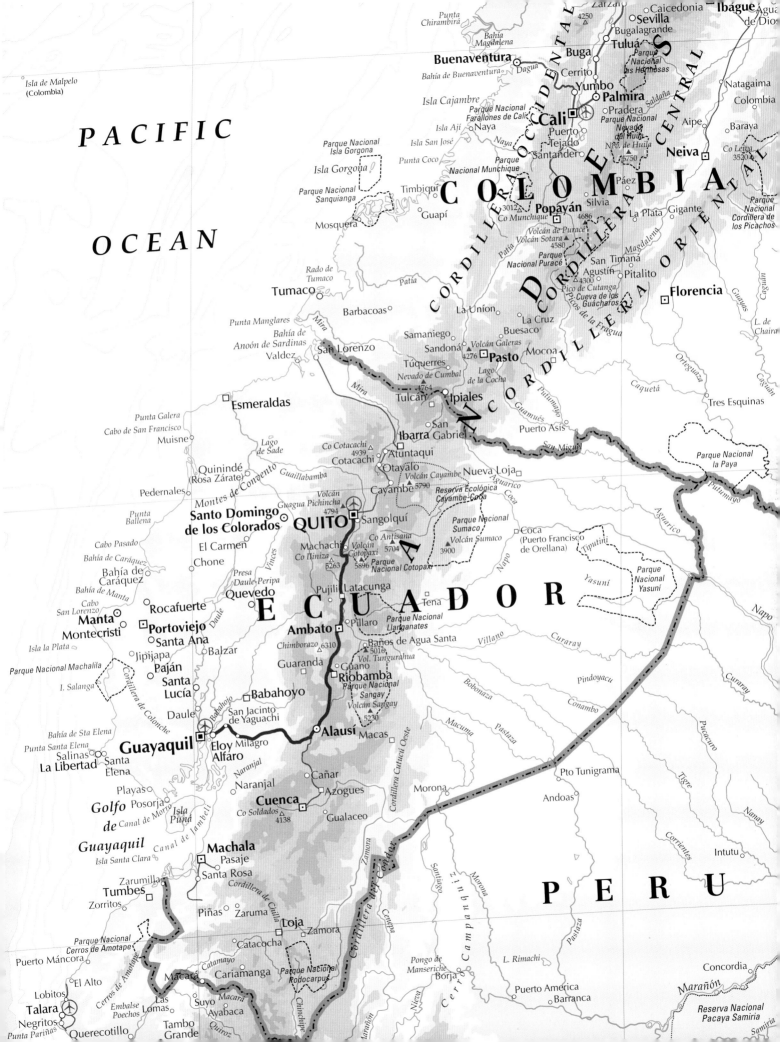

Once home to the Inca civilization, the South American country of Ecuador suffered 300 years of Spanish rule until becoming an independent republic in 1830. It is bounded to the west by the Pacific Ocean, to the north by Columbia and to the east and south by Peru. The low-lying coastal plain in the west soon gives way to the Andes mountain range which runs north-south through the centre and which contains some of world's highest volcanoes such as Cotopaxi (19,347 ft) and Chimborazo (20,564 ft). Ecuador's capital city, Quito (at 9,350 ft above sea level the highest capital city in the world) and its third-largest city Cuenca are both UNESCO World Heritage sites. On the west coast the port of Guayaquil is the largest city in the country and the embarkation point for the Ecuador-owned Galapagos Islands.

Ecuador's first railway was opened between Durán and Milagro in 1873 – the former, now named Eloy Alfaro, was then reached from Guayaquil by ferry across the Guayas River. Located on the coastal plain, the city of Milagro is an important agricultural centre best known for sugar cane and pineapple growing. The 3-ft 6-in.-gauge line reached Bucay at the foot of the Andes in 1888. Building the railway across the Andes to the capital Quito was a major engineering project and, with the aid of American engineers and financiers – notably the Harman brothers – and 4,000 Jamaican labourers, construction work started in 1897. As the railway pushed higher into the mountains it reached Sibambe where a series of zigzags at Devil's Nose (Nariz del Diablo) were built in 1902, allowing trains to gain height by climbing back and forth up the mountainside side on gradients as steep as 1-in-18. After the railway reached the ancient town of Alausí it turned northwards, climbing ever higher to the city of Riobamba, 9,035 ft above sea level and close to Chimborazo volcano.

From Riobamba the railway continued to climb to its highest point at Urbina, 11,841 ft above sea level, before descending through the 'Avenue of Volcanoes' to the capital, Quito. The line finally opened to great celebrations in 1908, reducing the journey time to the coast from over a week to just two days.

Two other railways were later opened in Ecuador; a 90-mile branch line from Chunchi, south of Alausí, to Ecuador's third largest city, Cuenca, was built between 1915 and 1965 and a 230-mile railway was opened between Quito and the northern Pacific coast port of San Lorenzo in 1957. All three railways were later nationalized under the umbrella title of Ferrocarriles del Ecuador Empresa Publica (FEEP).

In addition to being engineered and financed by Americans, the Guayaquil & Quito Railway operated powerful 2-6-0 and 2-8-0 steam locomotives built by the Baldwin Locomotive Works of Pennsylvania, the last of which was delivered in the early 1950s. French-built Alstom diesels were first introduced in 1957 with the last batch arriving in 1992. Self-propelled railcars, or

PREVIOUS PAGE: One of the most dramatic railway journeys in the world – the Guayaquil & Quito Railway's 2-8-0 No. 17, built by Baldwin in 1935, negotiates the Lower Reverse switchback with a 2-coach train in August 2003.

'autoferros', built from converted road buses, were also introduced for some shorter passenger journeys or used as tourist trains.

The Guyaquil to Quito railway was initially a great success and even in the 1980s steam-hauled tourist trains were still operating along stretches of its route. By then, however, almost all freight and regular passenger traffic had been lost to road transport and the appalling floods and landslides caused by El Ninõ that occurred in the early 1980s and late 1990s virtually closed the railway. By its centenary in 2008 only a few unconnected short sections remained open for tourist trains.

All traffic halts as G&Q Baldwin built 2-6-0 No. 7 proceeds slowly along Milagro's streets with a mixed train in November 1990.

Since 2008 the fortunes of the FEEP have been transformed, with previously closed sections being rebuilt and reopened in stages and stations restored to their former glory. In that year the ambitious $245 million project to reopen the line was given the green light by Ecuador's President Correa and the railway reopened completely on 4 June 2013. It now operates a tourist train, 'Tren Crucero', along the entire length of this spectacular route using six original restored Baldwin steam locomotives and more modern Alstom diesels for various sections. With a capacity for fifty-four passengers, each train consists of four modern air-conditioned red coaches built in Spain.

The entire journey in either direction now takes four days, with overnight stops in traditional haciendas and coach trips to places of interest such as the Cotopaxi National Park and indigenous markets. Shorter two- and three-day trips are also available. One of the most spectacular train journeys in the world crossing seven distinct climatic zones, the 'Tren Cucero' operates on selected days from January to February, June to August and in December each year. Shorter tourist trains using restored 'autoferros' or locomotive-hauled wooden clerestory coaches also operate between stations along the route, with similar services operating between El Tambo and Coyoctor on the southern Cuenca branch and between Ibarra and Salinas on the northern San Lorenzo line.

RIGHT: Gaining height in the Andes - G&Q 2-8-0 No. 17 gingerly negotiates the famous Devil's Nose switchback on 7 October 2006.

Llama country – G&Q Baldwin-built 2-8-0 No. 17 halts at Urbina (11,870 ft above sea level) with a short passenger train in October 2006.

OVERLEAF: A Guayaquil & Quito Railway diesel-hauled train makes its way towards the Devil's Nose switchback. This spectacular Ecuadorian railway reopened in 2013 after suffering severe flooding and landslides.

FERROCARRIL CENTRAL ANDINO
PERU, SOUTH AMERICA

GAUGE: 4 FT 8 ½IN. · LENGTH: 332 MILES ·
ROUTE: CALLAO AND LIMA TO HUANCAYO/CERRO DE PASCO

Built by American entrepreneur Henry Meiggs and Polish engineer
Ernest Malinowski, the Central Railway of Peru was a tremendous feat
of railway engineering that conquered the Andes Mountains with
numerous tunnels, zigzag switchbacks and viaducts. It remained the
highest railway in the world until the opening of the Qinghai-Tibet
Railway in China in 2006.

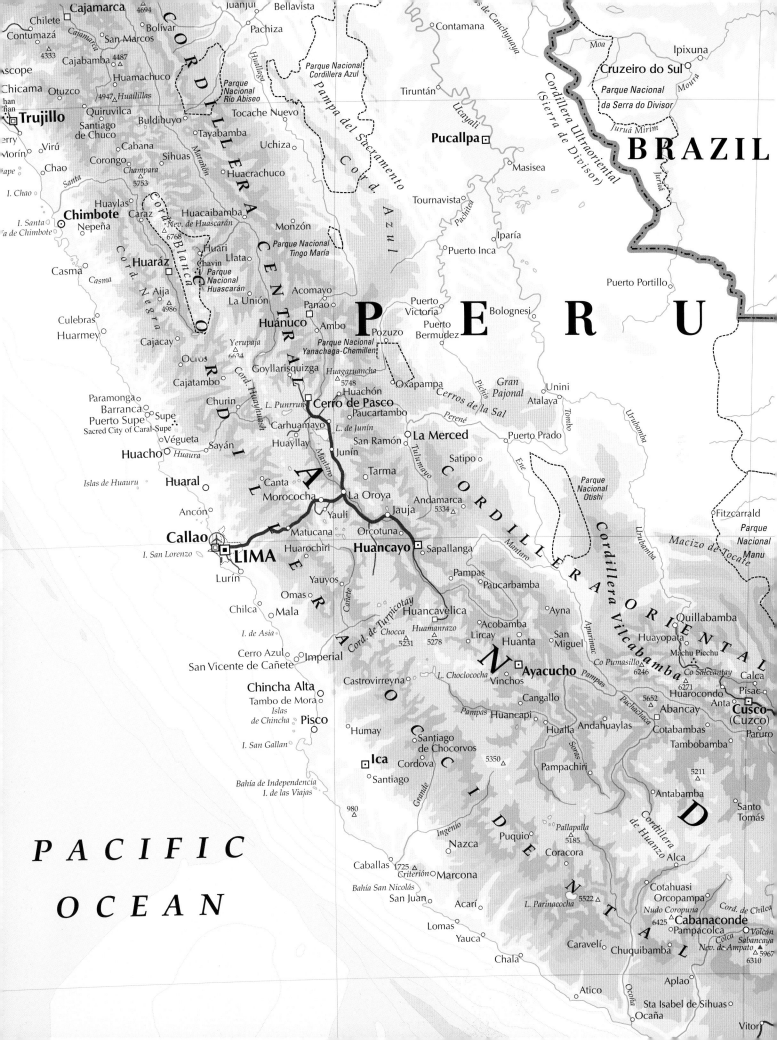

The Ferrocarril Central Andino of Peru is one of the most remarkable railways in the world. Built to the standard gauge of 4 ft 8½ in., it started life in 1851 with the opening of an 8½-mile section from the Pacific port of Callao to the country's capital Lima. As we have read on page 296, the American entrepreneur, philanthropist and railroad builder Henry Meiggs moved to Peru in 1868 after completing the construction of a railway in Chile. With the financial backing of the Peruvian Government and British investors, Meiggs went on to build both the Southern and Central railways, both of which were enormous engineering triumphs that took the two separate railways high up into the Andes Mountains in order to tap into valuable mineral deposits.

As an extension of the original 1851 line, the contract to build the Callao, Lima and Oroya Railway (later to become the Ferrocarril Central Andino) was entrusted to Meiggs together with the eminent Polish railway engineer Ernest Malinowski. Construction work on extending the original line eastwards from Lima into the Andes started in 1870 and by the spring of 1873 it had reached the Ticlio Pass, at 15,806 ft above sea level, the highest railway in the world. To achieve this, the railway builders had to excavate sixty-two tunnels though solid rock with a total length of over 3½ miles and build thirty bridges and viaducts. In places the railway gained height through a series of zigzags, or switchbacks, up steep mountainsides, with turntables installed at eleven locations so that locomotives could change direction.

Meiggs died in 1877 and the outbreak of a war between Peru and Chile in 1879 brought construction work to a halt. The war ended in 1883 leaving the Peruvian Government in enormous debt, especially to the railway's British investors. This problem was solved in 1889 when a new Peruvian Corporation was formed in London to take over the country's railways (see page 296).

The railway eventually reached La Oroya in 1893 and, following Malinowski's death in 1899, was extended southwards to Huancayo, opening in 1908. West of Oroya the line passed through the Galera summit tunnel, excavated under the appropriately named Mount Meiggs,

which at 15,692 ft above sea level was the highest railway tunnel in the world. It then passes through Galera station, then the highest station in the world at 15,673 ft above sea level. The railway held these records until the opening of the Qinghai-Tibet Railway in 2006.

Meanwhile a second standard-gauge line had already been opened northwards from La Oroya to Cerro de Pasca and coal mines at Goyllarisquizga in 1904, making La Oroya the highest railway junction in the world. From Huancayo a 92-mile 3-ft-gauge railway was completed to the mining district of Huancavelica in 1926 – in recent times this line has been converted to standard gauge, reopening in 2010.

Steam motive power on this demanding route came in the form of powerful American 2-8-0, 4-8-0 and 4-6-0 steam locomotives built by Baldwin and Alco along with 'Andes' Class oil-fired 2-8-0s supplied by Beyer, Peacock of Manchester in England. First introduced in 1963, Alco diesels gradually took over their workings although one of the 'Andes' Class has since been restored to working order.

Peru's railways were nationalized in 1972 as Empresa Nacional de Ferrocarriles del Perú but state control only lasted until 1999 when they were re-privatized, with the central section from Callao and Lima to Cerro de Pasca and Huancayo/Huancavelica taken over by American-led Ferrocarril Central Andino (FCCA).

The FCCA is primarily a freight line transporting smelted minerals from Peru's metallurgical capital of La Oroya down to the coast and building materials, fuel and foodstuffs in the opposite direction. Zinc bars, copper plate and lead bars are transported down to Callao on monster freight trains that can consist of up to eighty bogie wagons, each carrying seventy tons. Located 12,287 ft above sea level, La Oraya's smelter has earned the city the unfortunate reputation of being one of the world's most polluted places.

While the railway has not operated a regular passenger service for some years, it does run a twice-monthly tourist train between the capital, Lima, and Huancayo. The journey time on this spectacular route is twelve hours with stops at San Bartolomé, Matucana and Galera. Coaching stock for this service consists of a fleet of 68-seat 'Classic Cars' built in the UK in 1950 and in Romania in 1982 along with 48-seat 'Turistic Cars' built by the railway in 2006.

PREVIOUS PAGE: High in the Andes two passenger trains cross in the loop at Meiggs – the nearby Mount Meiggs is named after the railway's American builder, Henry Meiggs, with the railway burrowing under it via Galera Tunnel, 15,629 ft above sea level.

Founded by the Spanish conquistador Francisco Pizarro in 1535, Lima is served by the nearby port of Callao, one of the busiest and largest commercial ports in South America through which rail-borne minerals from the Andes such as silver, zinc and coal are exported. Located in the historic city centre (in 1988 declared a UNESCO World Heritage site for its high concentration of Spanish colonial architecture), Lima's Desamparados Station was completed in 1912 and, as befits a railway with so many superlatives, the grand 3-storey building has a classical façade and features an Art Nouveau vaulted stained glass roof above its concourse. From Lima trains climb eastwards from the flat coastal plain to the 15,629-ft summit in Galera Tunnel, a distance of 170 miles. So quick is the rise that oxygen cylinders are carried in each tourist train to relieve passengers suffering from altitude sickness.

Between Lima and Huancayo trains pass through sixty-nine tunnels, reverse along six zigzag switchbacks and cross fifty-eight bridges of which the most spectacular is the steel double-cantilever Verugas Bridge, 252 ft at its highest point above a ravine and 575 ft long. After halting at the highest point, Galera, trains descend to La Oroya before heading south along the fertile Mantaro River Valley to Jauja, Concepción and Huancayo. The last fifty or so miles – all between 10,000 and 11,000 ft above sea level – pass through the most important wheat-producing region in Peru. The historic town of Jauja briefly became Peru's provisional capital in 1534 after the Spanish conquistadors discovered huge amounts of Inca stores and wealth hidden there but its importance was later eclipsed by the city of Huancayo to the south. Although the end of the line for the tourist train from Lima, Huancayo is the starting point for a thrice-weekly passenger service along the recently re-gauged line to Huancavelica. This leisurely six-hour journey through the canyons of the Mantaro Valley on the Ferrocarril Huancayo-Huancavelica takes in spectacular mountain scenery.

The FCCA is primarily a freight line carrying minerals from La Oroya high in the Andes down to the Pacific coast. Here a mineral train headed by two General Electric Class C30-7 diesels slowly crosses a steel trestle bridge between Rio Blanco and San Mateo.

OVERLEAF: Hard at work in the rarified air of the Andes. FCCA GE Class C30-7 No. 1001 heads an empty mineral train near to the summit of the railway at Galera, 15, 673 ft above sea level.

FERROCARRIL DEL SUR
PERU, SOUTH AMERICA

GAUGE: 4 FT 8½ IN. • **LENGTH**: 536 MILES •
ROUTE: MATARANI AND AREQUIPA TO CUZCO AND PUNO

From Matarani on the Pacific Coast, the Southern Railway of Peru climbs high into the mighty Andes Mountains to reach Lake Titicaca. Although construction was started by the American entrepreneur and railroad engineer, Henry Meiggs, the railway was taken over by a British company after his death and completed. Today, the line remains one of the wonders of the railway world.

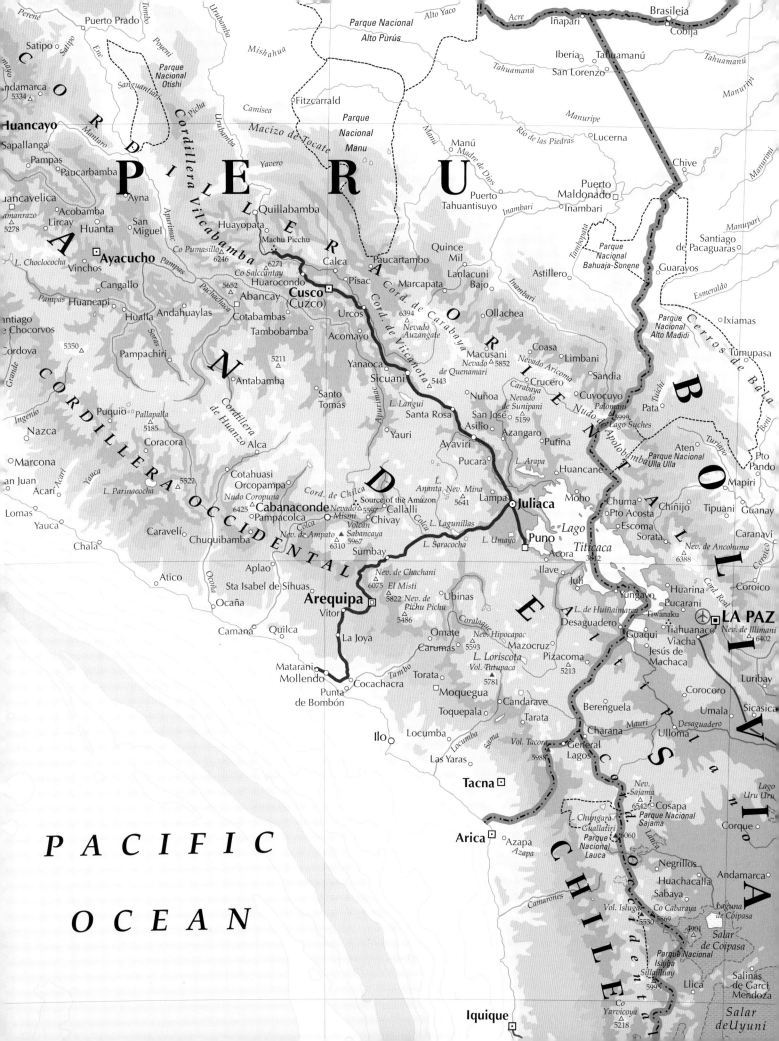

Once part of the Inca Empire, the South American country of Peru was colonized by the Spanish for nearly 300 years until gaining independence in 1821. Bordered to the west by the Pacific Ocean, to the north by Ecuador and Colombia, to the east by Brazil and Bolivia and to the south by Chile, the country can be divided into three main geographical regions: the narrow coastal plain in the west soon gives way to the Andes Mountains followed by the Amazonian tropical rainforests in the east. The Peruvian Andes contain rich mineral deposits as well as some of the highest peaks in South America including Huascarán, 22,205 ft above sea level.

The first railway to be built in Peru opened between the Pacific port of Callao and the capital, Lima, in 1851 – this line was later extended to Huancayo and Huancavelica in the Andes by the Central Railway (see pages 288–293). In the south of the country, construction of the Southern Railway inland from the port of Mollendo started in 1869 and by 1871 it had reached the city of Arequipa, 7,500 ft up in the foothills of the Andes. Both built to the standard gauge of 4 ft 8½ in., the Central and Southern railways were the brainchild of American entrepreneur, philanthropist and railroad builder Henry Meiggs. Born in New York State in 1811, Meiggs was a remarkable railroad builder, first constructing the line between Santiago and Valparaiso in Chile between 1858 and 1867. A year later he moved to Peru where he acquired interests in silver mining and persuaded the Government and British investors to part with huge sums of money to fund more railroad building – some say that Meiggs bribed politicians to obtain permission to build the railways.

With Meiggs in the driving seat, construction of the Southern Railway eastwards from Arequipa into the Andes was remarkably quick considering the mountainous terrain that needed to be crossed. Involving the construction of lofty steel trestle bridges, numerous tunnels and reversing zigzags up mountainsides to gain height, the railway reached Puno, 326 miles from the coast, on the west shore of Lake Titicaca in 1876. The railway's highest point was reached west of Juliaca at Crucero Alto, 14,666 ft above sea level. A railway-owned steamer and train ferry service was also

introduced across the lake, 12,500 ft above sea level, to the Bolivian railhead 120 miles away at Guaqui. A short coastal extension from the port of Mollendo to Matarani had also been opened by then. Construction of a second line from a junction at Juliaca, north of Puno, to the city of Cuzco was started in 1872 but its completion was delayed for over thirty years.

Meiggs died in 1877 leaving the Peruvian Government in great debt to railway bondholders in Europe, particularly in Britain. With Peru facing bankruptcy all railway building in the country ground to a halt and then, in 1879, the country became involved in a debilitating war with its southern neighbour Chile. The war ended in 1883 with Peru's finances in tatters. In order to appease its British bondholders the Government entered into an agreement in 1889 known as the Grace Contract, whereby a new Peruvian Corporation was formed in London to take over most of the country's railways for a period of sixty-six years in return for the cancellation of the debt. In return the new Corporation agreed to complete various railway extensions including the unfinished line from Juliaca to Cuzco.

Reaching an altitude of 14,150 ft above sea level at La Raya, the 210-mile line to Cuzco was eventually completed in 1908. Powerful 2-8-0, 4-8-0 and 4-6-0 steam locomotives, built by Baldwin and Alco, were the mainstay of operations on this demanding railway and lingered on until the 1980s, gradually being replaced by Alco diesels introduced between 1956 and 1963. Although Peru's railways were nationalized in 1972 as Empresa Nacional de Ferrocarriles del Perú, state control only lasted until 1999 when they were re-privatized, with the southern section from Matarani to Cuzco and Puno rebranded as PeruRail.

Formed in 1999, PeruRail is jointly owned by Orient-Express Hotels and a Peruvian holding company. Passenger services operate only on the 3-ft-gauge line from Cuzco to Aguas Calientes (see right) and on the standard-gauge route from Cuzco to Puno on Lake Titicaca, via the 14,150-ft summit at La Raya and the junction at Juliaca. The latter route is used thrice weekly by the luxury 'Andean Explorer' train for the 241-mile, ten-hour journey and oxygen is available for passengers at this high altitude. The company also operates regular freight services between the port of Matarani, Arequipa, Juliaca, Cuzco and Puno.

PREVIOUS PAGE: Passengers are treated to glorious vistas of the High Andes as they travel on the train between Puno, on the shores of Lake Titicaca, and the city of Cuzco.

CUZCO TO AGUAS CALIENTES (FOR MACHU PICCHU)

GAUGE: 3 FT · LENGTH: 68 MILES

A separate 3-ft-gauge railway was opened between Cuzco and Santa Ana in 1928 and later extended to Quillabamba in 1978. After suffering from floods and landslides in the 1990s the line was cut back to Aguas Calientes and now forms the principal means of transport for visitors to the fifteenth-century Inca site at Machu Picchu, which was discovered by the American historian Hiram Bingham in 1911. On leaving Cuzco the railway gains height over a short distance through a series of five zigzags before descending into the Sacred Valley to Agua Calientes, the station for Machu Picchu. Currently this first section has been closed due to landslides and flooding, with services now starting from Poroy station, an 8-mile taxi ride from Cuzco. Sadly, the sight of steam trains picking their way through the historic crowded streets of Cuzco is now a distant memory. The 'Belmond Hiram Bingham' luxury train that operates on this route was voted the best train in the world by UK readers of Condé Nast Traveller magazine in 2011.

For visitors to Machu Picchu the 'Belmond Hiram Bingham' train on the 3-ft-gauge railway from Poroy, near Cuzco, is by far the most luxurious way to travel.

OVERLEAF: Named after the American explorer who discovered Machu Picchu, the diesel-hauled 'Belmond Hiram Bingham' luxury train has two dining cars, an observation/bar car and a kitchen car and can carry 84 passengers.

INDEX

AUTHOR'S ACKNOWLEDGEMENTS

Befitting the subject this is a truly international production. Firstly I would like to thank the following for their unstinting creativity in producing this book: **Jethro Lennox**, **Keith Moore** and **Kevin Robbins** in Glasgow, Scotland; **Gavin James** in Queensland, Australia; **Ginny Naish** in Kent, England; printed in China.

Secondly, and in keeping with the international flavour, I would also like to thank the following individuals and organizations for the assistance they have provided during the making of this book:

Allison Haas, White Pass & Yukon Railroad, Skagway, Alaska
Bruno Hillion, SNCF, Montpelier, France

Kaagwana Ambambi, Desert Express, Namibia
Kylie Clark, Japan National Tourism Organization, London
Melanie Reid, Great Southern Rail, Australia
Peter Hughes, Port Moody, Canada
Simon Shimizu-Metcalfe, Kyushu Railway Company, Japan

Last but not least a big thank you to **Gordon Edgar**, English railway photographer *par excellence* who has not only supplied many of the photographs used in this book but has also filled several gaps in my knowledge of railways in Eastern Europe and China and tirelessly checked the proofs during its production.

PHOTO CAPTIONS

ENDPAPER FRONT
The steeply-graded Flåm Railway in western Norway is one of the most popular tourist destinations in the country.

CONTENTS 4-5
Hauled by a TransNamib diesel the 'Desert Express' crosses the arid Namibian landscape on its 220-mile journey between Swakopmund and Windhoek.

EUROPE 10-11
High summer at the lower end of the Jungfrau Railway in Switzerland. The railway features Europe's highest railway station: Jungfraujoch is 11,332 ft above sea level and is reached through tunnels deep beneath the Eiger and Mönch mountains.

AFRICA 110-111
Built by Ansaldo of Genova in 1938, Mallet 0-4-4-0 No. 442-55 approaches Tunnel No. 11 high up in the Eritrean mountains on the steeply graded Italian-built Massawa to Asmara narrow-gauge line in 2010.

ASIA 142-143
Hauled by several Class NJ2 5,100-hp diesel-electric locomotives a train on the Quinhai to Lhasa railway passes by the snow-clad peaks of the Nyenchen Tanglha Mountains in Tibet.

AUSTRALASIA 220-221
Headed by two 'NR' Class diesel-electric locomotives 'The Ghan' crosses the Fergusson River in the Northern Territory on its 1,851-mile journey across Australia between Adelaide and Darwin.

NORTH AMERICA 234-235
In bitterly cold conditions Canadian National diesel-electrics Nos. 2587 and 5780 head a westbound grain train along the frozen banks of Moose Lake as they approach Red Pass in the Canadian Rockies.

SOUTH AMERICA 272-273
Reopened in 2013 the Guayaquil & Quito Railway in Ecuador is one of the world's most spectacular railway journeys. A diesel-hauled train is seen here gaining height through the Andes by negotiating the famous Devil's Nose switchback.

ENDPAPER BACK
A double-stack intermodal freight train makes its way alongside the Bow River in the Banff National Park, Alberta, Canada.

PHOTO CREDITS